Praise for *FUSION*

"Leaders everywhere are trying to build great brands, but few realize how powerfully brands are shaped by the cultures of their organizations. This compelling book shows how to connect the image you present to the outside world with the values and norms that operate inside your world of work."

—Adam Grant, *New York Times* bestselling
author of *Originals* and *Give and Take*

"Denise Lee Yohn hit a home run with her first book, *What Great Brands Do.* Now she's written *FUSION* and it is just as provocative. Denise proves beyond a shadow of a doubt that great companies are powered by brand-culture fusion. I highly recommend this book!"

—Ken Blanchard, Coauthor, *The New One Minute Manager,*®
Coeditor, *Servant Leadership in Action*

"Denise Lee Yohn's *FUSION* should be on every business leader's reading list. It provides the much-needed antidote to the culture and leadership crisis corporate America is experiencing."

—Marshall Goldsmith, *Thinkers50*
#1 Leadership Thinker in the World

"Denise Lee Yohn's extensive research, insightful analysis, and gift of storytelling make *FUSION* a practical and inspiring guide to building a great brand and a great culture."

—Philip Kotler, S.C. Johnson & Son Distinguished
Professor of International Marketing,
Kellogg School of Management

"Denise Lee Yohn is back with another breakthrough! *FUSION* cracks the code on culture-building and reveals how outstanding companies use their corporate cultures as a competitive advantage. It's a must-read!"

—Verne Harnish, Founder, Entrepreneurs' Organization (EO),
Author, *Scaling Up* (Rockefeller Habits 2.0)

"Few really know how to create an outstanding corporate culture. Denise Lee Yohn takes you behind the scenes at some of the world's greatest organizations and pulls the curtain back on the strategies that enable them to attract and motivate the best talent."

—Tiffani Bova, Growth and Innovation Evangelist, Salesforce

"I have spent a lifetime creating and building brands based on ideas-based leadership cultures. *FUSION* explains it all. Bravo Denise."

—Kevin Roberts, Author, *Lovemarks*

"The relationship between internal and external brands and culture is a relevant topic which Denise Lee Yohn has thoroughly explored. *FUSION* presents great ideas and examples that can provide any leader or company an opportunity to rethink the way they go to market."

—Mark Levy, former global head of
Employee Experience, Airbnb

"Denise Lee Yohn has an uncanny knack for pulling the curtain back on the strategies that enable today's most-successful companies to consistently produce market-leading results. If you're an executive or leader who wants to take your organization to the very top, then you owe it to yourself to read this book and then share the lessons you learn with your team."

—Peter Economy, Inc.com's The Leadership Guy

"*FUSION* tackles one of the most important and surprising aspects of a strong brand: company culture. Yohn builds a compelling case that will make leaders everywhere want to achieve brand-culture fusion. Highly-recommended!"

—Skip Prichard, Author, *The Book of Mistakes*,
and Leadership Insights blogger

"Denise is the first brand expert to bridge two powerful, yet apparently disconnected areas of business and management: Culture & Brand...*FUSION* is a history-making book, an essential read for every businessperson driving change."

—Eduardo P. Braun, leadership expert, Author,
People First Leadership

FUSION

How Integrating Brand and Culture Powers the World's Greatest Companies

DENISE LEE YOHN

NICHOLAS BREALEY
PUBLISHING

BOSTON · LONDON

First published in 2018 by Nicholas Brealey Publishing
An imprint of John Murray Press

An Hachette U.K. company

23   22   21   20   19   18   1   2   3   4   5   6   7   8   9   10

A CIP catalogue record for this title is available from the British Library

Library of Congress Cataloging-in-Publication Data
Names: Yohn, Denise Lee, 1967– author.
Title: Fusion : how integrating brand and culture powers the world's greatest
    companies / Denise Lee Yohn.
Description: Boston, MA : Nicholas Brealey Publishing, 2018.
Identifiers: LCCN 2017053694 (print) | LCCN 2017054553 (ebook) |
    ISBN 9781473676992 (ebook) | ISBN 9781473677043 (library ebook) |
    ISBN 9781473676985 (hardcover)
Subjects: LCSH: Branding (Marketing) | Advertising—Social aspects. |
    Brand name products.
Classification: LCC HF5415.1255 (ebook) | LCC HF5415.1255 .Y63 2018 (print) |
    DDC 658.8/27—dc23
LC record available at HYPERLINK "https://protect-us.mimecast.com/s/
    qO54BOsp6leWtN?domain=lccn.loc.gov" https://lccn.loc.gov/2017053694

ISBN 978-1-47367-698-5
U.S. e-book 978-1-47367-699-2
U.K. e-book ISBN 978-1-47367-705-0

Printed and bound in the United States of America.

John Murray Press policy is to use papers that are natural, renewable, and recyclable
products and made from wood grown in sustainable forests. The logging and
manufacturing processes are expected to conform to the environmental regulations
of the country of origin.

John Murray Press Ltd   Nicholas Brealey Publishing
Carmelite House   Hachette Book Group
50 Victoria Embankment   Market Place Center, 53 State Street
London EC4Y 0DZ   Boston, MA 02109, U.S.A.
Tel: 020 3122 6000   Tel: (617) 263 1834

www.nicholasbrealey.com

TABLE OF CONTENTS

page

ACKNOWLEDGMENTS   ix

INTRODUCTION. Great Companies Are
  Powered by Brand-Culture Fusion   xi
  The Unsung Drivers of Business   xiii
  The Power of Fusion   xv
  Why Companies Fail to Build Great Brands and
    Cultivate Great Cultures   xviii
  A Blueprint for Brand-Culture Fusion   xxi
  Every Organization Needs Fusion   xxiii
  Lead Your Fusion   xxvi

PART 1: THE FOUNDATIONS OF
  BRAND-CULTURE FUSION   1

Chapter 1. Set Your Sole Purpose and Core Values   3
  Overarching Purpose: Your "Why"   5
  Core Values: Your "How"   13
  Unify Your Organization   24
  The Cornerstones of Culture   27

Chapter 2. Assess Your Brand-Culture Fusion   29
  Identify Your Brand Type   30
  Determine the Values You Need   37
  Assess the State of Your Brand-Culture Fusion   45
  Capture Your Company's Uniqueness   52

Chapter 3. Lead the Change   **55**

Different Culture, Different Outcome   58

Communicate, Communicate, Communicate   60

Actions Speak Louder than Words   64

Engage Every Leader   66

Reinforce Your Culture with the Right
    People Decisions   68

Brand-Culture Fusion Starts with You   70

PART 2: FIVE STRATEGIES TO ACHIEVE FUSION   **73**

Chapter 4. Organize and Operate On-Brand   **75**

From Talking about Culture to Operationalizing It   77

Design Your Organization Deliberately   78

Align Your "What" with Your "Why" and "How"   85

Inspect Your Brand Touchpoints   88

Culture Is Not "Soft Stuff"   93

**Chapter 5. Create Culture-Changing Employee
Experiences**   **95**

What Is EX?   98

Make EX a Priority   101

Design Your EX in Four Steps   103

Craft an EX that Is Right for *You*   112

Get Employees Involved   116

Integrate Your EX with Your CX   118

Fuel Fusion with EX   120

Chapter 6. Sweat the Small Stuff   **122**

Give Your Culture Life through Rituals   125

Make Your Culture Visible through Artifacts   131

Promote Your Culture through Policies
    and Procedures   134

Design Every Detail   140

Chapter 7. Ignite Your Transformation   **143**

Employee Brand Engagement Creates Culture
    Change   146

Stage Great Employee Brand Engagement
    Experiences   148

Carefully Craft Communications Campaigns   154

Develop Toolkits for Ongoing Engagement   158

A Worthy Investment   160

Chapter 8. Build Your Brand from the Inside Out   **163**

Put Your Purpose into Action   166

Leverage Your Values to Re-Define Your Brand   170

Showcase Your Culture to Differentiate Your Brand 176

Transform Your Brand and Culture Together   180

CONCLUSION. The Journey to Brand-Culture Fusion   **182**

END NOTES   **187**

ABOUT THE AUTHOR   **207**

INDEX   **209**

For Chris

ACKNOWLEDGMENTS

Expressing gratitude is always difficult for me because words never seem sufficient to convey my deeply felt thanks, but I would like to try to acknowledge some of the people who have helped me in my journey of writing this book. And if I fail to mention you, please know that your importance to me is greater than my forgetfulness.

I'm particularly grateful to Steve Morris as well as Ross Blankenship, Eduardo Braun, Lucy Gill-Simmen, Darci Poole, Mark Tomaszewicz, and Marnie Wilson for your instrumental help in reviewing my manuscript, assessment tool, and/or contributing to the content of this book substantively. I'm blown away by your generosity and insight.

Thank you to Martin Bishop, Barbara Cave Henricks, Peter Economy, Peter Fader, Annette Franz-Gleinicki, Kate Goodison, Verne Harnish, Juliana Smith Holterhaus, Zach Johnson, Sarah Marrs, Karen Murphy, Yvonne Nomizu, Christina Stahler, Jackie Waldorph, Curt Swindoll, and Nick Wiik for helping me with content, connections, and counsel.

The people who graciously allowed me to interview them for this book deserve my sincere appreciation: Stephan Aarstol, Alejandro Asrin, Vivienne Bechtold, Tina Chong, Jana De Anda, Rachelle Diamond, Arndt Ellinghorst, Jennifer Forman, Eric Jackson, MG Kristian, Kenzie Leas, Nicole Leverich, Mark Levy, Jeff Lindeman, Bryan Miles, Monique Mulbry, Garry Ridge, Scott Sabin, Gillian Smith, Rachelle Snook, Patricio Supervielle, Brian Takumi, Lilian Tomovich, Ari Weinzweig, Ardine Williams, and Darin Yates.

Genoveva Llosa, aka editor extraordinaire, thank you for making my manuscript exponentially better. And to Josh Bernoff, thank you for getting me started on the right track.

Thanks to the team at Nicholas Brealey: Alison Hankey, Melissa Carl, Giuliana Caranante, and Michelle Morgan. And to Giles Anderson for your representation.

Richard Boren, thank you for all your work on the assessment tool.

Several folks have gone the extra mile in supporting me with their friendship and advice during my journey: Tiffani Bova, Jim Canfield, Sally Hogshead, Mitch Joel, Danny Kim, Sondra Kissinger, Tamara Romeo, John Sarkisian, and Ed Wallace.

I'd like to acknowledge the members of the Great Brand Society who helped me launch my previous books and will most likely be the people I lean on again for this one—I'm so grateful for each one of you. Also thank you to those folks in my brand-as-business brief community who gave me feedback when I was developing the assessment tool—it was so helpful to get all of your comments. And thanks to the Write and Rant Facebook group for your inspiration, ideas, and answers.

Finally, my family: Dad, Viv, and Jim, thank you for being God's vessels of love to me. And Chris, I couldn't have done this book—nor anything else in my life—without you.

INTRODUCTION

GREAT COMPANIES ARE POWERED BY BRAND-CULTURE FUSION

"Bruising."
"Relentless."
"Painful."
"Frequent combat."
"Burn and churn."

No one would fault you for thinking a company with a workplace culture described in these harsh terms is destined for failure. Yet, one such company recently nearly doubled its operating income, increased its annual revenue by 27 percent, and turned in its eighth straight quarter of profitability.[1] What's more, the company tops the lists of many customer service awards, holds the No. 2 spot on LinkedIn's Top Companies list to work for,[2] and added more than 85,000 employees in 2016.[3]

That company is Amazon—and the scathing comments I quote above were part of a 2015 *New York Times* article examining its workplace. The piece reported on the "sometimes-punishing aspects" of Amazon's culture and its "purposeful Darwinism" approach to managing staff. It shared stories of employees crying at their desks, suffering from incredible stress, struggling to keep up with the intense pace at Amazon—or being fired for failing to meet the exacting standards and metrics set by management.[4]

Not surprisingly, the article stirred up an emotional response. Some readers and former employees called the retailer a workplace bully. But others came to Amazon's defense, notably some existing employees. Many commented on the thrill of working in such a fast-paced environment, on how much they learned in a short time, on how grateful they were to be pushed to excel; and on the pride they felt achieving innovations once thought impossible.[5]

Amazon's workplace culture is not for everyone—that much was exposed by the article. But its own employees' response revealed something else: a company's culture does not need to be "warm and fuzzy" to be effective. If you look beyond the attention-grabbing elements of the *New York Times* article, you see that the company's constant drive for innovation, rooted in a competitive, demanding, exacting organizational culture, has a lot to do with its success. What some describe as a "gladiator culture"[6] is the very way CEO Jeff Bezos and other company leaders ensure Amazon managers clearly define their goals and meet them. Standards that seem unreasonably high are the tools by which Amazon managers drive their teams to deliver ever-increasing levels of service to customers.

But Amazon doesn't succeed simply because of its supposedly "brutal" or high-demanding culture any more than a company would succeed by promoting a culture that coddles employees. The company succeeds because it has a single, unifying drive behind its internal culture and its external brand. Amazon's distinctive organizational culture fosters a performance-driven environment that fires up employees to innovate in pursuit of an outstanding, continuously-improving customer experience. Its brand identity is based on delivering that same disruptively innovative customer experience.

It is the fusion of Amazon's culture and brand that powers this amazing company. Everyone is singularly focused on one thing: excellence on behalf of the customer. No one needs to expend extra energy figuring out what to do or how to behave to achieve what Amazon wants its brand to stand for in the world. Customers have rewarded the organization's single determination with their esteem, loyalty, and more importantly, dollars. And employees have recognized Amazon's distinct culture by making it one of the most desired companies to work for.

Amazon is a perfect example of what I call *brand-culture fusion*—the full integration and alignment of external brand identity and internal organizational culture that explains the success of the world's greatest companies. Instead of treating brand and culture as separate entities, savvy business leaders like Amazon's Bezos power their companies' performance by fusing together their brand and culture. You can too.

THE UNSUNG DRIVERS OF BUSINESS

In nuclear physics, fusion is the reaction that happens when two atomic nuclei come together. Nuclear fusion releases large amounts of energy—it's what powers the sun. When fused, the two nuclei create something entirely new.

In the same way, you can unleash great power when you fuse together your organization's two nuclei: your culture—the way the people in your organization behave and the attitudes and beliefs that inform them (i.e., "the way we do things around here")—and your brand or brand identity, how your organization is understood by customers and other stakeholders. Culture involves so much more than perks and parties, and brands are built by so much more than ads and public relations. But until recently, culture and brand were often seen as the "soft stuff" in business, often relegated to human resources and marketing efforts, respectively. Today, many leaders are starting to recognize what astute ones have known all along: culture and brand are the nuclei of their organizations, the biggest drivers of the hard results they must produce every day.

Culture is not incidental or incremental to business performance—it is instrumental. In *People First Leadership: How the Best Leaders Use Culture and Emotion to Drive Unprecedented Results*, Eduardo Braun, former director of the World Business Forum, shares his experience interviewing business leaders from around the world. He was struck as he heard leader after leader—from Jack Welch, GE's former CEO, to Virgin Group founder Richard Branson—point to culture as their primary competitive advantage. Their common refrain, he writes, was, "Culture multiplies results."[7] Braun goes on to recount the words of Jim Collins, the best-selling author on leadership. In the prologue of *Dream Big* by Cristiane Correa, Collins explains that "culture is not part of the strategy. Culture *is* the strategy."[8]

When Herb Kelleher, founder and former CEO of Southwest Airlines, was asked what differentiated his airline—which had posted forty-four consecutive years of profits while never executing a layoff—from other companies, he pointed to Southwest's culture as its key competitive advantage. "Our competitors can get all the hardware," he said. "I mean, Boeing will sell them the planes. But it's the software, so to speak—the people—that's hard to imitate."[9] Data from the Great Place to Work organization supports all these leaders' beliefs in the power of a strong culture. The data shows great workplaces benefit from stronger financial performance, reduced turnover, and better customer satisfaction than their peers.[10]

Culture is a powerful antidote to the unprecedented threats most organizations face today. A large body of research has shown that a lack of employee engagement plagues today's business world. Most notably, in 2017, the Gallup organization found that 70 percent of workers are unengaged. A healthy culture helps increase employee engagement and productivity—and the likelihood employees will stay at a company.[11] Many businesses also operate in sectors where a war for talent rages, and ratings on websites like LinkedIn and Glassdoor greatly influence prospective employees' perceptions of companies. An attractive culture can be a powerful magnet to compel the best candidates to join a company.

As they have with culture, savvy business leaders are learning to see their brands as value creation tools. Companies with strong brands operate more profitably and are valued at levels much higher than their estimated future cash flows and assets alone would suggest. Having worked on some of the world's greatest brands, including Sony, Frito-Lay, and Oakley, I've witnessed firsthand how a strong brand can become the key weapon in a company's competitive arsenal. As market saturation has made it increasingly difficult for any one company to sustain product leadership over time and to differentiate its brand on product features or performance alone, a definitive brand identity expressed through superior customer experiences can help build long-term customer relationships and maintain higher profit margins.

Independently, culture and brand are powerful, often unsung, business drivers. But when you fuse the two—when you create an interdependent and mutually reinforcing relationship between how your organization thinks and acts on the inside and how it is perceived and experienced on the outside—you create new growth that isn't possible by simply cultivating one or the other alone.

THE POWER OF FUSION

Fully integrating and aligning your brand and culture produces meaningful, powerful results that affect your whole business. First, brand-culture fusion aligns your workforce, increasing the efficiency of your entire organization and the quality of your outcomes. Your people are less likely to function at cross-purposes or to use conflicting standards when working toward a clear, common goal.

Second, fusing together your brand and culture improves your organization's competitive advantage because it enables you to produce intangible value that is difficult to copy. Competitors may be able to match *what* you offer to customers and employees, but it's much harder for them to embody the unique *why* and *how* of what you do. As people increasingly make decisions about which companies to work for or to buy from based on meaning and shared values, deliberately linking your brand to your culture can increase your organization's perceived relevance, differentiation, and appeal.

Brand-culture fusion also ensures the authenticity of your brand. Customers are more savvy today. They see advertising rhetoric for what it is, and they no longer accept brands at face value. They are skeptical about the claims companies make. They want authenticity—brands that live up to their promises and stated ideals. But most companies simply slap "authenticity" on their list of brand attributes and try to engage customers superficially via social media to appear more humane or relatable. These efforts to create a more authentic brand image rarely convince customers. People don't want brands to *appear* authentic, they want brands to demonstrate that they actually *are* authentic in the way they operate and the customer experiences they deliver. By aligning and integrating your culture and brand, you truly are on the inside what you say you are on the outside—and you pass the customer test of brand authenticity.

Finally, and perhaps most important, brand-culture fusion allows you to move your organization toward its vision more successfully, since it provides a common motivation and focus for everyone in your organization. When you align the values and behaviors of your employees with what is expected and experienced by your customers, you attract and retain employees who feel an emotional commitment to your company *and* brand. They understand the meaning behind their work, so they work hard to fulfill the company's purpose. They feel more connected to other employees because everyone is united by common goals. And they feel more connected to your customers because they understand and believe in the ultimate value your organization wants to create for those customers.

As powerful as brand-culture fusion is to a company, its absence can affect an organization more strongly—even if that impact is less immediate and obvious.

When your brand and culture are not aligned and integrated, your culture-building efforts are likely to go to waste. Many leaders are led to think that they must pamper and pander to their staff because conventional wisdom says that employees are your greatest asset. But as Gregg Lederman, CEO of the employee engagement firm Brand Integrity, observes, they're not: "The right employees who have the passion and knowledge to do the *right* things at work are."[12]

Start-ups, for example, are notorious for taking extraordinary measures to create a "fun" workplace environment and to give "cool" benefits to employees—like providing free lunches, stocking their break rooms with beer kegs and foosball tables, or offering free gym memberships. There is nothing wrong with providing great perks for your employees and being generous with your benefits.* But while these

---

* Some perks aren't as effective at motivating employees as they might seem. A study on millennials in the workplace by Qualtrics, an experience research platform, found that free food is one of least important elements of culture. "Catered lunches might boost employee morale once in a while," Qualtrics CEO and founder Ryan Smith says, "but it's a losing strategy if you're trying to help your employees feel like they're an integral

perks might do a great job of making people feel good, they alone do not necessarily build a culture that cultivates the specific behaviors and skills that a company needs to succeed. Social media software start-up Buffer, for example, struggled to achieve profitability because its openhanded cultural practices, including offering extra vacation days and paying for yoga classes, ate away at cash flow instead of producing employees who were prepared to deliver great customer experiences.[13]

If your culture and brand are mismatched, you can also end up with happy, productive employees who produce the wrong results. Many well-known brands have engaged me to improve their brand position and increase their competitive advantage. I've helped many well-known brands build their brands and realize strong gains. But they're often held back from sustained success by a culture that's out of step with their desired brand identity.

At a large grocery store chain I worked with, for example, employees were steeped in a culture that valued efficiency and productivity. As the industry shifted toward customer service and merchandising, the company needed to make its brand known more for the service and experience it offered. But its employees were so focused on increasing inventory turns and sales per square foot that the company fell behind. The culture of this organization, though vibrant and vital, was holding it back from serving its customers well, evolving its brand image, and therefore thriving in the long run.

Ultimately, a disconnect between what your organization values on the inside and how it is perceived on the outside can damage customer relationships. This is precisely what happened when a former employee wrote a blog post exposing a culture of sexism and sexual harassment at Uber. Beyond being offensive in general, the revelations

---

part of a thriving organization." And Dennis Eusebio, design leader at Tuft & Needle, says that perks can end up being like a "siren song." They have "diminishing returns," he writes in *Entrepreneur*. Employees find, he says, that "you simply don't value a foosball table as much the tenth time you've played as the first time." (Sources: Smith, Ryan. "Free Food Is a Poor Excuse for Company Culture." *Fortune*, June 10, 2015. http://fortune.com/2015/06/10/ryan-smith-retaining-employees/. Eusebio, Dennis. "Why Office Perks Are Traps, Not Benefits." *Entrepreneur*, February 16, 2017. https://www.entrepreneur.com/article/289056.)

about Uber's organizational culture offended customers to such a great degree in part because they uncovered the disconnect between what they loved about Uber's brand identity—its populist ethos, progressive character, and heroic role—and the discriminatory, primitive, and predatory behavior that characterized Uber's internal operations. The lack of alignment and integrity between Uber's culture and brand eroded its customers' trust and esteem of the company. In comparison, the highly competitive culture that the *New York Times* exposed at Amazon ultimately made sense to customers who, whether they approved of it or not, could see how the company's culture produced the benefits they enjoyed.*

WHY COMPANIES FAIL TO BUILD GREAT BRANDS AND CULTIVATE GREAT CULTURES

I've been helping companies of all sizes and types accelerate their growth by building strong brands for more than twenty-five years. In that time, I've discovered that, despite the incredible value of an integrated and aligned brand and culture, most organizations not only separate them as if the two have nothing to do with each other, but also go about building and cultivating them the wrong way.

When it comes to building brands, leaders typically expect their marketing departments to promote awareness, create images, and send messages. The high visibility of advertising and promotions—and the pervasiveness of social media channels in recent years—gives them the impression that they should, indeed, elevate the brand communication function. But growth in brand equity and influence comes from an

---

* At the time of this writing, a new CEO at Uber has just been named. The new leader faces the formidable challenge of repairing Uber's brand identity and culture. Doing so will require balancing two potentially conflicting forces: restoring the stability the company needs to regain the trust of customers, employees, and other stakeholders, while reinvigorating the bold and convention-breaking culture it needs to fuel innovation and reclaim a leadership position. I will continue to provide perspectives on Uber and other companies in this book as new developments unfold. Go to **http://deniseleeyohn.com/fusion** for my latest insights.

entirely different way of thinking about and using brands: it comes from leaders driving everything their organization does with a clear, focused, distinctive brand identity—what they want the brand to be known for.

In other words, great brands are built from the inside out. The power of a business to create value in the world is unleashed from inside the organization, not by promoting an image on the outside. You build a great brand by operationalizing it—by using your brand purpose, values, and positioning to develop strategy and guide operations, so that your brand isn't just what you *say*, it's what you *do*.

My first book, *What Great Brands Do: The Seven Brand-Building Principles that Separate the Best from the Rest*, unpacked this powerful "brand-as-business" management approach to brand-building. I explained that when you start brand-building *inside* your organization, you unleash your brand's full potential. After the book was published, I heard from so many leaders who had discovered that closing the gap between building their brands and managing their businesses was the secret to brand success they had been searching for.

With *FUSION*, I hope to crack the code to culture-building for you in a similar way. Culture-building is all too often misunderstood. As I've spoken to executives around the world over the past decade, I've met leaders who incorrectly assume that there is a "right" kind of culture—a warm and benevolent one—that works in all companies to produce happy, productive employees. I've met leaders who champion culture-building tactics that don't align with or even seem relevant to their business goals. Leaders who think culture-building is exclusively the purview of the human resources department to work on through recruiting, training and development, compensation, and benefits. Leaders who try to improve their culture by giving employees perks and throwing parties, which these days are mere table stakes for most employees. Leaders who believe culture is out of their control—that it grows organically—so they shrug off any responsibility for cultivating it at all.

It is true that culture can't be imposed. As a leader, you can't force people to think or behave a certain way. And the role of culture is changing. Paul Michelman, editor in chief of *MIT Sloan Management Review*, argues in a piece titled "The End of Corporate Culture as We

Know It" that "when we look ahead to life in the digital matrix, there is reason to question culture's role. Our relationships to institutions will become increasingly defined by the activity in which we are engaged at any given time.... We will weave in and out of relationships, working interchangeably with those who belong to the same organization and those who do not." He concludes that such an environment has less need for conformity and that the tools meant to reinforce consistency of behavior can transform culture "from a motor to an anchor."[14]

His point raises an important distinction: Your culture should produce unity, not uniformity, within your workforce. You want to set up your organization to operate in a particular, but not necessarily predictable, fashion. Your approach should be to lay down guardrails that prescribe boundaries, not tracks that dictate behavior. But you absolutely can and should set the conditions to cultivate an organizational culture that deeply influences the way your employees perform daily.

If you have responsibility and oversight for the core operations of your business and set the tone and direction for your company—either as a leader or C-level executive of your organization—then this book is for you. I hope *FUSION* will change the attitudes about building brand and culture of managers at all levels of an organization, but as with all corporate priorities, leadership is required from the top. While human resources and marketing executives, who see an opportunity to make a bigger impact on their companies can use the insights and tools in this book to integrate their efforts, they alone cannot drive the change of the scope that's required to achieve brand-culture fusion. Only you at the top of your organization can make brand-culture fusion a priority by setting top strategies to support it, directing resources and attention to it, and holding your people accountable for achieving it.

You must accept the challenge to lead your organization to greatness. That doesn't mean, though, that you need to cultivate a "nice" culture or the one "right" culture that helps every company succeed—there's no such thing. Every organization is different and so is its culture. A culture that fuels one company's brand-culture fusion might backfire completely at yours. Amazon's Bezos explained it best in his 2015 letter to shareholders. He wrote, "If it's a distinctive culture, it will fit certain people like a custom-made glove.... We never claim that our approach is the right one—just that it's ours—and over the last two decades, we've collected a large group of like-minded people. Folks who find our approach energizing and meaningful."[15]

You must cultivate a distinct culture that is fully aligned with your brand identity—that is so well integrated with it that it is hard to distinguish what you do internally from who you say you are externally. Cultivating such culture will allow you to achieve the kind of brand-culture fusion that has propelled companies like Amazon to greatness.

I wrote this book to show you how.

A BLUEPRINT FOR BRAND-CULTURE FUSION

FUSION examines some of the world's greatest organizations and reverse engineers their greatness. By unpacking case studies, sharing insights from interviews with industry leaders, reporting on findings from respected academic research, and drawing on my experience working with extraordinary brands across a broad range of sectors, including retail, healthcare, packaged goods, and technology, I explain how great companies achieve the brand-culture fusion that creates extraordinary results and growth so that you can, too.

In Part 1, I show you how to lay the groundwork for brand-culture fusion, starting with identifying and clearly articulating a single overarching purpose and one set of core values of your organization, the focus of Chapter 1, **Set Your Sole Purpose and Core Values**. In Chapter 2, **Assess Your Brand-Culture Fusion**, I then explain how to determine your "desired culture"—the culture you ought to cultivate to support and advance your brand identity—or the brand identity you'd like to evolve to. You'll also have an opportunity to assess how far off you are from your desired culture and to pinpoint where you need to make changes in your brand or culture (or both) to fuse them together.

The final step in laying the foundation for brand-culture fusion—taking ownership of the process—is laid out in Chapter 3, **Lead the Change**. As a leader of your organization, you must take responsibility for achieving fusion. Even if implementing specific changes to produce fusion falls to the leaders of functional areas, you must initiate and champion them across the board. And you must ensure all other leaders and managers are actively engaged in and accountable for cultivating the desired culture and making on-brand decisions.

In Part 2, I provide five strategies for aligning brand and culture. If your company is like most, your culture is probably less developed or defined than your brand. That's why the first four strategies focus on cultivating your desired culture by aligning it with your existing brand identity as the main path to achieve brand-culture fusion. The final strategy—designed with companies that have a well-entrenched or powerful culture in mind—focuses on leveraging your existing culture to change your brand and thus align both. The five strategies are:

1. **Organize and Operate On-Brand:** Implement an organizational design and run your operations to give your organization the structure and processes necessary to operationalize your culture.

2. **Create Culture-Changing Employee Experiences:** Deliberately design and manage your company's employee experience—just as you would customer experiences—so that every facet of an employee's journey throughout his or her connection to your organization encourages and enables your desired culture.

3. **Sweat the Small Stuff**: Ensure even the most mundane or minute aspect of your organization—from its "rituals" and "artifacts" (things your organization regularly does and creates to commemorate or symbolize important achievements or events) to its policies and procedures—advances and supports your desired culture.

4. **Ignite Your Transformation:** Use employee brand engagement tactics—stage employee brand engagement experiences, launch creative communications campaigns, and develop and deploy employee brand engagement toolkits—to kick-start the fusion process and then to regain focus and momentum when necessary.

5. **Build Your Brand from the Inside Out**: If your culture is so powerful or established that it doesn't make sense to try to change it to achieve brand-culture fusion, leverage your existing culture to define or re-define your brand identity.

For each of these strategies, I'll provide analyses and tools and share the stories of great organizations—including Airbnb, Adobe, Nike, MGM Resorts, Salesforce, and many more—that have successfully integrated their brands and cultures, so you can be inspired and equipped to achieve brand-culture fusion at your company. Leading companies like Starbucks, Southwest Airlines, and Virgin Group have been implementing these strategies for years, but no one has examined their successes through the lens of brand and culture alignment and integration, nor has anyone deconstructed the process for achieving it...until now.

After reading *FUSION*, you will know how to cultivate a unique, flourishing culture that:

- Creates continuity and consistency by perpetuating key norms across your people and over time
- Reduces uncertainty and confusion by establishing a guide to action for your people
- Creates social meaning and order within your organization by making clear what is expected of your staff and why
- Builds a collective identity and commitment by binding your employees together
- Produces the capability for customer experience excellence by fostering the necessary mindset, decisions, and behaviors
- Makes possible your vision of the future by energizing your organization and moving it toward your goals

I'm excited to lay out the complete blueprint for brand-culture fusion that I've discovered.

EVERY ORGANIZATION NEEDS FUSION

Certain circumstances present a clear call for brand-culture fusion:

- You're being outperformed in your category.
- Your brand value seems to be declining.
- You're experiencing high turnover or low recruitment success.

- Your employee or customer surveys show lots of room for improvement.
- Your financial performance is shaky or unpredictable.

Perhaps you are experiencing some—or all—of these issues right now. They usually result from a weak culture, weak brand, or both—and you can fix the problem by building strong brand-culture alignment and integration. To get started, you need little more than an awareness of your situation and the conviction to remedy it. But organizational readiness for change and resources that can be redirected to the cause will accelerate your ability to produce results.

Virtually every type of organization can benefit from fusion. Although larger, B2C (business-to-consumer) companies have been more likely to engage in brand- and culture-building in the past, the importance of brand and culture as vital components of any organization has been gaining wider ground. If you don't think integrating brand and culture is important to your company, think again. Brand-culture fusion has the potential to improve the competitiveness and accelerate the growth of almost any organization, regardless of its size or type, including:

B2B (business-to-business) companies: The integration and alignment of brand and culture is critical in B2B organizations because employees are highly involved with customers during the sales process and throughout the product service and support cycle. In the case of consulting and other professional services firms, employees often *are* the product themselves. In fact, Laurie Young, author of *Marketing the Professional Services Firm*, has concluded that the day-to-day client-facing activities of employees are "probably the most influential aspects of building a professional services brand."[16] So in many B2B companies, culture is on display to customers much more clearly through people's attitudes and behaviors. That's why B2B organizations may need brand-culture fusion more than most. You'll learn how B2B businesses including Salesforce, GE, and others have recognized their need to integrate their brand and culture and pursued it.

Start-ups: Culture-building isn't something that only large, established companies need to attend to. David Cummings, cofounder of marketing automation company Pardot, believes "culture is insanely important for startups." He should know: Pardot was on *Inc.* magazine's fastest-growing-company list in 2012 and was acquired for just under $100 million only five years after its founding. "[Culture] is the cohesion that holds you together. For a lot of startups, culture is haphazard, and then all of a sudden they have 20 employees. The employees start grating on each other and they don't work well together. To be sustainable, culture has to be intentional."[17] As I share the stories of companies such as Airbnb and Nike, you'll see that their leaders made brand-culture fusion a priority from their earliest days.

Small businesses: If you own or a lead a small business, there are two primary reasons why brand-culture fusion can benefit your organization. First, the limited resources that constrain most small businesses require that everything you do be more productive. When your organization's culture and brand are aligned and integrated, a single effort—a piece of communication such as a newsletter or a special event like a community-service activity—can produce results inside and out. And second, brand-culture fusion can help you get greater clarity on your priorities and navigate the countless new ideas and ventures that present themselves to small-businesspeople. By using your brand and culture as decision-making filters, instead of simply reacting to challenges or opportunities that rise unexpectedly, you can drive more sustainable growth. You'll learn from small businesses such as BELAY, a virtual staffing firm based in Atlanta; Traction, an interactive agency in San Francisco; and Tower, a beach lifestyle company in San Diego.

Nonprofit organizations: Brand-culture fusion is particularly important for nonprofit organizations that must align the needs of beneficiaries, donors, volunteers, and sometimes governments or regulatory groups in addition to employees. Brand-culture fusion transcends and unites all of these groups and can be further leveraged if you design and manage explicit experiences for each of them. By introducing you to City Year, an organization that helps students stay in school and on

track to graduate, and Plant With Purpose, which helps reverse deforestation and poverty around the world, I will demonstrate the power of
integrating brand and culture in the nonprofit sector.

Brand-culture fusion even accelerates the success of organizations in
which the traditional notion of "brand" doesn't seem to apply. Brands
are not the sole purview of commercial enterprises—they can be used
by all sorts of organizations to engage the people involved with them
inside and out. Whether yours is a highly technical company or a
scientific institution, a public-sector agency, or even an academic or
faith-based organization, your culture should still be integrated with
your external identity—your brand—to help you achieve your goals.

LEAD YOUR FUSION

Integrating brand and culture can help your organization thrive and
grow over time—but only if you actively nurture and continually reinforce it. Often leaders turn to culture- and brand-building only after
their organization has experienced a crucible or crisis. But the time to
integrate your brand and culture is now, while you have the bandwidth,
resources, and employee goodwill necessary to do so. Brand-culture
fusion acts like glue, binding your organization together; it may be the
only thing that can get it through hard times.

Brand-culture fusion is a never-ending responsibility—a leader's
responsibility. My sincere hope is that this book will fundamentally
shift how you think of brand- and culture-building—from side tasks
to be delegated as marketing and human resources functions to fundamental business priorities that deserve your attention and care.

Achieving brand-culture fusion is a journey. Start today.

PART 1

THE FOUNDATIONS OF BRAND-CULTURE FUSION

Just as you can't build a great building on a weak foundation, you can't build a great organization without a strong foundation that's established by setting your purpose and values, understanding the current state of brand-culture fusion in your company, and taking charge.

CHAPTER 1

SET YOUR SOLE PURPOSE AND CORE VALUES

Read this chapter to learn:

- Why your organization needs an overarching purpose and how to develop a powerful one
- Why your organization needs one set of core values for its internal culture and external brand identity
- How to evaluate and activate your core values

Why do we exist? This is the most important question an organization must ask itself—and the question that got Phil Knight through some of his darkest days when he started the company that would become Nike. Faced with mortgaging his house, making a "deal with a devil" (a hostile supplier), and begging for yet another loan from his bank, Knight kept coming back to why he was willing to sacrifice so much. "I believed in running," he writes in his memoir, *Shoe Dog*. "I believed that if people got out and ran a few miles every day, the world would be a better place, and I believed these shoes were better to run in."[1]

Even as a young, scrappy entrepreneur selling shoes out of his parents' basement, Knight understood the importance of having a compelling purpose that would not only sustain him through Nike's early days but eventually inspire millions of Nike's customers and employees. Today that purpose continues to inform what Nike calls its "mission," the driving force behind its brand and corporate culture: "Bring inspiration and innovation to every athlete* in the world. *If you have a body, you are an athlete."*[2]

Nike's renowned advertising tagline, "Just Do It," translated that mission into a brand message that has bonded customers to the Nike brand for years. Just as important, the mission—and the company's "11 Maxims," which include guiding principles such as "simplify and go" and "evolve immediately"[3]—have served as the core of the organization's internal culture through the years as well.

Today Nike executives use its mission and maxims to set the tone within the organization. When issues of race, violence, and policing rocked the U.S. in 2016, for instance, CEO Mark Parker referenced the company's mission in a letter he penned to employees to explain Nike's response to the events. He wrote, "To serve *every* [emphasis mine] athlete individually and completely, across hundreds of countries where we do business, we need teams that reflect the diversity of our consumers and a culture of inclusivity that respects the communities in which we live and work."[4]

Nike's mission and maxims also pervade its designers' thinking. Tinker Hatfield, one of Nike's most influential and esteemed shoe designers, explains, "Our future really revolves around how we can improve the lives of athletes and just people running around in the streets. So we're asking ourselves all the time: What can we do to improve what we've done in the past?"[5] And Nike's innovating and inspiring spirit isn't only embraced by people working on its products. "We've consciously tried to be innovative in all areas of the business," Knight once said, "and right now that means advertising. We need a way of making sure people hear our message through all the clutter...

---

* The asterisk and corresponding footnote is based on Nike cofounder Bill Bowerman's belief that "everyone has a body and is therefore a potential athlete" and expresses how universal the company believes its mission is. (Source: Nike. "Mission Statement." Accessed August 22, 2017. https://help-en-us.nike.com/app/answer/a_id/113.)

that means innovative advertising—but innovative in a way that captures the athletes' true nature."[6]

Just as Nike's mission is to bring inspiration and innovation to every athlete, Andre Martin, the company's chief learning officer, says his mission is to bring inspiration and innovation to every employee. He wants "to unleash human potential and help employees own their own career and get them ready for key transitions so everyone in the organization can do more work that matters." To achieve this goal, training at the company is designed around Nike's mission and maxims, not only to reaffirm them to every employee but also to ensure the training develops employees who keep them—and therefore the culture—alive.[7]

Nike has used its unifying purpose (its mission) and its motivating core values (its maxims) to grow from Phil Knight's fledgling business on the brink of bankruptcy into a $100 billion global enterprise[8] and the world's most valuable sports brand.[9] They are the foundation of both Nike's brand identity *and* its organizational culture—the crux of Nike's brand-culture fusion—and the key to its success.

While Nike's example shows the power of having one overarching purpose and one set of values that inform both the organization's culture *and* its brand identity, few organizations have achieved this level of alignment and integration. In fact, most business leaders often separate their business and organization's purpose and values from those of their brand. The result is a disconnect between how the organization behaves on the inside and how it is perceived on the outside.

To make brand-culture fusion happen, you must articulate a single overarching purpose and one set of core values to drive, align, and guide everything your company does internally and externally. In this chapter, I'll show you how to develop them the right way.

OVERARCHING PURPOSE: YOUR "WHY"

A company's purpose is its why—*why* it does what it does, *why* it exists. Having a meaningful purpose or being a "purpose-driven" company has become a popular notion in business today, and with good reason. In today's cluttered, ultracompetitive, choice-overloaded world, each company must have a clear reason for being. You need to play an invaluable, irreplaceable role in people's lives, and you must live out that purpose convincingly or your customers can easily be lured away by any one of your more deliberate competitors.

Likewise, many employees—especially millennials, who comprise the largest group of workers today—want to work for companies that have a strong sense of purpose beyond making money.[10] When explaining why her company has been included on *Fortune's* 100 Best Companies to Work For list, Autodesk's human resources chief Jan Becker, says people usually praise her company for the employee benefits it offers, such as six-week paid sabbaticals and its extraordinary office designs. But when she meets with Autodesk employees, she says, "I commonly hear that they're most excited about having meaningful impact on the world around us, the innovation occurring every day in our offices around the world, and how they are developing technology that is helping everybody imagine, design, and create a better world."[11]

When articulated and implemented well, a compelling purpose shapes culture by engaging employees, even those prone to be skeptical or apathetic, and making their work more meaningful. And purpose can unite even the most diverse and distributed workforce by serving as a driving force that transcends the silos and divisions that inevitably form in organizations. Virgin Group founder Richard Branson believes purpose is essential to engaging employees who are expected to work longer hours and with greater commitment. "Purpose is no longer a buzzword. It's a must-have," he says. "Passion and purpose will keep people focused on the job at hand, and ultimately separate the successful from the unsuccessful."[12]

Most business leaders know they should promote a purpose for their organization, but most also go about it the wrong way. The typical mission statement outlines the scope of the business—what the organization does, produces, or sells—and sets a goal to achieve certain financial targets or create value for shareholders. For example, a typical mission statement might read, "To build shareholder value by delivering pharmaceutical and healthcare products, services, and solutions in innovative and cost-effective ways." Often these same organizations will express a separate purpose or essence for their brand that describes what they want it to be known for. For example, that same company might want their brand identity to stand for safety and trust-worthiness. Both purposes describe worthy aspirations but they don't seem to have anything to do with each other.

Another example: A bookstore chain claims, "Our mission is to operate the best specialty retail business in America, regardless of the product we sell," but its brand purpose "to promote a love for books and reading" reveals a narrower interest. Or consider a company that aspires to industry-leading profitability as a business and yet prom-ises generous service to all customers as a brand. These disconnects between business and brand purpose often cause confusion for people in the organization, especially when they seem at odds.

Setting financial targets and clarifying your business footprint are necessary to set the expectations of investors, business partners, and other stakeholders, but you shouldn't separate them from the way you engage and motivate your primary ones: customers and employees. The purpose of your business and the purpose of your brand should be seamlessly inte-grated, tightly aligned, and articulated as a single overarching purpose.

Traditional management theory differentiates between an organi-zation's purpose (its reason for being), vision (its desired future), and mission (how it achieves its vision or fulfills its purpose). But it's not necessary to articulate all three of them in separate statements, which can be quite confusing to your employees. A single statement that articulates a single purpose for your business and brand works best. It's clear, simple, and easy to remember.*

One way to arrive at a sole overarching purpose is by examin-ing your company's higher purpose—its purpose beyond making money. Sometimes this might lead you to articulate a socially- or environmentally-conscious purpose, as has been the case with the new generation of leaders who have taken the helm of some of today's leading companies. For example, in a 2016 *Fast Company* article about the role of business in society, Facebook founder and CEO Mark Zuckerberg

---

* To keep it simple in this book, I use "purpose" to refer to any one of the three types of statements in the examples I discuss, regardless of the term that the organization might use.

explains, for example, that his company "was built to accomplish a social mission—to make the world more open and connected."[13]

But a higher purpose doesn't necessarily have to be a socially-responsible one. Nike's purpose to "bring innovation and inspiration to every athlete" and Amazon's purpose to become "Earth's most customer-centric company"[14] transcend their profit-making goals without claiming to create a benefit for society in general.

Note that embracing a higher purpose doesn't dull your organization's ability to create a high-performing, profitable business. In fact, several companies with a higher purpose prove just the opposite: Amazon's market value increased 1,934 percent between 2006 and 2016, while every other major retailer's value declined.[15] Starbucks, whose purpose reads "to inspire and nurture the human spirit—one person, one cup, and one neighborhood at a time,"[16] is one of the most profitable companies in its industry. "Caring for the world, one person at a time"[17] has guided Johnson & Johnson's business and brand through the years—and helped it consistently outperform the U.S. stock market since its IPO in 1944.[18]

It's not enough to simply state an overarching purpose by identifying the mark you want to make in the world; you must operate your company so that it becomes known—internally and externally—for it. Zuckerberg has achieved this coherence with his company purpose—"to make the world more open and connected." It's one of the cornerstones of the company's culture as well as how he runs the business. "We believe that a more open world is a better world because people with more information can make better decisions and have a greater impact," Zuckerberg explains. "That goes for running our company as well. We work hard to make sure everyone at Facebook has access to as much information as possible about every part of the company so they can make the best decisions and have the greatest impact."[19]

With a single overarching purpose, Zuckerberg creates enduring inspiration and motivation for people inside Facebook and out. Similarly, Henry Ford started his company to "build a car for the great multitude," and the company continues to thrive over 100 years later because the ethos of democratizing transportation resonates with employees and customers. The purpose of the *New York Times*—to be the news authority—has also fueled that company's culture and brand for over 160 years.

An overarching purpose can power your company to sustained success too.

Pinpoint Your Purpose

To identify your overarching purpose, go deep and think big. Steve Jobs wanted to put a dent in the universe.[20] What difference in the world are you being called to make? What do you want your organization's legacy to be? Sometimes it's helpful to go back to your company's founder and revisit why he or she started it in the first place. And consider what would be missing—or how the world would be worse off—if your organization no longer existed.

You can use several established exercises and approaches to formulate your overarching purpose:

Five Whys exercise. Jim Collins and Jerry I. Porras, authors of the seminal book *Built to Last*, recommend getting at your purpose by starting with a descriptive statement such as "We make X products" or "We deliver X services," and then asking, "Why is that important?" five times, each time asking the question in response to the previous answer. In a *Harvard Business Review* article, Collins and Porras describe using this technique to help a market research company uncover its deeper, richer purpose. In a working session with company executives, they started the process by describing what the company's most basic purpose was: "To provide the best market-research data available." Then they asked them *why* providing the best market-research data available is important. After continuing to ask "Why?" in response to their answers, the executives concluded that their company's ultimate purpose was "to contribute to our customers' success by helping them understand their markets." Porras and Collins observe, "The five whys can help companies in any industry frame their work in a more meaningful way."[21]

Random Corporate Serial Killer game. In this exercise, also designed by Porras and Collins, you are challenged to think about what would be lost if your company ceased to exist—and why it's important that it endures. Gather colleagues and ask them to imagine that you could sell your company to someone for a fair price while guaranteeing stable employment for your employees after the sale. Ask them also to imagine that the buyer plans to completely kill the company after purchasing it—its products and services would be discontinued, operations would be shut down, brand names would be dropped, etc. Then ask them if they would still be willing to sell the company, and why or why not. This exercise, Porras and Collins write, is a particularly powerful technique to help you uncover your company's purpose beyond that of merely maximizing shareholder wealth.[22]

Think. Feel. Do. exercise. Think. Feel. Do. is a Thematic Apperception "Test" (TAT) borrowed from the world of psychology that helps to reveal underlying motives, appeals, and concerns. Most TATs use ambiguous pictures of people and ask participants to make up narratives about the images. To use a TAT to help you uncover your company's purpose, convene a working session of your key executives and other stakeholders. Give each person two pictures of a stick figure, one representing a customer before your brand existed and another representing the customer after the brand launched (or before and after the customer becomes aware of your brand and tries it). Ask participants to come up with narratives about what the customer is thinking, feeling, and doing before and after. Ask participants to consider how the brand might have changed the customer's life—how he might relate to himself, other people, and his environments differently; what decisions he might make differently; and how he might spend his time or money differently. Review everyone's narratives, discussing the similarities between them and the reasons why they differ. The discussion will help you extract key themes that lead to an articulation of your purpose.

Whatever method you use, once you pinpoint your purpose, codify it. Collins and Porras argue that a company's purpose ought to be a way for you to put a stake in the ground about who you are, what you stand for, and what you're all about.[23] Don't assume that your people know it—write it down and share it.

Craft a Meaningful Purpose Statement

To codify your company's newfound purpose, craft a purpose statement that describes the impact you want to make on others—inside and outside your company. Your overarching purpose statement should be clear, pithy, and externally oriented. The purpose statements that drive some of the world's most admired brands reveal how a short, powerful phrase can aptly convey a company's reason for existing:

> Zappos: To deliver happiness to the world.[24]
> Sony: To create technologies that inspire people to dream and find joy.[25]
> Apple: To make a contribution to the world by making tools for the mind that advance humankind.[26]

These companies' aspirations are bold and inspiring yet definitive. They are not about changing the company by making better products or improving its service; these companies aim to make a bigger impact. But you don't have to be a large corporation or operate in emotionally-resonant sectors to have a compelling purpose. Consider examples from companies whose products or services may seem more mundane:

> Squarespace, a software-as-a-service-based content management system: Giving voice to ideas.[27]
> Xradia, provider of microscopy products for life sciences and materials research: To advance innovation, science, and industry by providing unique insight through superior X-ray imaging solutions.[28]
> Hagerty, an automotive insurance company: To protect the physical connections to the best moments in your life.[29]

Finally, ensure your purpose is relevant to your employees and resonates with them emotionally. Collins and Porras say, "A good purpose should serve to guide and inspire the organization."[30] To gauge how well your purpose would guide your people, consider whether or not you can explain how discrete business goals and strategies would help you achieve it. Evaluate its *focus*—how well does it direct everyone's efforts in a specific direction—and its *flexibility*—how much does it allow people to explore new opportunities and evolve your business as circumstances require. For example, the focus in Sony's purpose, "technologies that inspire people to dream and find joy," is to tap people's imagination and hopes and to lead them to enjoyment. Its purpose is also flexible because "technologies" doesn't connote any specific product, service, or solution. It suggests the company will take certain directions with its product development and marketing but it doesn't hem itself in.

Toronto-based marketing consultant Hilton Barbour captures the precise prescriptive nature of a powerful purpose: "The real opportunity doesn't lie in articulating what is allowed . . . but what is possible."[31]

....

YOUR OVERARCHING PURPOSE STATEMENT SHOULD BE:

- Clear
- Pithy
- Externally oriented
- Relevant
- Emotionally resonant
- Focused *and* flexible
- Guiding
- Inspiring
- Enduring

....

To gauge how inspirational your company's purpose is, Aston Business School professor Leslie de Chernatony suggests asking yourself what your employees would do if they won the lottery—would they quit their jobs or would they continue working to fulfill your company's purpose?[32] Mark di Somma, founder of change management firm the Audacity Group, recommends running the "tell me again" test. He advises imagining a time in the future when your grandchildren come to you and ask you to explain why you spent so much of your life working. Think about what answer they will most want to hear; what story will they want to hear again and again? "Will their interest match your purpose?" he challenges you to consider. He concludes, "A purpose that is not worth sharing is not worth having."[33]

One final note: Your company's purpose should be enduring—you shouldn't plan to change it. Porras and Collins studied companies such as Disney, Boeing, and Sony and observed that they have been pursuing their same purposes for decades, even as the companies' product offerings, markets of operation, and business models have changed dramatically from their inceptions. This is another reason why your purpose shouldn't be tied to a specific product or service.

Steve Morris, founder and CEO of brand strategy firm Mth Degree, recommends paying special attention to your purpose during times of change and transition, since that's when you need it to keep you focused and on track. "Change creates chaos," he says. "Chaos breeds fear. Fear can get you off course from your purpose."[34]

Sometimes, however, a deliberate change in your purpose is called for, as Facebook's founder Zuckerberg discovered in early 2017. In a speech, he explained that the scale at which his company grew and the global opportunities and challenges it faced required it to expand its purpose. "I used to think that if we just give people a voice and help some people connect that that would make the world a whole lot better by itself," he said. "[But] look around and our society is still so divided. We have a responsibility to do more, not just to connect the world but to bring the world closer together."[35]

So, set your purpose with the intent of using it as a North Star to orient your organization over time. But unlike an internally-focused, finance- or operations-driven purpose, an overarching purpose that aligns and integrates your business and your brand may eventually and naturally need to be reconsidered when the context in which you operate changes.

CORE VALUES: YOUR "HOW"

Once you have an overarching purpose in place to express the *why* of your company, you need core values to express the *how*. Core values are the essential and enduring principles and priorities that prescribe the desired mindset and behavior of everyone who works at your company.

Just as most business leaders understand the usefulness of having a well-articulated purpose for their organization, they also understand the importance of setting values for it. But all too often leaders develop a list of internal workplace values that are intended to guide employees' behaviors and decisions, and separately they come up with a list of desired brand attributes and values that describe the way they want their brand to be perceived by customers. The former is usually filled with generic platitudes, such as "we operate with integrity" or "we value respect and teamwork." The latter tends to be either so abstract (e.g., attributes such as authentic, fresh, cool) that most employees don't understand what it has to do with them or it is so aspirational that employees don't believe it.

It simply doesn't make sense to specify the values through which you engage your employees if those aren't linked to the way you want your employees to engage customers. Instead, you should bridge the gulf between organizational and brand values by using one set of core values to describe the unique way you do things on the inside and the outside.

Your values should function as the "operating instructions" of your organization—that is, they should inform, inspire, and instruct the day-to-day mindset and behaviors of your people. Your values should describe the collective attitudes and beliefs that you desire all employees to hold, translate those into specific actions and decisions that they should make, and then in turn show how those behaviors produce customer experiences that define and differentiate your brand.

Having a single set of core values results in tangible benefits. As researchers from Booz Allen Hamilton and Aspen Institute's Business and Society Program found, companies usually think of values as tools to improve employee retention and recruitment and to bolster corporate reputation. But their research also found that values can directly affect earnings and revenue growth if they're linked to the way the company actually operates. Companies they qualified as financial leaders tend to ensure their values are "prescriptive and explicit," are aligned with their strategies, and foster specific attitudes and behaviors that influence the company's growth and performance.[36]

The benefit of a single set of core values that is aligned with your external identity goes well beyond profits: it offers organizations clear guidance in the midst of a crisis or a crucible moment, as it did for Cincinnati, Ohio–based megachurch Crossroads Church. In 2008, during the opening night of its elaborate annual Christmas show, which attracts nearly 100,000 people, a young woman performing an aerial stunt fell to her death. The tragic incident stunned everyone at the scene, including the church's senior leadership team, who had been working backstage and throughout the auditorium. They didn't know what to do. "You're never prepared for those moments," recalls Darin Yates, chief operating officer.

After clearing the auditorium and notifying the woman's family, the team gathered in a conference room and spent the night praying and asking themselves "What is the right thing to do?"[37] They eventually decided to cancel the remaining performances and hold a "worship and celebration of life" ceremony the following night, inviting anyone who wanted to attend. Senior pastor Brian Tome led the event, which was attended by hundreds of people. Yates described how Tome, with tears falling, admitted to the attendees that the incident had shaken his faith. Tome recalled to local newspaper *WCPO*, "It had me questioning God."[38] His comments were a visceral display of one of the church's core values—authenticity—which Crossroads' "Culture Guide" defines this way: "Whether it's what happens on stage, within our serving teams or in our homes, we need to be able to share our faults and weaknesses."[39]

Tome told *WCPO* that "his public expression of how [the person's] death rocked his sense of faith drove some people away from Crossroads."[40] It was not the kind of response the church needed, especially after such a tragic event. But his decision to share his doubts and stay true to his organization's core value reinforced Crossroads' authentic identity to people inside and outside the organization. The church could not claim to be authentic if its people weren't willing to live that value and suffer the consequences. Hopefully the alignment of your values and brand identity won't be tested in a situation like this, but it should nonetheless be as resolute.

Identify Unique Values that Work Inside and Out

Setting your core values is a process of both identification and aspiration. Although values serve as general standards that your people should apply to specific situations while using their best judgment, you cannot dictate how employees should think or act. They're people, not robots. Trying to impose values on employees—especially millennial workers and those even younger who expect to participate in shaping their workplaces—is not particularly effective. Instead, your goal should be to illuminate the beneficial attitudes and behaviors that currently exist in your organization and to envision new ones that will help you align your internal culture with your external brand.

For example, when Sam Palmisano took the reins at IBM, he led a cultural renewal by first asking employees to identify IBM's enduring values, and then he activated newly-inspired values by conducting tests and collecting feedback from employees on how well they served the company. With the similar goal of capturing the values that operate within its walls, Zappos publishes an annual "Culture Book," a collection of unedited submissions from employees about what the culture at the company is really like and what it means to them. By sharing this Culture Book, everyone can learn which of its core values are strong and being lived out—as well as those that are not and need to be revisited or reinforced.

In Chapter 2, I will show you how to determine the core values that are right for you—including new values that do not currently exist in your organization—and introduce you to the Brand-Culture Fusion Assessment, an online tool to help you get started in doing so. But here, we'll go over how to evaluate the values that exist in your organization or those you eventually develop.

Effective values share a few common characteristics, starting with uniqueness. There isn't one *right* set of values for every organization. Instead, each organization should operate by *unique* values that contribute to its desired culture. What do I mean by unique?

First, *core* values should differ from *category* values, which all brands in any given category must adopt to be viable competitors. For example, all fast-food restaurants must embody the values of speed and convenience; all software makers must value reliability and ease of use. A fast-food restaurant that says it values speed...well, it's not saying anything different from any other fast-food restaurant. Differentiation is the key driver of brand power. Your company's core values must embody what makes your company uniquely "you"—what makes you stand out from others.

Second, for your company's values to be unique, the words or manner in which you choose to describe them must be distinctive. According to the Booz Allen Hamilton and Aspen Institute's Business and Society Program researchers, most corporate values incorporate similar words and ideas. Ninety percent of them reference ethical behavior or use the word "integrity," 88 percent mention commitment to customers, and 76 percent cite teamwork and trust.[41] Don't default to these overused terms. You can also differentiate your core values by expressing them differently from other companies who might hold somewhat similar beliefs. Use a style or voice that uniquely represents your organization. Doing so provides more than a veneer of differentiation; it makes your values more distinct because they embody the spirit and personality of your organization. If your core values are not expressed with distinct words and in a unique style, how likely are your employees to pay attention to, much less care about, values that seem commonplace and conventional?

Finally, your core values should also incorporate words that are active and actionable. Ann Rhoades, former chief people officer of Southwest Airlines, recommends spelling out behaviors that start with an action word and are "observable, assessable, trainable, hireable, and rewardable."[42] If your values are this explicit, they will most certainly impact employees' and ultimately customers' experiences.

Consider the way the following companies, large and small, B2B and B2C, articulate their core values distinctively to guide their employees and describe how they want customers to experience their brands:

- The WD-40 Company declares, "We value creating positive lasting memories in all of our relationships," and "We value making it better than it is today." [43] These statements are far more motivating and directive than the more commonplace values of "commitment" and "continuous improvement" that most companies default to.

- Google calls its values "Ten Things We Know to Be True." Even in the way it describes values as "things we know to be true," Google distinguishes itself. Instead of stating its commitment to customers in a generic way such as being "customer-focused," Google's values proclaim "focus on the user and all else will follow." In place of "have fun," Google's values statement declares "you can be serious without a suit." And instead of stating it values "quality," Google declares, "Great just isn't good enough." These differences are more than semantics. They reflect the spirit and personality with which the values were conceived— and are intended to be lived out.[44]
- Instead of simply listing "teamwork" as one of its values, Illumina, a life science technologies company, describes its commitment to it this way: "Deep collaboration allows us to compete in ways others cannot." In place of listing "transparency" as a value, Illumina's values statement explains, "We are open— physically and philosophically."[45]
- The values at Gazelles, a strategic planning consulting and coaching firm, include "practice what we preach" and "first class for less."[46] With such clear and cleverly-articulated values, Gazelle conveys its priorities and its unique personality.

As a litmus test of whether a core value represents the unique principles that shape your internal culture and external brand, ask yourself the following question: Could another company claim this value as its own and live it out in the same way we do? Many companies list "passion," "innovation," and "caring" as their values—and embody those values every day in expected ways such as developing new products and serving their customers with care. But if one of your values is to "deliver WOW Through Service," as is Zappos', you're claiming unique territory. "WOW" conveys the organization's personality and spirit. Your people know to deliver—and your customers expect to receive—service that is above and beyond what's called for and that triggers a visceral, emotional response.

Alternatively, ask yourself: Would any company select the opposite of your company's value as its own? Some companies might take the position that "done is better than perfect," while Google believes "great just isn't good enough." Both points of view are valid—and valued by different companies. If the opposite of your value is one that an organization would find inspiring or instructive, then that value you've identified can distinguish you in a powerful way.

Your company's core values must also work well as a collection; they must complement and support each other. "It's important to remember that values work in combination," advises Jörgen Andersson, former marketing director of international retailer H&M, in the book *Living the Brand* by Nicholas Ind. H&M's values—which include common sense, initiative, faith in individuals, cost awareness, and constant innovation—are highly correlated. For example, Jörgen explains, "There's no point in being very cost conscious if you don't apply common sense."[47] Think of your core values as pieces of a puzzle. Two values might contrast with each other like concave and convex puzzle pieces (e.g., humility and confidence, inspiration and pragmatism) but actually serve to balance each other and ultimately contribute to a cohesive culture.

Finally, like an overarching purpose, your values must inform both your culture as well as your brand. Consider how the companies mentioned above have embraced values that apply internally and externally: they don't expect their employees to adopt one set of attitudes and behaviors when they work with each other and another set of standards for the experiences they create for customers. The employees at the WD-40 Company value "creating positive lasting memories" when they run meetings and develop their teams, as well as when they create and deliver products to customers—even if those products are simply cans of lubricants that fix common problems so people are no longer bothered by them. As a core value, "creating positive lasting memories" aligns and connects what the company does on the inside to what it does on the outside.

....

YOUR CORE VALUES SHOULD BE:

- Unique
- Active
- Actionable
- Complementary

...and above all,

- Correlate with the customer experience you want to deliver

....

Once you've drafted your set of core values, here are some simple questions to ask yourself:

- Do these core values capture the essence of our culture and brand?
- Do they set us apart from companies like us?
- Do they help our employees understand how they are expected to think and act?
- Do they inspire behaviors that will differentiate our brand?
- Are they credible and can they be consistently applied?
- Do our employees want to be true to them? Will they want to stay true to them as our organization grows and markets change?

However well you set and define your unique core values, you shouldn't assume that your employees will understand what they mean or that everyone will interpret the same value into the same behavior. It's critical that you establish the desired behaviors or behavioral norms associated with your values so employees know what your values look like in action.

At Argentinian bank Banco Supervielle, Patricio Supervielle, chairman, CEO, and president, knew it was not enough to state his company's core values as "agile," "simple," and "friendly"—especially if he wanted to turn such common notions in the banking industry into a differentiating competitive advantage. So he and his colleagues engaged in a year-and-a-half road show to meet with all their managers and executives and flesh out what the core values meant. They defined the behaviors they expected employees to demonstrate for each value. For "simple," they specified "make decisions as close as possible to the customer" and for "friendly," they spelled out "respect the agreements reached." They also defined those behaviors they would not accept. For "agile," they spelled out that "setting unchallenging goals" and "ignoring mistakes and not learning from them" is unacceptable.[48] Supervielle acknowledges that "it is very hard to be consistent, to really walk the talk in every circumstance," but by so explicitly defining and describing the company's core values, he has made it a little easier.[49]

Live Out Your Values

Writing in a *Harvard Business Review* post, renowned business book author Patrick Lencioni explains the impact that values should have. "When properly practiced, values inflict pain," he says of the difficult decisions that values should lead companies to make, e.g., to exit a profitable business because it conflicts with the company's values or to let a top-performing sales representative go because she doesn't conform to them. "They make some employees feel like outcasts," he continues. "They limit an organization's strategic and operational freedom and constrain the behavior of its people. They leave executives open to heavy criticism for even minor violations. And they demand constant vigilance."[50]

Lencioni purposefully describes the seemingly negative consequences of living by your values because he's found—as have I—that far too many leaders take them lightly. They don't consider what it would require for their organizations to actually take their values to heart. But once you've set your core values, its not enough to simply espouse them—that is, claim or speak about them. You must also enact them.

Psychologists use the term "value congruence" to refer to the extent to which an individual can behave at work consistent with their own values and self-image. Applying this concept to an organization, "core values congruence" is the extent to which a company practices its values and behaves consistently with its external image. As such, it is one of the keys to aligning and integrating your culture with your brand—that is, to achieving brand-culture fusion.

To determine if your organization has core values congruence—that is, if it behaves internally in ways that are true to its external image—Professor de Chernatony recommends examining it for three types of inconsistencies:

1. **Action inconsistency**. Your company says it values one thing but doesn't support it with actions. Example: Your company's leaders constantly talk about the importance of customers, but they reject an opportunity to reduce customer complaints because of the cost involved.
2. **Symbolic inconsistency**. Your company promotes a value externally but doesn't appear to authentically live it internally. Example: Your company runs a healthy grocery store chain, but the vending machines in the employee break room are stocked with junk food.
3. **Ideological inconsistency**. Your company claims to take an ideological stand on an issue but then behaves contrary to that stand. Example: Your company is an investment firm that claims a policy of ethical investments but accepts an invitation to consult with a company with human rights violations.[51]

Netflix, the video streaming giant, offers a cautionary example of the importance of values congruence—and the danger of "action inconsistency." In 2010, the company was enjoying tremendous growth and success, with its shares more than tripling in a single year.[52] Only a year later, however, the company was in crisis, losing 800,000 subscribers and watching its stock price plummet 77 percent in four months.[53] What happened to precipitate this fall?

At the time, the company had published a much-talked-about 124-page manifesto called "Netflix Culture: Freedom & Responsibility," which described the company's unique cultural philosophies and practices. Communications—and particularly listening—was listed among the company's core values. The manifesto claimed: "You listen well, instead of reacting fast, so you can better understand."[54] But while that value statement might have described how Netflix leaders *expected* their employees to work with each other, their actions revealed an inconsistency in how they actually behaved.

When Netflix CEO Reed Hastings announced a plan to do away with a popular subscription plan that combined access to DVD rentals and on-demand streaming video and replace it with two separate services, each at a higher cost, customers were outraged. CNET's coverage of the incident started with a clear diagnosis: "Reed Hastings stopped listening, and that's when the trouble started."[55] The article revealed Hastings hadn't listened to customers before he decided to make the change and he also failed to listen to his colleagues who had expressed concern about it.

In the end, Netflix listened to its customers and dropped its plan to separate the DVD and on-demand streaming video subscriptions—but by then the brand had taken a huge blow and the company had lost one-third of its value. Netflix has since turned around, but the debacle shows how even a popular brand like Netflix can quickly lose customer dollars and goodwill if doesn't practice its core values and behave consistently with its external image.

When you are in the process of identifying your core values, keep this lesson from Netflix in mind. While you'll be able to identify some values that already exist in your organization, even if they were not recognized as such, you'll likely have to set values that aren't currently lived out in your organization but must be for your company to transform into the brand that you desire. This is when core values congruence is most at stake. Setting aspirational values is okay, but you must be careful to set values that are believable and achievable. If you don't, your company, like Netflix, can easily fall into one of the three types of inconsistencies.

For example, I once had to push back on a CEO who wanted to include "we respect and serve one another" as one of his company's values. His people were notorious for yelling at each other, so I was concerned the company would only pay lip service to this value, while employees would continue behaving disrespectfully with each other—a clear action inconsistency (and, not to mention, just wrong).

I explained to the CEO that he could articulate aspirational values but he must also show how the organization is going to achieve them. In the end, he personally committed to championing the change to a more respectful and service-oriented culture. The company included respect and service in its list of core values as well as implemented an action plan, including communication training and leadership coaching, to move its culture more in line with the CEO's vision.

Achieving and sustaining core values congruence requires discipline and diligence. But by adopting a single, central set of core values that you consistently live out, you increase the likelihood of operating in a way that is consistent with the image you want to project and, ultimately, be esteemed in today's business context which rewards authenticity and transparency.

UNIFY YOUR ORGANIZATION

While individually a sole overarching purpose and a set of core values can help you realize some gains at your company, together they help create a high-functioning organization that is poised to produce significantly better business outcomes.

Your employees will understand that they and their contributions matter at a higher level than their job descriptions might suggest. Your organization won't just be a great place to work; its work becomes great. An integrated purpose and values instills in employees a sense of pride in the brand and makes them want to enhance their skills and capabilities to make the brand even stronger. They will be more attuned to each other, customers, the competition, and the market as a whole. They will work together more efficiently and require less oversight, not only lowering costs but also making the organization more attractive to younger employees who prefer to be empowered instead of managed.

But most important, a properly developed and implemented overarching purpose and set of core values unifies your employees, counteracting the divisions that naturally occur in work environments that are increasingly diverse, divided, and distributed. In fact, these days, it's rare to find an organization that isn't composed of newly combined or loosely connected groups—and people who have little in common with each other and rarely interact in person.

De Chernatony cites research by Andrew Brown, a Nottingham University professor, that identifies three types of organizational subcultures—groups of people within an organization who share a common experience—that arise today:

- *Enhancing subcultures* usually adhere to and advance the broader organization's culture.
- *Orthogonal subcultures* align with the larger organization but also accept separate yet nonconflicting values. They usually arise in companies spread across different regions or countries or in those made up of units that operate somewhat independently such as a remote call center or restaurant and retail stores that are part of chains.
- *Countercultures* embrace values that contrast with the desired culture of the entire organization. They usually form after a merger or acquisition or when a new senior leader is appointed and different factions exhibit different allegiances.[56]

Both orthogonal subcultures and countercultures can create friction and confusion that take a toll on employee productivity and, ultimately, company performance. A clear and compelling overarching purpose and values can be used as powerful antidotes to these subcultures. A definitive overarching purpose unifies people with a higher calling that transcends functions, geographies, and even histories. Core values convey expectations that are universally relevant and applicable. When a merger or acquisition or significant reorganization is involved, an overarching purpose and core values set clear expectations for the transition and create greater alignment on the end goal. In every instance, they establish non-negotiables—the standards to which everyone will be held.

FedEx discovered the unifying power of core values in the mid-2000s after acquiring several businesses, including freight transportation company RPS and Kinko's office services centers. Eric Jackson, who served as vice president of worldwide corporate communications for the company, known then as FedEx Express, during that critical time, described to me how the culture had been so deep, rich, and unique, its leaders had assumed that it would be adopted across the board. But the company struggled to align all its existing and new employees and operations across such disparate business models and working environments.[57] Eventually it rolled out a new set of values under the banner "Operate independently. Compete collectively. Manage collaboratively." The cultural change initiative specified how the organization would work together moving forward and stand "as one brand worldwide" while allowing each business unit to focus on meeting the distinct needs of their customers. It also helped FedEx retain its industry leadership.[58]

At LinkedIn, Nicole Leverich, senior director of corporate communications, credits her company's vital values for making it possible to acquire numerous businesses (between 2010 and 2017, LinkedIn made nineteen acquisitions including lynda.com for $1.5 billion in cash and stock[59]). "If values are not accepted, understood, and embraced," she told me, "it's easy in an acquisition for them to disappear." But through all of the transactions, LinkedIn demonstrated the same commitment to its values, including transparency, and its vision never changed. "When you keep all those things the same, it's easier for acquisitions to be successful," she observes.[60]

Ardine Williams, Amazon's vice president of people operations, explained to me how "leadership principles" that serve as the core values for her organization make it easier for employees to take on new roles in different business units. Although operations in Amazon's e-commerce business couldn't be more different from operations in its on-demand cloud computing business, Amazon Web Services, the company's values are embraced and applied across both and all other businesses. "Every business is very different, but how we measure, innovate, evaluate, and interact is consistent," she said. As the company continues to expand its footprint, thereby producing more opportunities for employees to move between business units, a cohesive purpose and set of values will become increasingly important.[61]

It's not just large enterprises like FedEx and Amazon that need an overarching purpose and single set of core values to unify employees.

Organizations of any size must align and unite their workforces if they include employees who work from home or a remote location. Bryan Miles, CEO and cofounder of BELAY, a virtual staffing company, believes all leaders must be "maniacal" about communicating their organization's purpose, but particularly those who have remotely located employees. "We've been intentional about our purpose from day one. It's not an afterthought, it's always top of mind,"[62] he told me. Miles employs seventy people who all work remotely and are hired by clients as virtual assistants doing remote work. "'Why' is the best thing to leave somebody with when you're not around. If your people know why they're doing something, they can fill in the blanks on what and how to do it."

THE CORNERSTONES OF CULTURE

Your organizational culture is largely shaped by its purpose and values. After all, culture, or "the way we do things around here," is made up of people's attitudes (beliefs and ideas) and actions (behaviors and decisions)—and purpose and values influence both. In fact, your purpose and values are so foundational to your culture that renowned management guru Peter Drucker framed his consulting advice around them. Figuring them out was the essence of some of the questions he outlined in his influential book *The Five Most Important Questions You Will Ever Ask about Your Organization.*[63]

This chapter has started you on the journey to brand and culture integration and alignment at your organization by taking you through the what, why, and how of setting an overarching purpose and a single set of core values. These are the foundations upon which you build your desired culture—the culture you need to support and advance your brand identity and ultimately unleash the growth-inducing power of brand-culture fusion. The next chapter points you toward your desired culture and helps you assess how far off you are from achieving brand-culture fusion.

Key Takeaways from This Chapter:

- The purpose of your business and the purpose of your brand should be seamlessly integrated and tightly aligned.
- Your overarching purpose statement should be clear, pithy, and externally oriented.
- Use one set of core values to describe the unique way you do things both as an organization and as a brand.
- To achieve core values congruence, your company must behave consistently with its external image.
- An overarching purpose and core values counteract the divisions that naturally occur in increasingly diverse, divided, and distributed work environments.

CHAPTER 2

ASSESS YOUR BRAND-CULTURE FUSION

Read this chapter to learn:

- How to identify the optimal brand-culture fusion for your organization
- How well-fused your brand and culture are today and what are specific areas for improvement
- How engaged your employees are on three critical dimensions

Leaders of great organizations have tremendous clarity about their brand identity and about how to cultivate an organizational culture that enables them to achieve it. Jeff Bezos has made the Amazon brand synonymous with innovations that delight customers by cultivating a culture that doggedly pursues those innovations. Richard Branson has created a disruptive brand by running his Virgin enterprise to "screw business as usual."[1] And Starbucks has always been about more than the coffee it serves because Howard Schultz conceived the brand as an experience, not a product, and enrolled his staff in that vision.

To build your own great organization, you must have that same clarity about your brand aspiration and how to align your organizational culture to it. But if you're like most leaders I come across, you lack that certainty. And because you don't know your destination, you don't know how far away it is nor how to get there.

In this chapter, I'll help you get the clarity you need. First, I'll help you determine the kind of core values and culture—your *desired* culture—you should be cultivating to successfully support your brand identity. Then I'll help you understand how far your *desired* culture is from your *current* culture—that is, how well-aligned, or not, your culture and brand identity are today. Finally, I'll show you how to diagnose the existing state of brand-culture fusion at your organization so you can pinpoint the areas that need the most improvement.

To help you in your journey, I've designed an online tool that makes this process easy. To get the most out of this chapter, I encourage you to read it first, then go to **http://deniseleeyohn.com/fusion-assessment/** to take the Brand-Culture Fusion Assessment. When you're finished with both, you'll have a clear picture of your brand-culture fusion destination and what kinds of cultural transformations you need to get there.

IDENTIFY YOUR BRAND TYPE

In the previous chapter, I explained that every company should have, at the heart of its culture, a distinct and overarching purpose and a set of core values that guide how it operates inside and how it is perceived outside. I also showed you how to develop your overarching purpose. If you're as thoughtful as most of the leaders I encounter, I'm confident you'll be able to set your purpose without too much difficulty.

I'm guessing, though, that you might find identifying a suitable, single set of core values more elusive. Your company certainly has values it follows already—every organization operates with values either explicitly or implicitly. These values might be proudly listed on your company's website or they might lurk undefined, influencing under the radar your employees' behaviors and how customers experience your brand.

But are these values—implicit or explicit—serving your company well? Are they helping you create an organizational culture that is strategically aligned and integrated with your brand identity? If they're not, what values should you be encouraging in your organization to achieve brand-culture fusion?

To arrive at the core values that successfully link your culture and brand, I recommend starting with identifying the brand type that your brand falls into. If you know the general type of your brand, you'll then be able to isolate the kinds of organizational values needed to support it.

Brand types are categories of brands that share the same strategic approach or take similar stances to shape their positioning. They differ from brand archetypes, which are concepts that classify brands according to storytelling character types like the Hero, the Joker, and the Innocent. While brand archetypes can be helpful particularly in creating a narrative and tone of voice to use in advertising campaigns and other communications, the brand types I'm referring to identify the various ways that brands compete and are positioned relative to each other. For example, while the Apple and Nike brands target different customers, offer different benefits, and express different personalities, both fall into the "innovative brand" type because they are characterized by their relentless pursuit and introduction of new products. Likewise, Ritz-Carlton and USAA are both "service brands" because they consistently deliver superior service, but their identities and competitive brand strategies couldn't be more different.

Having worked on a broad range of brands for more than twenty-five years—large and small, local and international, B2C and B2B, start-ups and well-established enterprises—I've concluded that there is a finite number of brand types, or ways that brands compete and position themselves. Although no two brands share the exact same brand *identity*, there are only nine general brand types:

1. **Disruptive brands** challenge the current ways of doing things and introduce new concepts that substantively change the market.

2. **Conscious brands** are on a mission to make a positive social or environmental impact or enhance people's quality of life.
3. **Service brands** routinely deliver high-quality customer care and service.
4. **Innovative brands** consistently introduce advanced and break-through products and technologies.
5. **Value brands** offer lower prices for basic quality products or services.
6. **Performance brands** produce products or services that deliver superior performance and dependability.
7. **Luxury brands** offer higher quality at higher price.
8. **Style brands** are differentiated by the way their products or services look and feel, as much as or more than by what they do.
9. **Experience brands** are differentiated by the experiences they provide, as much as or more than by their products or services.

Some of these brand types overlap, and some characteristics are—or should be—embraced by all brands. All brands should offer good service, for example. But a brand that falls into the service brand type always makes delivering high-quality customer care and service its top priority. Its strategies, operations, and ultimately customer value propositions are all centered around delivering great service first.

Although your brand might seem to fall into two or three brand types, it's critical that you identify a primary one. All too often companies are unable to make a choice about what their brands stand for. They vacillate between brand types with widely different strategic approaches. The result is a brand that is unfocused and generic. Establishing a single, focused, differentiated brand identity starts with picking a primary brand type—and that brand type should be the one that aligns best with your overarching purpose, resonates most with your organization, and gives you the most impact with your customers. (When you take the online Brand-Culture Fusion Assessment, you'll get an even clearer picture of your brand type.)

A company's brand might evolve from one type to another as its customers, competitors, and other outside influences like technology change. But usually a brand builds equity by sticking to a single brand type over time. The nine brand types are broad enough to allow for that. Even if a company's products or services change in scope; or the company targets new customers; or it grows its footprint into new markets, channels, and organizational configurations; the brand type it falls under will likely remain the same. For example, Disney is now an enterprise that extends well beyond its original video cartoon production house, but it has remained an experience brand.

The nine brand types are also broad enough that they don't confine any one brand's unique identity or precise positioning in a market. Consider the differences in purpose, scope, target customer, and personality between three different performance brands: BMW, FedEx, and American Express. All three brands are characterized by superior performance and dependability, but that's where the similarity between them ends. BMW's brand is about a superior driving experience, FedEx's is about dependable delivery, and American Express is rooted in a world-class reliable service brand identity. The brazen personality expressed in BMW's advertising contrasts with FedEx's unceremonious tone and American Express' sophistication. And while BMW and American Express might both target higher-end customers, FedEx's target audience is mainstream consumers and businesses.

Each of the nine brands types is distinguished by two main characteristics. The first one is its point of reference, that is, the standard the brand is positioned relative to. The second one is its tone and manner—how the brand usually behaves or expresses itself. Take a look at the description of each of the brand types, their point of reference, and their tone and manner—and then consider what type your own brand falls under. I've also included some examples of each brand type, although I recognize that there's an element of subjectivity when determining the brand type of brands that are not your own.

Here are the nine brand types:

Brand Character: *what characterizes the brand*	Description:	Point of Reference: *what the brand is positioned relative to*	Tone and Manner: *how the brand usually behaves and communicates*	Examples:
Disruptive Brand	Challenges the current ways of doing things and introduces new concepts that substantively change the market	Category leader	Rebellious, confident, daring	Virgin, Airbnb, Dr. Pepper
Conscious Brand	Is on a mission to make a positive social or environmental impact or enhance people's quality of life	Higher purpose	Inspiring, thoughtful, transparent	Seventh Generation, SoulCycle, Patagonia
Service Brand	Routinely delivers high-quality customer care and service	Customer need	Humble, predictable, friendly	Nordstrom, USAA, Ritz-Carlton
Innovative Brand	Consistently introduces advanced and breakthrough products and technologies	Possibility	Risk-taking, imaginative, progressive	Apple, Nike, Amazon
Value Brand	Offers lower prices for basic-quality products or services	Higher-priced brands	Down-to-earth, practical, straightforward	Walmart, IKEA, Subway

Brand Character: *what characterizes the brand*	Description:	Point of Reference: *what the brand is positioned relative to*	Tone and Manner: *how the brand usually behaves and communicates*	Examples:
Performance Brand	Produces products or services that deliver superior performance and dependability	Performance standard	Precise, competent, reliable	BMW, FedEx, American Express
Luxury Brand	Offers higher quality at higher price	Populist brand	Discriminating, refined, glamorous	Tiffany, Mercedes-Benz, Hermes
Style Brand	Is differentiated by the way its products or services look and feel, as much as or more than by what they do	Functional brand	Creative, stylish, contemporary	Target, JetBlue, Mini Cooper
Experience Brand	Is differentiated by the experience it offers, as much as or more than by the product or service	Customer emotion	Exciting, energetic, imaginative	Disney, American Girl, Wegmans

BRAND TYPES DIFFER ON TWO DIMENSIONS

If you are having a difficult time identifying the primary brand type that your brand falls under, thinking about your brand on the following two dimensions might help you narrow your choices.

Brand types vary in the degree to which they are oriented to change: Some brand types embrace it. Disruptive, experience, and innovative brands tend to emphasize novelty and are oriented to what's next. Other brand types eschew change and are built through consistency. Style, service, and value brands tend to establish themselves by being reliable and unchanging. Some brands types like conscious, luxury, and performance fall somewhere in between.

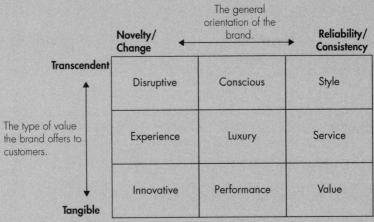

Figure 2.1   The Change & Value Dimensions of Brands

The brand types also vary by the type of value they offer to customers. The value of conscious brands tends to transcend a specific product or service while performance brands usually create value that is very tangible and material, and most luxury brands create value that is somewhere in between.

Look at Figure 2.1 and identify where your brand might fit best.

As you consider which brand type your brand best fits under, try to be as objective as you can. When it comes to building your brand identity, perception is as important, if not more than, reality. For example, your organization may develop what you think are innovative products, but if your customers don't perceive you or your products as innovative, then your existing brand probably doesn't fall in the innovative brand category. Whenever possible, involve other leaders in the process of identifying your brand type, and if you have conducted customer research recently, consult their findings to get the full picture on how your brand is currently perceived.

After going through this exercise, you might find that, while your brand currently fits under one brand type, you aspire for your brand to be another type. If that's the case, your aspirations for brand transformation should be realistic. It's unlikely that a value brand that offers low prices for basic quality will become a luxury brand that delivers higher quality at higher prices, for example. But if you choose to make a sensible shift from one brand type to another, success is entirely possible if you make changes to your values and culture. The next step in this assessment process helps you identify the kinds of values that most support your current or desired brand type.

DETERMINE THE VALUES YOU NEED

Each brand type requires a specific organizational culture to thrive. If you want to be an innovative brand, for example, then your culture must encourage a test-and-learn mentality among your employees. If you've set your sights on being a style brand, then you need to infuse your culture with design and creativity.

Once you know the type of brand you have or desire to build, the next step is to identify the kind of culture required to deliver on it. Organizational cultures are not as easily classified as brand types, though. Many researchers and consulting firms, including OCAI, Denison, Human Synergistics, and Organizational Culture Profile, have developed tools and constructs that classify organizational cultures. Each offers insights into the common drivers and indicators of cultures. But

I've found that too many variables distinguish an organization's culture, so any attempt to classify cultures ends up producing categories too broad to be meaningful or actionable. Most of these approaches are also limited because they are based on the internal dynamics of an organization and do not take into account important external influences on culture such as brand identity or customer needs.

Instead of culture types, I focus on organizational values. Distilling culture down to core values is at once a more robust *and* a more streamlined approach than classifying different types of culture. Along with an overarching purpose, core values are the cornerstones of culture. They reflect what's important to your organization, shape your people's attitudes and actions, and drive how your organization shows up and operates in the world. If you know the types of core values you need to deliver on your particular brand type, you can design the other aspects of your culture to align with, build on, and reinforce them. In short, you have a starting point for designing your *desired* culture.

To identify the core values you should cultivate as the foundation of your desired culture, look at the chart below and find your brand type. Next to your brand type you'll find a list of the three top values that are most likely to help it thrive (for a definition of each value, see page 42):

Brand Type: *what characterizes the brand*	Top Organizational Core Values: *what shapes the way the people in the company think & behave*
Disruptive Brand Challenges the current ways of doing things and introduces new concepts that substantively change the market	Competition, standing out, risk-taking
Conscious Brand Is on a mission to make a positive social or environmental impact or enhance people's quality of life	Purposefulness, high commitment, transparency
Service Brand Routinely delivers high-quality customer care and service	Caring, humility, empathy

Innovative Brand Consistently introduces advanced and breakthrough products and technologies	Inventiveness, experimentation, continuous improvement
Value Brand Offers lower prices for basic quality products or services	Accessibility, fairness, pragmatism
Performance Brand Produces products that deliver superior performance and dependability	Achievement, excellence, consistency
Luxury Brand Offers higher quality at higher price	Sophistication, distinction, status
Style Brand Is differentiated by the way its products and services look and feel as much as or more than by what they do	Design, discernment, creativity
Experience Brand Is differentiated by the experience it offers as much as or more than by the product or service	Entertainment, enjoyment, originality

Once you've identified the values you need to support your desired culture, you then need to ascertain whether the values that currently exist in your organization—explicitly or implicitly—align with those that correspond with your brand type.

To do so, start by assessing your culture as it actually is and the core values that are currently in play in your organization every day—not necessarily the values that are stated in your company's mission statement. When I work with my clients on their culture, we start by performing a thorough culture audit to fully understand the existing state of their organizational culture. We do an anthropological study, walking around their offices and taking note of what we see and hear. We observe how people interact with each other and their environment. We collect materials from all areas of the business and analyze them, applying semiotics—the study of signs and symbols—to uncover hidden meanings. And then we discuss our findings with employees to get their take on the culture.

A culture audit is best conducted by a cross-functional team working together with outsiders who can offer fresh perspectives. Doing so ensures the audit is objective and thorough. If that approach is out of reach for you, or if you want to make progress while you shore up the resources for that kind of effort, you can still do your own informal audit by taking stock of the following:

Communications. What, when, where, why, and how your organization communicates to employees, other stakeholders, and customers reveals a great deal about your culture and values. For example, when a CEO sends a handwritten thank-you note, it suggests a personal, perhaps even informal culture, whereas a weekly all-hands web chat signals a tech-savvy, democratic one. Founding stories, legends, and customer anecdotes that are regularly shared around the office also contain clues about the values of your organization. A story about someone going to great lengths to satisfy a customer, for example, speaks volumes about the company's service-oriented culture.

Employee policies and procedures. Consider the policies and procedures that dictate employee behaviors in every area. What are the policies for:

- Your dress code (is the dress code more professional or casual?)
- The use of technology and social media (are they more restrictive or open?)
- Taking vacation, sick, and personal leave (are they more flexible or strict?)
- Safety (are they more proactive or free-handed?)

Compensation, benefits, and retirement packages. How you pay and reward your employees illuminates whether your company values an individual's performance over team or company performance, outcomes vs. effort, tenure vs. merit, and more.

Office location, architecture, design, and layout. Companies usually identify with the region or area they're based in—Silicon Valley for technology companies, New York for financial firms, etc. Location says a lot about how a company sees itself. An automotive company that

selects a city other than Detroit for its U.S. headquarters may be signaling a rebellious or disruptive identity and culture. The architectural
style and interior design of an organization's building often expresses
its personality (e.g., modern vs. old-fashioned, flashy vs. understated).
Office layouts reflect how employees work together. The open floor
plans at many technology start-ups suggests their organizational cultures are open and collaborative.

Rituals. Organizational rituals are ceremonies, rites, and other regularly occurring events and activities such as annual awards or weekly
meetings. If, when, and how your organization gives out awards, celebrates milestones, and carries out traditions indicates what it values. For
example, an organization that prides itself on its family-oriented culture
probably celebrates employees' work anniversaries with a party of some
sort, or invites employees' families to company picnics and holiday
gatherings. An organization that thrives on healthy competition might
stage an annual sales contest in which reps are encouraged to one-up
each other.

Artifacts. The objects that your organization creates, keeps, and
distributes, such as awards, tchotchkes, pictures, and devices, also
symbolize what is important in your culture.

Informed by insights from your audit, you should be able to identify
from the following list the top values that exist at your organization.
The list is, I admit, a generic collection of broad values. As explained
in the previous chapter, every company has—or should have—values
that are distinct to it or at least expressed in a unique way. But offering
a more comprehensive or nuanced list of values would be impossible,
given that the possibilities for *unique* values are endless. My hope is
that you'll use the list as a springboard, and that you'll see your unique
values represented here by some of these general ones. Also, as is the
case with brand types, you might find many of these values in your
organization, but you should focus on the degree to which your organization embraces a value to determine the three most salient and influential ones.

For some of you, the culture at your organization is either nondescript or so negative that it might be difficult to see any values from the list at work in your organization today. That's okay. If you find yourself in this situation, skip this exercise. You've already laid the most important groundwork by clearly identifying the type of brand you're building and learning the core values you'll need to cultivate to deliver on it.

Here are the twenty-seven common organizational values:

Accessibility—people at your company make themselves easy to understand and engage with, regardless of rank or role.

Achievement—people at your company focus on the successful attainment of goals typically by effort, courage, or skill.

Caring—people at your company consistently display kindness and concern for others.

Competition—people at your company strive to win or be more successful than others.

Consistency—people at your company adhere steadfastly to the same principles, course, or form.

Continuous improvement—people at your company engage in ongoing efforts to improve products, services, or processes.

Creativity—people at your company rely on imagination or foster original ideas.

Design—people at your company focus on the look, style, or fashion of everything they do or produce.

Discernment—people at your company emphasize using acute judgment and discretion.

Distinction—people at your company like to set its brand apart from the competition clearly and deliberately.

Empathy—people at your company try to put themselves in other people's shoes—especially those of other employees and customers.

Enjoyment—people at your company go out of their way to have fun and seek out delight.

Entertainment—people at your company emphasize amusement or celebration.

Excellence—people at your company try to be outstanding or to meet the highest standards.

Experimentation—people at your company experiment with new methods and approaches, knowing some will fail.

Fairness—people at your company go out of their way to act without bias or partiality.

High commitment—people at your company believe in acting with intense and ironclad dedication to a purpose.

Humility—people at your company believe in adopting a modest or low view of one's own importance.

Inventiveness—people at your company like to create new things with imagination.

Originality—people at your company champion independence, creativity, and fresh perspectives.

Pragmatism—people at your company deal with things sensibly and realistically and try to find the most practical way to do things.

Purposefulness—people at your company pursue its goals with intention and determination.

Risk-taking—people at your company engage in activities that involve danger or risk in order to achieve a goal.

Sophistication—people at your company rely on social or esthetic standards to discriminate between options.

Standing out—people at your company attract attention to it by being particularly noticeable or different.

Status—people at your company care about the relative social standing of people and things.

Transparency—people at your company do things openly and in a straightforward way.

Once you've identified the top three core values that currently exist in your company, use the chart on pages 38 and 39 to compare them with the top three values associated with your brand type. For example, if you've identified your values as excellence, design, and creativity, then you can see on the chart that these values are associated with the performance brand type (excellence) and with the style brand type (design and creativity).

The difference between your existing values and those of your current or desired brand type provides a good indication of how far off your organization is from your desired culture—the culture that will enable you to support and advance your brand identity (or the brand identity you'd like to evolve to.) For example, if you've determined that your brand type is a performance brand, then the chart shows that the core values that typically support that brand type are excellence, achievement, and consistency. In your culture audit, you've determined that excellence is indeed one of your top three values—but the other two top values in your organization align best with a style brand type. Therefore, in your case, there's a clear misalignment between the core values at play in your culture and the ones needed to support your current brand type. You'll need to foster and cultivate the values of achievement and consistency if you want your organizational culture to help your performance brand truly thrive.

Now that you know the top values that you need as the foundation of your desired culture—and whether they currently exist in your organization or you need to cultivate them from scratch—you must make them your own. The top three values listed in the chart are only a starting point for drafting your unique core values. As I noted previously, these values are expressed in the most general terms. Apply them to your organization by fleshing them out into a full set of core values, articulating them in unique ways, defining what they mean in your organization, and tying them to specific behaviors, as described in Chapter 1.

ASSESS THE STATE OF YOUR BRAND-CULTURE FUSION

Once you know the types of core values you're aiming for, it's time to examine how well your culture and brand are aligned and integrated today. You need to know how much work you have to do and diagnose where the biggest disconnects are so you know which areas of culture-building you should focus on.

To understand the current state of brand-culture fusion at your organization, it's important to "begin with the end in mind," as business guru Dr. Stephen R. Covey advised.[2] Understanding what it looks like when an organization successfully achieves brand-culture fusion will help you see if and how fusion is lacking in your organization.

When culture and brand are completely in sync, their alignment is manifested visibly in four primary areas:

- Purpose and values integration
- Employee experience–customer experience integration
- Internal brand alignment
- Employee brand engagement

As you read about each area, consider whether the indicators listed under each are present in your organization. Whenever possible, invite other leaders and employees—particularly from various parts of and at different levels in your organization—to participate in this exercise and contribute their perspectives.

Purpose and Values Integration

Purpose and values integration is the extent to which your overarching purpose and your core values are woven into your business and organization. Here are the ways in which purpose and values integration is most visible:

- Your company has an overarching purpose that unites its business ambitions and brand aspirations.
- Your company uses a single set of core values to describe its internal culture *and* desired brand image.
- Your company's purpose and values have a real impact on how it operates.
- Most employees clearly understand what your company stands for, why it exists, and what it values.
- The gap between the values your company claims to hold and the actual values lived out by your employees every day is very small.
- Your company leaders usually act, make decisions, and communicate in ways that are consistent with your company's overarching purpose and core values.
- Your people use your overarching purpose and core values as filters when recruiting, training, and evaluating employees.
- Your operations processes (e.g., supply chain, product development, labor management, etc.) are designed and implemented in line with your purpose and values.
- Your organizational design (i.e., the units, hierarchy, and roles in your organization) supports and promotes work that is aligned with your purpose and values.
- The perceptions among your customers about your company are accurate—that is, your company's brand image is pretty much what your organization is really like.
- Your company has translated its purpose and values into differentiators that distinguish your brand from competitors or create value for customers.

If you believe your company needs help achieving purpose and values integration, you might revisit Chapter 1 to reflect on how to develop and activate a strong overarching purpose and set of core values. Pay close attention to Chapter 3, which explains the fundamental role of leaders in integrating what you do and say internally with what you do and say externally, and to Chapter 4, which explains how to design and run your organization in line with your purpose and values. Chapter 8 shows how to translate your culture—including your values and purpose—into brand differentiators.

Employee Experience–Customer Experience Integration

The next area is the extent to which your employee experience and your customer experience are aligned and integrated. When your culture and brand are interdependent and mutually reinforcing, there is a strong connection between how employees experience every aspect of work life during their tenure in your organization—from being hired to going through training, from working in a particular space to having tools for and information about their jobs and the company—and how customers experience your brand. You engage your employees in the way you expect them to engage your customers. Indicators of this integration include:

- Your managers treat employees in ways that are consistent with how they expect them to treat customers.
- You design the employee experience at your company with the same principles used for your desired customer experience.
- You design and manage your organization to facilitate the collaboration and shared accountability you need to excel in crafting and delivering customer experience.
- Your company's physical workplace environment—a key influence on employee experience—embodies your brand attributes.
- Your company engages employees through rites, rituals, and symbols that reflect and bring to life your overarching purpose and core values.

If you find that your current culture falls short of engaging your employees in the way you expect them to engage customers, then turn to Chapter 5. There, I'll show you how leading companies are able to deliver superior customer experiences *because* they weave them together with employee experiences. I'll also teach you how to achieve strong employee experience–customer experience integration at your company. And in Chapter 6, I will explain how to use small experiences in your organization such as rituals and artifacts to reinforce your desired culture.

Internal Brand Alignment

Internal brand alignment is the extent to which your people are aligned with each other on brand matters. For your culture to be fully aligned with your brand, everyone in your organization must share one common understanding of your brand identity. There are two ways in which this alignment is manifested in your culture:

- Your company's brand identity and positioning have been clearly articulated to everyone inside your organization.
- The key stakeholders at your organization consistently agree about what's "on brand" and what's not.

If your organization fails at either of these, direct your attention to Chapter 7, where I provide a wide range of examples of experiences and tools that can increase internal brand alignment and explain the best approaches to develop them.

Employee Brand Engagement

Employee brand engagement is the extent to which your people are aligned and engaged with your brand. This area of brand-culture fusion deserves a lengthier explanation because people often conflate employee *brand* engagement with employee engagement in general (employees' commitment to the company and their jobs). But you can't afford to miss the particular importance of employee brand engagement when your goal is brand-culture fusion.

The lack of brand and culture alignment and integration is a key driver of most organization's engagement shortcomings. As with culture overall, employee engagement can't be pursued in a generic, unfocused way. If your engagement efforts are intended simply to make employees feel valued and satisfied, employees might be more inclined to perform their jobs better, but they're not necessarily going to help your organization go after its purpose, live out your core values, or create customer experiences that express either.

Only when you engage your employees with your *brand* will they think and act in the specific ways that produce the specific results you're looking for. General employee engagement is manifested in employees' relationships with their managers and co-workers, their view of their job responsibilities, and their participation in work activities. Employee *brand* engagement, meanwhile, shows up in these three brand-specific ways:

1. **Personal and emotional engagement with the brand**
   - Employees' personal values and your company's core values are well-aligned.
   - Employees act as brand ambassadors, sharing positive information about your company with their friends, families, and communities and recommending it to them.
   - Employees believe that your company delivers on its brand promise.
   - Employees feel an emotional connection to your company and your brand.
   - The company's overarching purpose makes employees feel their job is important.
   - Employees exhibit a clear preference to work at your company instead of its competitors.

2. **Day-to-day engagement with the brand**
   - Your leaders expect everyone, not just the marketing department, to do what they can to build your brand.

- Employees have appropriate access to tools and data about how your brand is perceived in the marketplace relative to your competitors.
- Employees tend to make decisions by thinking about what's right for your company's brand in the long term instead of what's likely to produce short-term results.
- Employees believe they are responsible for nurturing and reinforcing your brand on a daily basis, at every touchpoint.
- Employees clearly understand their roles within the company and the impact they have on making the brand successful.

3. Engagement in your company's brand strategy
- Employees understand what makes your brand different and special from a customer perspective.
- Employees clearly understand who the company's target audiences are and their primary wants and needs.
- Employees have the skills and resources they need to ensure they deliver on the brand promise.
- Employees would say they are empowered to deliver on the brand promise to customers.
- All employees—even those who don't have direct customer contact—understand how they contribute to a great customer experience.
- Employees consistently demonstrate the behaviors that help create loyal relationships with customers.

For this area of brand-culture alignment, more than any other, it's critical that you include in your assessment your employees' perspectives so that you gain an accurate understanding of the current state of your employee brand engagement. (If you conduct an employee engagement survey, consider incorporating these measures of brand-specific engagement in it. If you don't, Chapter 5 will introduce you to a complete toolkit of survey methods that you can use to glean employee insights on these and other important topics.)

Should your findings reveal that your employee brand engagement is not as strong as you'd like, you'll find relevant insights and action steps throughout Part 2 of this book. Chapter 7 will be particularly helpful, as I show you how to produce experiences, communications strategies, and brand toolkits that develop employee brand engagement and cultivate your desired culture.

ASSESSMENT RESULTS REVEAL WIDESPREAD LACK OF BRAND-CULTURE FUSION

If, as you read through the areas of integration, you realize your culture and brand aren't as well-integrated and aligned as you had hoped, you are not alone. Prior to the publishing of *FUSION*, 250 business leaders pre-tested the online assessment tool, which asks participants to assess their organizations on each of the four areas of brand-culture integration. Their responses indicate that few companies have strong brand-culture fusion across the board. While a few bright spots exist—B2C organizations tend to enjoy stronger employee brand engagement than do B2B companies, for example—most indicators in each area received a favorable rating from around half of the respondents or fewer. Take the online assessment to receive a personalized report that will show you specifically how your results compare to others'.

Now that you've assessed your organization on the four areas of brand-culture alignment and integration, the remainder of this book provides the roadmap, tools, and approaches for the rest of your journey to brand-culture fusion. Use your findings to guide you as you read through Part 2 of this book, referring to the chapters that correspond to the integration areas where you see the biggest disconnects in your organization.

BRAND-CULTURE FUSION AREA	ACCESS INSIGHTS AND INSTRUCTIONS IN:
Purpose & Values Integration	Chapter 1 Set Your Sole Purpose and Core Values
	Chapter 3 Lead the Change
	Chapter 4 Organize and Operate On-Brand
	Chapter 8 Build Your Brand from the Inside Out
Employee Experience–Customer Experience Integration	Chapter 5 Create Culture-Changing Employee Experiences
	Chapter 6 Sweat the Small Stuff
Internal Brand Alignment	Chapter 7 Ignite Your Transformation
Employee Brand Engagement	Chapter 7 Ignite Your Transformation

If you want to get the most value out of the findings from this chapter, then take the online Brand-Culture Fusion Assessment (**http://deniseleeyohn.com/fusion-assessment/**). Once you complete it, you will receive a personalized report that shows your results and compares them to the average of everyone who has taken the assessment as well as to companies with similar characteristics. The report also totals your responses into a Brand-Culture Fusion Score to represent the overall strength of brand-culture fusion at your organization. After you've implemented some of the strategies outlined in this book, take the assessment once more to see how much progress you've made.

CAPTURE YOUR COMPANY'S UNIQUENESS

In this chapter, I've shown you how to start cultivating your desired culture by identifying the core values that are most likely to support your brand aspiration. But before you begin the task of transforming your current culture to achieve your desired one, let me remind you one more time: there is no single right or wrong culture. It might be tempting to grab on to the top values recommended for the type of brand that best fits your company and to stop there. But it is up to you to identify and flesh out all the specific core values that create your company's unique and powerful culture.

Amazon, for instance, might fall under the innovative brand type whose top values encourage inventiveness, experimentation, and continuous improvement—values that are shared by most brands that are innovative. But Amazon has adapted these general values into distinctive, core ones that capture the unique way it expects its people to embrace innovation, including "invent and simplify" and "learn and be curious." The other values that round out its complete set of core values also define the distinct way Amazon expects its people to *achieve* its innovations. For example, to ensure the company delivers the highest level of customer experience, every employee at Amazon is expected to embrace the value of "taking ownership of results." According to former Amazon executive John Rossman, this means everyone is expected "to function as both owners and leaders. [CEO Jeff Bezos] wants you to drive the business as if it were your own car, not some weekend rental."[3] This core value not only fuels Amazon's unique innovative brand, it sets its culture apart from others.

Like Amazon's culture, your culture must be as distinct as your brand. It doesn't matter if your company culture is friendly or competitive, nurturing or analytical. There is no single right type of culture, just as there isn't one best type of brand. Salesforce is known for being inspiring; Southwest Airlines, fun; Starbucks, sincere. All three of these companies are leaders in their fields and they got there in part by employing a unique overarching purpose and distinctive core values that are woven together with a differentiated brand. Following their lead, your goal should be to identify the specific cultural elements that enable you to achieve your desired brand identity and then deliberately cultivate them.

This chapter has laid the groundwork for you to do just that. The next chapter is about the remaining foundational element of brand-culture fusion: leadership.

Key Takeaways from This Chapter

- There are nine types of brands and each requires certain organizational core values.

- You should determine your desired brand type and corresponding values to identify your desired culture—one that is fully aligned and integrated with your brand.

- Successful brand-culture fusion manifests itself in four areas: purpose and values integration, employee experience–customer experience integration, internal brand alignment, and employee brand engagement.

- Employee brand engagement shows up in three brand-specific ways: emotional and personal engagement with your brand, engagement in the day-to-day, and engagement with your brand strategy.

CHAPTER 3

LEAD THE CHANGE

Read this chapter to learn:

- How leaders support and advance brand-culture fusion in their communications *and* their actions
- How one group of employees might stall your efforts to integrate brand and culture
- Why decisions about hiring and firing are among the most important and visible ways you can live out your core values

The story of how the venerable Ford Motor Company managed to recover from the Great Recession of 2008 is considered one of the greatest corporate turnarounds in U.S. history. Not only did Ford recover, but it ended up thriving and achieving heights once thought impossible for an American carmaker.

With its sky-high gas prices and financial industry meltdown, the Great Recession was the worst crisis to afflict the American automobile industry in eight decades. Ford's stock dropped to $1 a share from its high of $57 in 2000[1], and the company posted a $14.6 billion loss in 2008[2]. Three short years later, though, Ford posted annual profits of $6.6 billion, making it the most profitable automobile company in the world at the time.[3] Its stock price rebounded to $12–$14 per share,[4] its U.S. market share increased for the third consecutive year,[5] and its sales surpassed Toyota, which had previously knocked Ford down to the number three automaker in the U.S.[6] Most significantly, Ford achieved this remarkable recovery without the U.S. government bailout money that resuscitated General Motors and Chrysler.

Who was responsible for leading Ford's recovery from its near-death experience? Alan Mulally, the former Boeing executive who was recruited to save the company. Mulally led the automobile giant to develop industry-leading products and partnerships with technology and consumer electronics companies. He also revived the Taurus brand, consolidated global operations into a single business unit, and decided against the government bailout. But of all his moves, the most instrumental to the turnaround was to lead a brand-inspired cultural revolution inside the organization.

When Mulally arrived at the struggling company, he set his sights on dismantling the toxic culture that had metastasized within it. In *American Icon: Alan Mulally and the Fight to Save Ford Motor Company*, Bryce Hoffman writes about the lack of transparency, fractious business units, and a preoccupation with self-preservation that had come to define Ford's culture. Meetings resembled mortal combat, with executives regularly looking for vulnerabilities among their peers to exploit.[7]

Given the state of internal affairs at the company, it's no wonder its brand was struggling on the outside. With its leaders distracted by playing politics and defending turfs, the Ford brand had become listless and unfocused. Ford's product lineup faltered, as it did not appeal to customers who were looking for smaller, more fuel-efficient vehicles. And different regions pursued different automobile configurations, which further diluted the brand identity around the world.[8]

Mulally challenged this dysfunction head on and made championing "One Ford," a single, clear vision for the organization, his top priority. One Ford entailed reviving the Ford brand by promoting, as a *Fortune* article explains, "the critical ingredients that made a Ford a Ford" and then working as one team "to create great products on a global scale using those ingredients."[9]

One Ford was grounded in the original purpose that prompted Henry Ford to start the company—to "build a car for the great multitude"—and inspired by a painting he had commissioned eighty-eight years earlier. Mulally recalls coming across the image, which was titled *Opening the Highways to All Mankind* and featured in a *Saturday Evening Post* advertisement. It depicted a Norman Rockwell–style scene of a young family at the top of a grassy hill overlooking a road filled with automobiles and the shadows of a Ford factory in the distance. Mulally immediately sensed its potential impact: Henry Ford's original vision could serve as the vision for Ford going forward. He believed the vision would help everyone—employees, suppliers, even stakeholders in the communities in which Ford did business—understand "what Ford stood for, and everybody could align themselves and their work to create an exciting, viable, profitable, growing company...you can imagine the innovation and the creativity that that compelling vision enabled. It just unleashed everybody to deliver this plan," he said in a *Fast Company* interview. One Ford conveyed that Ford was back in the business of "serving all around the world a complete family of cars that are best-in-class," Mulally explained.[10]

With One Ford, Mulally was able to put the purpose and values of the Ford brand at the center of the organization and unify the company's people, plans, operations, and products to restore the brand to automotive leadership.[11] He instituted weekly business performance review (BPR) meetings that required a new level of rigor, scrutiny, and detailed analysis from the company's leaders. While his executives initially bristled at Mulally's demands and resisted the changes, over time they began to see that the transparency he enforced effectively united them to work together on the company's business and brand goals and that the commitment he expected was not in service to himself but to the "phenomenally powerful" Ford brand, as he would describe it.[12]

He also drove them to define Ford's "DNA," as Derrick Kuzak, Ford's global product chief, called it—the "genome that was designed to and engineered to convey quality, innovation, and style." *Fortune* reported that Ford executives ended up identifying "300 different characteristics—from the chirps on the electronic key fob to the clunk of a closing door—that define the personality of its vehicles."

These not only served as a common design language that made it easier to create single products to sell in all markets, but also it helped build the Ford brand. Mulally wanted a Ford to be recognizable around the world and to elicit a strong, visceral, emotional reaction.[13]

Mulally also continually hammered home adherence to Ford's core values of honesty and accountability, which had been eroded in previous years. He knew that if his executive team embraced and lived them out, the rest of the organization would follow suit. Then they could all get back to working together—rather than splitting into warring territorial factions—to streamline operations, develop new technologies, and design cars that embodied the broad appeal the Ford brand had been built upon.[14]

It worked. Within a year, Ford's top executives had embraced the One Ford vision, and at every level of the company managers began to emulate Mulally's focused and data-driven approach. Equally or more important, he reinvigorated everyone's energy toward the Ford brand.[15] In 2010, *Motor Trend* named one of Ford's newest cars, the Ford Fusion, "Car of the Year." Ford, the company, was restored to profitability and Ford, the brand, to preeminence.

Ford's turnaround demonstrates the transformative power of a culture steeped in an overarching purpose and integrated with the brand. But more than that, it shows how leadership sets the tone and pace of its adoption for the entire organization.

DIFFERENT CULTURE, DIFFERENT OUTCOME

The leadership actions at Ford sharply contrast with how the executives at Volkswagen tore apart their organization and their brand. The scandal in which engineers programmed engine systems to fool U.S. government emissions testers ended with VW recalling hundreds of thousands of cars and agreeing to a $14.7 billion government settlement. It also revealed an organizational culture completely out of line with its brand.

A former VW executive explained to me that, as the cheating scheme came to light, American customers who had previously banded together like "tribes" over a common affection for the brand felt betrayed by the company's deceit. It was like "finding out your cousin is stealing from you," she noted. Diesel buyers, who consider themselves a "unique breed" and had previously identified with VW's outsider brand ethos, especially felt deluded.[16] The scandal revealed that the values of honesty and humility that had once distinguished the brand were just a facade. It turned out the self-deprecating humor that Volkswagen's ads conveyed and the countercultural spirit that its car designs embodied were not authentic representations of the organization that produced them.

Instead the company's leaders had fostered a culture that was in complete opposition to the honest, transparent, and straightforward brand image they had created. We can trace the lack of integration of corporate culture and brand back to Ferdinand Piëch, VW's chief executive from 1993 until 2002, and to Martin Winterkorn, the chief executive from 2007 until his resignation after the scandal became public. Critics charge Piëch and Winterkorn with cultivating a culture of arrogance and superiority.

"There is a self-righteousness which led down this terrible path," said David Bach, a senior lecturer at the Yale School of Management who followed the case.[17] In a *Financial Times* article, Arndt Ellinghorst, a former VW management trainee, corroborated Bach's assessment explaining, "VW was an organization full of hubris, you know, dominate the world and walk-on-water type of thinking."[18] When I interviewed Ellinghorst recently, he shared that VW's German leaders were particularly condescending toward American consumers. "They should be happy to get our superior cars," they thought.[19] The disrespectful attitude toward American consumers brewing among executives inside the company was a contradiction to the relationship the brand had built with them on the outside. American's affection for the VW brand and its role as an emblem of freedom during the 1960s cultural revolution had helped VW succeed as a company—if anything VW should have felt lucky to have American customers' brand loyalty.

Now an automotive industry analyst with Evercore ISI UK Ltd., Ellinghorst believes that the emissions scandal was particularly damaging to the company because it revealed an organization-wide culture of cheating. It would have been different, he explained, if the scandal had been contained within the ranks of management. But because the deception involved a multitude of people from low-level engineers to the board of directors, it signaled something was "fundamentally wrong" at the company.[20]

VW's leaders had set an arrogant tone throughout the entire organization that was permissive of cutting corners and deceiving customers—and it eventually came to a head. That's how leadership works. Leaders at VW shaped the organization's culture by the priorities they set, the decisions they made, and the behaviors they modeled. And in doing so, they sealed the company's fate.

In the previous chapter, I pointed you toward your desired culture—the culture that best aligns with and enhances your brand identity and enables you to achieve brand-culture fusion. The next step is to take leadership responsibility for cultivating it. Brand-culture fusion starts with you. You cannot delegate it to your HR or marketing leaders. They—and everyone in your organization—need you to champion it, so they can carry it out.

As I will show in this chapter, it's imperative to align what you and your top executives say and do with your desired culture. The degree of alignment of those two factors determines the viability of brand-culture fusion more powerfully than any other factor. But that's not enough: leaders in the middle layers of your organizational hierarchy also need to be thoroughly engaged in cultivating your culture because of their tremendous influence on the rest of your workforce. I'll also shine a light on the importance of leadership decisions about people—such as hiring, firing, and promoting them—in laying the groundwork for brand-culture fusion. It all starts with the example you set for others with your words and your actions.

COMMUNICATE, COMMUNICATE, COMMUNICATE

"Aharai!" is the motto Israeli military officers use when leading their forces into combat. The battle cry means "follow me" and it reflects a doctrine that all great leaders embrace. Great leaders—the ones

praised in history books, admired by colleagues, and followed by many—know that leadership is the practice of going first and setting an example. I've seen great business leaders live out this doctrine by casting a vision and then showing others what it looks like to pursue it with drive and determination.

"Leadership is about changing reality in some way," explains Eduardo Braun, author of *People First Leadership*, "so setting the vision is explicitly recognizing that you can change reality, and clearly stating in which ways you want to do so."[21] He outlines three levels in which leaders communicate their vision. The first level involves communicating ideas and information, the stuff of day-to-day business operations. The second level involves communicating emotions—empathizing with and inspiring others. And the third level involves communicating with concrete behaviors—"practicing what you preach, walking the talk, and delivering on your promises."[22]

Although strong communication is well-recognized as the key to great leadership,* most business leaders don't communicate well. At least that's what their employees say. According to talent management firm Aon Hewitt, only 46 percent of employees feel management communicates effectively.[23] And human resources firm Towers Perrin has found that just over half (51 percent) of employees believed that their leaders generally tell them the truth.[24] These findings are not entirely surprising if you consider that most leaders don't receive formal training in communications, so often they don't know what to say or how to say it in a way that effectively engages their people.

The keys to successful leadership communication—especially as you are trying to cultivate a culture that aligns and integrates with

---

* Among the leaders who recognize the importance of communication as a core leadership skill are Jack Welch, former GE CEO, and Kip Tindell, chairman of the board and cofounder of The Container Store. Welch defines a leader as someone who is able to communicate successfully, while Tindell goes so far as to say, "Communication and leadership are really the same thing." (Sources: Braun, Eduardo. 2016. *People First Leadership: How the Best Leaders Use Culture and Emotion to Drive Unprecedented Results.* Columbus, Ohio: McGraw-Hill Education. Location 1815, Kindle. Tindell, Kip. 2014. *Uncontainable: How Passion, Commitment, and Conscious Capitalism Built a Business Where Everyone Thrives.* New York: Grand Central Publishing. Page 138.)

your brand identity—are consistency, simplicity, storytelling, and relevance.

Consistency. When it comes to cultivating your desired culture and weaving it into the daily ethos at your company, you must first consistently and relentlessly communicate your company's overarching purpose and core values and why they're important. It's not enough to talk about these foundational elements of your culture when they're first being set or on an annual basis. You must regularly weave messages about your purpose and values into your presentations, memos, and conversations with employees and other stakeholders. You may tire of talking about the same topics over and over again or think you're being repetitive, but studies have shown repetition and consistency are critical to comprehension and traction.

Simplicity. Strive to make your communications simple and accessible. Some leaders try to be charismatic or come across as impressive whenever they speak or share information, so they get caught up in conveying a message that sounds exciting or that is full or jargon or complex terms instead of one that has substance and can be easily understood by everyone. A Morgan Stanley analyst once noted, "One of Alan Mulally's greatest skills was his consistent communication of the goals and the progress made in a strikingly simple way that inspired the entire organization from board down to factory line worker."[25] Keep your communication as simple and straightforward as possible—but that doesn't mean you have to "dumb it down" or make it boring. Mulally did neither.

Storytelling. Illustrate your message with engaging stories. Giving examples and telling stories helps people relate to abstract ideas like culture and values. For example, stories about great successes achieved in the face of great odds or of people who have pushed through challenges will cultivate values like perseverance and performance. Storytelling creates high levels of interest and feelings of authenticity—and a compelling narrative gets people to see themselves in the story so they become personally engaged.

Relevance. Make your communications relevant to your organization's overarching purpose and core values. Carefully choose what to talk about because it can speak volumes about the kind of culture you're trying to cultivate. If your desired culture is one that is familial and casual, you'll want to talk about your employees in a personal way and reference the things going on in their lives outside of work. If you're seeking to cultivate a culture of innovation and creativity at your organization, you can infuse your communications with references to cutting-edge ideas and iconic geniuses. You should also align the methods you use to communicate with the culture you want to promote. If you want to cultivate a culture of experimentation, try new communication channels and technology. If one of your core values is "adding the personal touch," send handwritten notes to your people.

KEYS TO EFFECTIVE LEADERSHIP COMMUNICATION:

- Consistent
- Simple
- Accessible
- Story-driven
- Relevant

Leadership communication is as much about listening as it is about talking. When Melissa Daimler headed the global learning and organizational development team at Twitter, she wrote a piece for the *Harvard Business Review* outlining three levels of listening:

1. Internal listening—pretending to listen to the other person but only focusing on your own thoughts, worries, and priorities
2. Focused listening—focusing on the other person but still not fully connecting with him or her
3. 360 listening—listening not only to what the other person is saying, but *how* they're saying it and what they're *not* saying

Daimler believes 360 listening is "where the magic happens.... There's energy. There's the reminder of what's possible if we focus on what the other person has to say."[26] By truly engaging with your employees with 360 listening, you can enroll them in your desired culture as much as you can by speaking with consistency, simplicity, storytelling, and relevance.

"Communication is responsible for transmitting the DNA of the company's culture," Braun sums up in *People First Leadership.* "Communication connects each member of the corporate body so they can trust each other and work toward the same vision."[27] But however important communication is to cultivating your desired culture, your work can't end there. As a leader, you must deliver on and embody your desired culture in your actions and decisions.

ACTIONS SPEAK LOUDER THAN WORDS

What you *say* matters, but just as important, what you *do* provides models of action for your people and telegraphs how committed you are to aligning your culture with your brand. As a leader, you must be a paragon of your desired culture. In a study by the American Management Association and Institute for Corporate Productivity, 61 percent of managers said that actions by leaders were the most likely to influence the behavior of others in the organization. Ann Rhoades, former head of people for Southwest Airlines, believes leaders should "leverage [this] very persistent tendency of employees to follow the leader."[28]

Alan Mulally certainly did. *American Icon* author Hoffman describes how he used his behaviors to promote a more open, unified culture at Ford. At the weekly BPR meetings with his executive team, for example, he introduced a color coding system for their reports that used colors to indicate the status of every program or project—green for those that were on track or ahead of schedule, yellow for those at risk with potential issues or concerns, and red for those that were behind schedule or off-target. The idea was to make it easy to track changes in status and pinpoint problems. Consistent with Ford's core values of honesty and transparency, he assured his team that the meetings were a safe environment where they could raise problems for the group to work on together. Nonetheless, at the beginning, his executives insisted on labeling all their charts green for weeks.[29]

American Icon author Hoffman describes how Mark Fields, president of Ford's U.S. business at the time, finally decided to test Mulally's words of assurance. Hoffman says that Fields thought "somebody has to figure out if this guy is for real." At the next meeting, Fields began his presentation with some preliminary data and then moved on to a chart that showed a new product launch was delayed; it was marked with a red flag. He paused and waited in silence, along with the rest of attendees, expecting to get chewed out and possibly fired for admitting a problem. That's what would have happened under previous leadership. Instead, Mulally started clapping and commended him for the "great visibility" he shared. Turning to the rest of the group, Mulally then asked who could help Fields address the problem and facilitated a discussion among the group that identified potential solutions. The meeting served as a turning point for Mulally and his people. They learned he was true to his word.[30]

Sometimes even a leader's seemingly small actions speak volumes. After Marvin Ellison took on the task of turning around JCPenney in August 2015, he chose to wear clothes bought at the company's stores, signaling to employees, customers, and the public at large a strong endorsement of the brand's quality and style.[31] Moreover, to reinforce the solidarity that the company would need to pull off such a dramatic turnaround, he instituted a rule requiring all executives to wear JCPenney–made clothes whenever they visit the stores.[32]

While actions—big and small—speak louder than words for everyone but especially for leaders, a lack of action can be just as powerful. You can't expect your employees to act in ways that you don't or won't.

Once, while I was facilitating a brand engagement session for a client, one of the employees pulled me aside during a break. I had just taken the group through an exercise to reinforce safety as the primary core value for the company. The employee told me he appreciated the focus on safety but he had a favor to ask: could I talk to the CEO about his personal engagement in safety training sessions—or rather, the lack of it. You see, over the years the CEO had never once attended a safety session, and his absence was noticed by employees, who took it to mean that the training was unimportant. It didn't matter that the CEO had declared safety as a core value and made it part of the company's tagline, nor that he had hired a dedicated safety trainer or built the very facility we were meeting at exclusively to be used for onsite safety training. Without walking the talk and making safety training sessions a priority on his calendar, his credibility had been shot.

ENGAGE EVERY LEADER

While it's essential that top leaders talk and walk when it comes to communicating and living out the core values of the company, you won't succeed unless every person in a leadership role, no matter their level, is on board. Organization-wide alignment is critical to integrating your culture and brand. Executives at the top of an organization must hold accountable their direct reports for cultivating the desired culture, those managers in turn must do the same for theirs, and so on. No managerial position is too small or too remote to ignore the impact it has on the attitude and behaviors of employees around it.

The adage "people leave managers, not companies" speaks to the central relationship between direct manager and employee—particularly for frontline employees who rarely interact with their organization's top executives. Leaders in the middle layers of an organization's hierarchy, like department managers, store managers, and program leaders, wield the most influence on an employee's daily experience and therefore are a critical group in any culture transformation effort.

But middle managers in many organizations are not engaged to the degree that higher-level leaders are. Aon Hewitt found that in companies rated as "best employers," engagement steadily declined, as you'd expect, along with the level of responsibility of the person surveyed—that is, top leaders were the most engaged, team members were the least, and in between there was a linear correlation going down through the organization. But at all other companies, there was sharp drop-off in engagement at the middle management and team leader level.[33] Why the drop-off?

Most often middle managers are burdened with day-to-day operations that make it challenging for them to focus on tasks that may seem longer-term or less defined. Sometimes top leaders view middle managers as employees to influence rather than as the powerful influencers that they are, so they don't engage them properly. When it comes to cultivating culture, these are missed opportunities since mid- and lower-level managers are uniquely positioned to show employees what the organization really values, which attitudes and behaviors are on-brand, and why they and their actions matter.

"Managers who buy into the vision of the company can make daily decisions that guide the firm in the right direction," observe business school professors George Serafeim and Claudine Gartenberg in an article for *Harvard Business Review.* They conclude, "[Purpose] only matters if it is implemented in conjunction with clear, concise direction from top management and in such a way that the middle layer within the firm is fully bought in."[34] If you don't engage, empower, and equip this management layer to cultivate the desired culture as much as you do with their higher-level counterparts, your efforts to align and integrate brand and culture are likely to be stalled by what one of my clients called the "frozen middle."

This client's company had hired me to help it achieve more traction on its diversity and inclusion (D&I) efforts and more tangible improvements in the results these efforts produced. At the very top levels of the organization, support for the D&I efforts was clearly evident: The CEO set it as a top priority and, together with the executive team, actively championed it in his communications. Grassroots support was also strong, with employees across the company participating in affinity groups, forums, and trainings dedicated to advancing D&I in the company.

Despite all that forward movement, middle management had been left behind. It was particularly hard for middle managers at the company, who were predominantly white males, to internalize the value of D&I. Even those who understood it intellectually didn't understand how to operationalize those values on a daily basis. This "frozen middle" was holding the company back from tapping into the innovation and fresh thinking that greater D&I would deliver—and that, in turn, was limiting the company's ability to address the changing landscape in which its brand operated.

To thaw this frozen middle, we had to think about, and then convey, the value of D&I from a middle manager's perspective. First, we broke down for them the business case for D&I and other data that tied D&I to the results the managers were accountable for. To win their hearts and motivate them emotionally, we assembled inspiring, relevant success stories from their peers. And to instruct them on how to embed D&I into their daily operating activities and reap its benefits, we offered them tools such as diversity action plans. By increasing adoption of D&I in this middle tier of management, we were able to shift attitudes and generate increased momentum for D&I among all levels at the company. Lower-level employees were informed and affirmed by the role modeling they experienced from their managers, and higher-level executives became even more engaged when they started to see improved results in their units. Every leader at every level is a link in the leadership chain that connects culture to results.

REINFORCE YOUR CULTURE WITH THE RIGHT PEOPLE DECISIONS

One reason it's critical to empower leaders at all levels to cultivate your desired culture is that leaders are responsible for the most important tasks in any organization: hiring, firing, and promoting employees. People decisions are perhaps the most visible way leaders can build their culture and align it with the company's brand identity.

When it comes to hiring employees, companies that are committed to cultivating and maintaining their desired culture don't simply use their core values to screen potential employees—they prioritize them. QuikTrip, a $9 billion regional chain of convenience stores in the U.S., relies heavily on the company's core values such as "work with teams to constantly improve" and "encourage continuous self-improvement" in its recruiting efforts.[35] But since, as a *Harvard Business Review* article observes, it's difficult to accurately and fairly assess a person on these intangible dimensions, the company puts applicants through "a rigorous, structured screening process" that includes administering a personality assessment and asking each interview question in several different ways. They've found that candidates can't game the system, and the test reveals their true fit with QuikTrip's values.[36]

To make core values a critical element of every hiring decision, you must first make it a leadership responsibility. Former Southwest Airlines executive Ann Rhoades explains, "Everyone in leadership must understand that this step, perhaps more than any other, is a *strategic business responsibility*, not an HR function. This sense of responsibility needs to permeate everyone's consciousness and be constantly reinforced by leaders." In her book *Built on Values,* she shares how one organization went so far as to make hiring and retaining "A players" part of the calculation for leaders' bonuses. Doing so produced clear and significant benefits—employee turnover fell dramatically while customer satisfaction rose just as considerably.[37]

When you rely on your core values to make choices about not only whom to hire, but also whom to *fire* and *promote*, you make sure the right people are on your bus—and you send a powerful message to your organization about the importance of its values.

Jack Welch, former CEO of GE, is known for having executed "public hangings," the term he uses to explicitly call out executives who do not align with the company's values. In a *Fortune* article, Welch and his wife and business partner, Suzy Welch, explain, "If your company's culture is to mean anything, you have to hang—publicly—those in your midst who would destroy it." They go on to explain that leaders should classify their people into one of four categories and decide their fates based on the classification:

- Employees who produce good results and behave in ways that align with your company's values should be promoted.
- Employees who are not a fit with your company's values and perform poorly should be fired.
- Employees whose behavior aligns with your company's values, but whose performance is mediocre deserve a second chance and coaching.
- Employees whose actions don't align with your company's values but who produce great results should be let go.[38]

The Welches believe that the employees who most threaten their organizations—who most undermine the culture of the company—are those in the fourth category. And yet managers typically give employees in this category a pass because of their great performance. Keeping these employees, they argue, sends "a big fat message to every other employee: Our company's values are a joke." The Welches' language may be harsh, but it describes spot-on why a leader's decisions about people are critical. "'Values drift' is pervasive in companies of every ilk," they write. "Employees either don't know their organization's values, or they know that practicing them is optional. Either way the result is vulnerability to attack from inside and out."[39]

The hiring and firing decisions you and your fellow leaders make may be the ultimate litmus tests for the strength of leadership commitment to cultivating your desired culture.

BRAND-CULTURE FUSION STARTS WITH YOU

"In order to be a successful leader in the twenty-first century," writes Braun, summing up his findings from hundreds of interviews with some of the world's most respected leaders, "one must lead through emotion, which means fostering a strong culture. That is the lesson I have learned."[40]

Leadership is critical to a thriving culture. But leadership is even more important if you want to *transform* that culture either because your current one is not serving the company well or because it has never been shaped or guided in a deliberate way in the first place. Building an internal culture that is aligned and integrated with your external brand, therefore, starts with you. You must prioritize brand-culture fusion and take responsibility for achieving it. You can't take it for granted, you can't delegate it, and you can't take a day off from it.

A leader functions like a rocket booster for the rest of the company. You provide the main thrust to lift the organization up and propel it toward brand-culture fusion. Without that initial boost, the company would have no chance of reaching its goal. Eventually, though, the organization develops its own power and takes off to even greater heights—but you must equip and empower it to soar. Part 2 shows you how to do so by laying out the five key strategies for achieving brand-culture fusion.

Key Takeaways from This Chapter:

- The integration of culture and brand is a key leadership responsibility—your responsibility.
- You must consistently communicate the purpose and values of your organization and why they're important, and do it in ways that reinforce their distinct characteristics.
- Small decisions and behaviors telegraph to your organization the strength of your commitment to brand-culture fusion, so model behaviors you want embraced organization-wide.
- Your efforts to integrate brand and culture are likely to be stalled by the "frozen middle"; ensure middle managers are just as engaged and empowered as top leaders to cultivate culture.
- Rely on your core values when making decisions about whom to hire, fire, and promote.

PART 2

FIVE STRATEGIES TO ACHIEVE BRAND-CULTURE FUSION

The roadmap for your journey to brand-culture fusion comprises strategies to nurture your desired culture by infusing it with your brand, or vice versa.

CHAPTER 4

ORGANIZE AND OPERATE ON-BRAND

Read this chapter to learn:

- Why your culture must be *operationalized* throughout your organizational design and operations
- How to use design thinking to match your organizational design to your desired culture
- How to use your brand purpose and core values to shape operations

When the leaders at Adobe, the maker of Photoshop and other popular software, took an honest look at their company a couple of years ago, they realized a deficit in its customer service and support. The company had experienced great success in a highly competitive market because it employed extremely creative people and actively nurtured their growth and development—which led them to produce superior products. But since Adobe products were originally sold almost entirely through channel partners like computer manufacturers and retailers, developing a strong support function to directly help their customers had not been the company's top priority.

As their business model evolved to include more direct-to-customer sales, their brand identity had to evolve too: Adobe needed to be known not just for its excellent products and how they enable creativity, but also for providing excellent customer support. To transform their brand, they had to inject more customer-focused thinking into of every one of their employees, regardless of role. Senior vice president Donna Morris explained, "We realized we needed to be as great to work with as we are to work for. That required cultural change."[1]

Morris and her colleagues started by combining previously disconnected parts of the company into single entities. First, they married the support functions for personal and enterprise products, which had previously operated independently, into one unit. Doing so produced a more holistic view of customers throughout the company.[2]

Second, they created a new department—a combined customer and employee experience organization—bringing together the support people on the front lines of helping customers with the HR team responsible for supporting employees. In her new role leading customer and employee experience, Morris' responsibility is to ensure everyone—employees and customers—has a positive experience with Adobe. At the time of the change she explained, "[My role] is making sure people are successful and we grow our relationship with them. If they're an employee, that means attracting and developing them and helping them grow. If it's a customer, it's the same thing."[3] The intent was that this new department would be able to leverage the company's expertise in creating great experiences for employees to produce excellent experiences for customers as well.

Finally, as Adobe transitioned to a cloud-based subscription model, it needed a more agile and adaptive workforce culture to meet the new needs of its customers. Morris and her colleagues assessed the number of Adobe work locations and reduced them from eighty to sixty-eight. They found that having so many offices had added complexity to the way Adobe employees worked and hindered its desired culture. Consolidating geographically, she said, "was a very deliberate decision to ensure that our employees had the opportunity to work together in close proximity."[4]

FROM TALKING ABOUT CULTURE
TO OPERATIONALIZING IT

Adobe's leaders approach culture change as a strategic business change. Most business leaders don't. Research from Korn Ferry, an executive search and recruiting firm, reports that while 72 percent of executives agree that culture is "extremely important" to organizational performance, only 32 percent say their culture aligns with their business strategy.[5]

That disconnect might be explained by the research conducted by Booz Allen Hamilton and the Aspen Institute, which shows that a vast majority of executives see their core values—and by extension, their culture—affecting only their corporate reputation and their employee recruitment and retention efforts. Far fewer believe that values and culture influence their organization's adaptability to changing conditions, operational efficiency and productivity, risk management, and growth in revenues and earnings.[6]

It's a chicken-or-the-egg problem. If business leaders don't see how culture impacts business performance, then they don't operationalize—that is, put into action and use—their core values throughout their business and, therefore, they don't see any definitive results from them. The researchers conclude, "The next set of imperatives is for business leaders to move from talking about values and viewing them defensively to embracing them in order to drive corporate performance and change."[7]

In other words, it's not enough to set an overarching purpose and core values for your organization without considering how you are actually going to pursue them:

- How does your purpose stretch your organization?
- What operational changes are needed to enable employees to live your values?
- How do your people need to work together differently?
- What must your organization start or stop doing to make your purpose and values a core part of the way you do business?

To tap the full value and growth-creating potential of your desired culture—one that is fully aligned with your brand—you must operationalize it through strategy (the company's business objectives and budgets), management (its leadership responsibilities and support), communication (its internal and external messages), employee experience (its daily employee interactions), organization (its structure), and operations (its systems.) These last two areas—(1) your organizational design: the units, hierarchy, and roles in your organization; and (2) your operations: the different business functions and day-to-day processes and practices at your company—are critically important because they undergird all the others. If your organizational design and your operations aren't supporting and advancing your desired culture and brand, they're probably detracting from it. You send mixed messages and dilute efforts by not aligning the two.

That's what this chapter is about. I'll explain why your desired culture cannot be cultivated only through human resources efforts—you must *operationalize* it. I will show you how to apply design thinking to match your organizational design to your desired culture and will share a range of examples that prove the effectiveness of doing so. Then I'll discuss the importance of your operations on culture and show how Brazilian personal care company Natura redesigned its processes to affirm and advance its overarching purpose and core values. I'll close the chapter by explaining how you can unify your people and processes by identifying, assessing, and optimizing key brand touchpoints using a tool I call the Brand Touchpoint Wheel. With these insights and methods, you'll be equipped to lead a successful culture change.

DESIGN YOUR ORGANIZATION DELIBERATELY

The culture at Southwest Airlines is widely admired, but what few people realize is that the company's agile, efficient, and fun culture is rooted in a unique organizational design. This design features a high managers-per-employee ratio, distributed leadership, and a boundary-spanner role (responsible for bringing together information from different operating units of the business).[8]

In fact, writing in *The Southwest Airlines Way*, Brandeis University professor Jody Hoffer Gittell attributes Southwest's success largely to the "organizational relationships" the company cultivates between managers and frontline employees, between employees themselves, and with outside parties. Southwest sees these relationships "as the foundation of competitive advantage, through good times and bad," Gittell reports. "They see the quality of these relationships not as *a* success factor, but as the *most essential* success factor."[9] Southwest shows that by developing and implementing a distinct organizational design, you can produce a distinct organizational culture. But most business leaders aren't deliberately designing their organizations these days.

Executive coach Gill Corkindale observes in the *Harvard Business Review* that organizations are being forced to rethink their strategies and change the way they operate more quickly and frequently, leading them to lose sight of the big picture. In turn, Corkindale writes, this "can result in lots of piecemeal change initiatives rather than looking at the overall organizational design. I rarely come across leaders who advocate wholesale organizational redesign or use it as a way to support their people and business."[10]

To reclaim control over your organization and implement a design that invigorates employees and builds distinctive capabilities, the consulting firm Strategy& recommends adhering to several design principles. These include, "Declare amnesty from the past"—that is, reflect on your desired outcome instead of getting stuck in your current state. Then set a new "bold direction" and "make the most of top talent"—design positions to optimize the strengths of the people who will occupy them. The following three principles, in particular, address how your design choices can facilitate brand-culture alignment and integration:

Benchmark sparingly, if at all. Instead of looking for best practices from other organizations, design your organization to leverage its unique capabilities. There are strengths that only your organization has which produce results that others can't match. They're probably the source of whatever brand advantage you've enjoyed to date. Design your organization to emphasize these.

Fit your company purpose. Design the spans of control and lay-ers of management to reflect your strategy, desired differentiation, and vision. Your organizational design should help your organization do the kind of work that is necessary to pursue its purpose.

Accentuate the informal. Acknowledge the intangible ways peo-ple think, feel, communicate, and act. In other words, consider how your existing organizational design has produced the core values that are currently being lived out, and then develop a new design that pro-motes the ones that correspond to your desired brand type and discour-ages the ones you want to change.[11]

Applying these design principles will ensure you don't simply design your organization in a way that's typical in your industry or produce a merely functional organization. It will also help you avoid a common mistake leaders make: assuming that an organizational design that has worked for them at one company will work in another one.

Eddie Lambert, who is CEO of Sears Holdings at the time I'm writ-ing this, learned this lesson the hard way when he decentralized the management of the Sears and Kmart organizations and created over thirty silos of business lines such as women's wear, shoes, and home furnishings, each with its own leadership and board of directors. A *New York Times* article chronicling the downfall of the company explained that this strategy is sometimes used at hedge funds, the kinds of firms Lambert had managed previously. But while the organizational design that emphasizes intracompany competition worked brilliantly in Lambert's financial firms, it was a complete disaster in a department store company where cross-functional cooperation and a collaborative culture are required to create a seamless customer experience. The orga-nizational design led to infighting among department heads and manag-ers who would "tell their sales staff not to help customers in adjacent sections, even if someone asked for help." The article suggests it was one of the reasons why the company was headed toward bankruptcy.[12]

Your goal should be an organization that's designed specifically to cultivate your desired culture—not someone's else—so that you can ultimately achieve brand-culture fusion. With this goal in mind, consider how you might use the three primary elements of organizational design: structure, standards, and roles.

Organizational Structure

The structure of your organization—its hierarchy, divisions, and organizing logic—determines who works together and how. You can use organizational structure to facilitate the relationships that will promote your desired culture and advance the priorities that you want your culture to embody.

The renowned Cleveland Clinic uses a particular organizational structure to support and advance its desired culture and brand. It is organized into different specialty centers focused on diseases such as diabetes, cardiac care, etc. Harvard Business School professor Frances X. Frei explains that this structure fits the unique demands of the organization. Because Cleveland Clinic attracts the most severely afflicted patients, its doctors operate in challenging environments that require innovative solutions. She observes, "Organizing into disease centers rather than narrower, more traditional lines of specialization (such as kidneys or blood) sets the stage for cross-disciplinary collaboration—and thus for novel perspectives—within those centers."[13]

Organizational Standards

Organizational standards—rules that are applied company-wide when forming departments, units, work groups, or teams—are another element of design that can help you create an organization that supports your desired culture. For example, the leaders of Google implemented "the rule of seven" throughout the company. In *How Google Works*, former CEO Eric Schmidt and former SVP of products Jonathan Rosenberg explain that, when designing their organization, they wanted to create an environment where "smart creatives" (multidimensional workers who have technical expertise, business savvy, *and* creative flair) could succeed. Knowing that smart creatives are oriented to getting things done and need direct access to decision-makers, Schmidt and Rosenberg encouraged managers to have a minimum of seven direct reports—instead of adding layers between smart creatives and decision-makers—to produce less managerial oversight and more employee freedom, the kind that allows smart creatives to thrive.[14] Thus, the standard or organizational "rule of seven" was born at Google.

Organizational Roles

When designing your organization, you should also carefully consider how creating certain roles can advance your desired culture. The unique role held by Donna Morris, who led the cultural transformation at Adobe described at the beginning of this chapter, serves as an example of how this element of organizational design can be used strategically. In her newly combined role as head of both the company's customer experience team and its human resources and facilities teams, Morris helps to cultivate a culture in which customer-focused thinking is in the DNA of every employee.[15]

Another example of a unique role comes from LinkedIn. There, "Culture Champions" are employees who volunteer to promote the company's culture and ensure employees have a great experience on a daily basis. The company's 250 Culture Champions, who are distributed across thirty offices worldwide, organize an average of forty-eight employee events a year, including "InDays," the days given to employees each month to "invest in themselves, the company and the world."[16] LinkedIn's communications leader, Nicole Leverich, explained to me that since, at its highest level, the company's brand stands for creating opportunities, it "sure as heck better create amazing professional opportunities for its employees. We should be at the forefront of benefits, learning, training....Otherwise, we're not walking the walk."[17] Because culture and brand must be so tightly intertwined at LinkedIn, the role of a Culture Champion is a critical element of its organizational design.

San Diego Regional Airport Authority created a new role to support its desired culture by combining responsibilities historically segregated into marketing and human resources departments. Jeff Lindeman served as the head of the Vision, Voice, and Engagement department *and* the Talent, Culture, and Capability department for the public agency, which manages the day-to-day operations of San

Diego International Airport. His role facilitated the transformation the organization undertook in 2016. It promoted the "Let's Go" campaign to position the airport externally as an international gateway and improve its competitiveness by creating a unified, seemingly larger identity. "Let's Go" was also used internally to rally the organization and help employees embrace the idea that the Airport Authority was a global competitor, not just a county or regional agency, and make decisions consistent with that identity. Lindeman told me, "The campaign became a catalyst inside the organization for being better."[18] The success of the campaign can be attributed in part to Lindeman's role which uniquely joined external and internal efforts.

Structure, standards, and roles are the primary elements to consider when you design or redesign your organization. Other design building blocks include information flows (how the organization processes and shares data and knowledge), decision rights and accountabilities (who makes what decisions and who has what responsibilities), networks (how people connect and work together outside the formal organization chart), and norms (what behaviors and actions are expected). All of these are variables for you to use to set the right design for your organization.

Once you have an initial design draft of your organization, examine it for redundancies, making sure responsibilities are allocated exclusively to the person or teams best suited to fulfill them. Determine if the design is flexible enough to evolve and adapt as your culture and brand do. Test it for feasibility—does the design take into account constraints that are out of your control (e.g., available technology)? Make certain that responsibility for key metrics of brand performance and culture health (e.g., customer and employee retention, Net Promoter Score, and employee engagement) are shared across the organization, as they should be.

Most importantly, determine if your design is a good fit with your culture—does the design promote your overarching purpose, core values, and desired culture? Think about how your employees' ability and proclivity to live out your purpose and values is cultivated or curtailed by your organization design. For example, if you want a culture that is less paternalistic and operates more democratically, does the hierarchy

MARKETING & HUMAN RESOURCES: COLLABORATION, NOT COMPETITION

One aspect of organizational design deserves special attention: the relationship between marketing and human resources departments. Hilton Barbour, partner at Toronto-based consulting firm Global Brand Leaders, writes about potential conflicts between the two groups. In a piece entitled "HR versus Marketing—The Next C-Suite Confrontation," he predicts a battle between the two functions over employees. "If creating a world-class brand experience remains the remit of CMO's, and without fully-engaged employees that's not possible, it stands to reason that employee experience and engagement should fall under that remit too." He recognizes though that, as a "marketing veteran," he is biased, so his final recommendation is to marry marketing and human resources.[19]

Consider the arrangement at Umpqua, a regional bank in the Northwest, that Tyler Laird-Magee describes in her doctoral thesis. The senior officers for Cultural Enhancement (human resources) and Creative Strategies (marketing) have their corner offices at either end of the executive floor and their employees work side-by-side in between.[20]

The Cultural Enhancement head explains, "It's really not two different departments because brand is culture and culture is brand.... We see ourselves as being on the same team—we share work, we share ideas." And the head of Creative Strategies adds, "I need and have to support what she [the head of Cultural Enhancement] is doing and vice versa since we are really playing off of each other. What I do helps her recruit really great people. What I do creates

> reputation, but what she does is deliver to that customer so that word of mouth is there.... There are no dotted lines.... We're constantly in each other's space." Laird-Magee observes, "To a visitor it is impossible to know where one department ends and the other begins."[21]

in your organizational structure reflect that? Or if your purpose is about inspiring people to be more creative, do you hinder that by restricting creative development to a single department?

Your culture is like a vine that requires a trellis to provide support and structure to grow in the right direction. The right organizational design provides that trellis.

ALIGN YOUR "WHAT" WITH YOUR "WHY" AND "HOW"

When it comes to fully integrating and aligning your culture and brand, how you *run* your organization is just as important as how you *design* it. Unfortunately, when most companies take on the task of operationalizing culture, they usually only consider changes to human resources processes such as recruiting, on-boarding, training, and rewarding employees. These processes are indeed critical to cultivating the culture you desire. But your core operations—that is, your company's business functions and day-to-day processes and practices—also help create the environment in which your desired culture can thrive and align with your brand identity.

But oftentimes, the processes and practices that employees engage in on a regular basis—planning, budgeting, sales, fulfillment, service, etc.—are the very ones that prohibit employees from executing on your core values. For example, mandating extensive budget and project approval processes will prevent a company from cultivating a less risk-averse culture. Insisting on detailed strategic planning will prevent a company from cultivating an agile culture.

But if you craft them the right way, your operations can help your organization cultivate the right culture. For example, if you want to undergird your performance brand identity with a more competitive organizational culture, give employees access to the company's key performance metrics and competitive intelligence and enroll them in a process of regularly engaging with that information. If you want to encourage a culture of experimentation to align with an identity as an innovative brand, develop a process for rapid prototyping.

When assessing the alignment of your company's current operations with your desired culture, consider the following: what do your product processes (e.g., designing, engineering, manufacturing, delivering, and servicing products) convey about your culture? That it is agile, original, or predictable? How about your sales process (e.g., goal-setting, prospecting and qualifying customers, closing deals, attribution), or your annual planning and budgeting process? If these processes are not in sync with where you want to take your culture—that is, if they don't help align your culture with your brand—then it's time for some process reengineering.

Culture-aligned operations can be achieved at any degree. On the more tactical end of the continuum, consider how Marvin Ellison instituted "Project Simple" as part of his efforts to turnaround JCPenney. To enable store employees to become more customer-service oriented, he reduced the number of emails managers get[22] and sent weekly instructions that streamlined what action items managers had to tackle so they could spend more time with customers rather than reviewing and filling out tons of paperwork.[23]

At a more strategic level, consider how Brazilian corporation Natura used new innovation processes to promote its desired culture. Antonio Luiz da Cunha Seabra founded Natura in a garage in Sao Paolo in 1969, and the company has since become a $4 billion global beauty care brand by operating as a different kind of company. Through the years, the company had been recognized as an innovation leader, including being named the eighth most innovative company in the world by *Forbes* magazine in 2011.[24]

But starting in the mid-2000s, Natura faced intense competition from around the world and it determined it needed to fortify its innovative brand identity. So the company leaders decided to double down on innovation in its strategy and culture. They renewed emphasis on innovation as a core capability and primary approach to product development and added it as one of their culture drivers, defining it as "being entrepreneurial, taking the lead, doing what has never been done and assuming the risks."[25]

To bring about this culture of innovation, Natura leaders revised many of the company's innovation processes and introduced new ones. They revamped their product development process to develop new competencies, integrating what they call a "Technology Funnel" to identify new materials and alternative methodologies for product testing and for measuring impact on the environment, with an "Innovation Funnel" to identify customer needs and market opportunities. They also implemented a new portfolio management process, which put more emphasis on analyzing the intangible value of new products[26], and they created new input, processing, and output metrics to assess the effectiveness of these new processes.[27] These changes required employees to embrace more innovative actions and decision-making, and as a result, they also embraced a more innovative mindset.

Between 2007 and 2011, Natura increased revenues from 3 billion to 5 billion Brazilian Real.[28] Three of its managers concluded in a case study showcasing the company that Natura achieved its remarkable results because it had adopted the view that innovation was "a complex process permeating all of the company, strongly influenced by internal processes and corporate culture."[29]

Their last observation makes an important point about the interplay between process change and culture change. So far I've described the role that operations can play in advancing culture, but the relationship between the two is less cause-and-effect and more symbiotic. Operations impacts culture by shaping how people work, and culture impacts operations by making that work effective and efficient. When aligned and integrated, operations and culture work together in a virtuous cycle that produces your desired business and brand outcomes.

INSPECT YOUR BRAND TOUCHPOINTS

One way to identify which organizational areas and which operational processes and practices are ripe for cultural transformation is to work on brand touchpoints.

Brand touchpoints are ways that people in the outside world come into contact with your brand. Some touchpoints can be a single element, such as a product or a piece of communication; other touchpoints are interactions or experiences that combine multiple elements, such as the installation of equipment or participation in a customer event. Touchpoints exist throughout the entire customer journey, from discovery (an email invitation, an in-store display, or a business card) to purchase (a salesperson at the register, a website check-out process, an invoice), to use (a button on a device, a project plan, a mobile app), and to service and support (a call center agent, the furniture in a waiting room, a loyalty program).

Most organizations have hundreds of brand touchpoints. For example, when I headed brand and strategy at Sony's electronics company, we identified over 240 brand touchpoints, not including all the different products we offered. A FedEx research project found more than 200 customer touchpoints, and John Deere Financial discovered 529 spanning multiple product lines.[30]

It's quite common to overlook or underestimate how back-office functions or employees in non-customer-facing roles affect brand touchpoints. A large construction company realized that its stringent contractor invoicing process was a touchpoint that directly affected building quality issues. When it switched to a shorter payment schedule and required contractors to fill out fewer forms, it began to attract better contractors, who in turn built better-quality homes. RightNow, a customer relationship management software company, identified areas in its contracts that often resulted in protracted negotiations with clients. By eliminating many of those sticking points, it was able to shorten its sales cycle, benefiting both the company and its customers.[31]

By identifying and assessing your brand touchpoints, you can pinpoint which ones impact brand perceptions the most. To improve the ones that have a negative impact as well as leverage the most positive ones, you also need to identify the people and processes within your organization that are responsible for them. Here's how.

Visualize Your Touchpoints with a Brand Touchpoint Wheel

With a Brand Touchpoint Wheel, you can catalog and visualize all the brand touchpoints at your company—and all the organizational elements that must come together to ensure each touchpoint is on-brand. It is a powerful tool to help you integrate and align your internal workings and external brand identity.

There are four steps to creating your Brand Touchpoint Wheel.

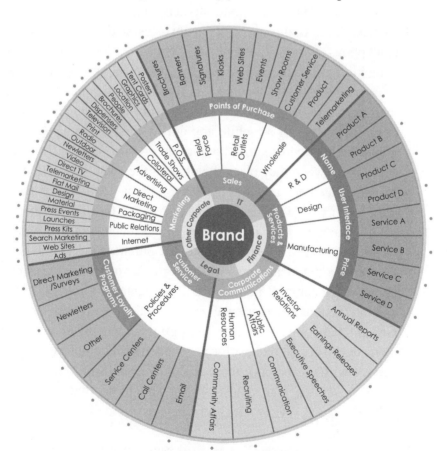

Figure 4.1 Brand Touchpoint Wheel Example

Step one, audit. Conduct an audit of all the ways your company communicates with the outside world and all the experiences you provide customers and other external stakeholders. This might seem like an overwhelming task, but assembling a cross-functional team to conduct the audit makes it more manageable—and you'll also end up with more comprehensive results.

Step two, organize. Organize your touchpoints by following one of these approaches:

- Classify them according to the stages in your customer experience journey, e.g., pre-purchase, purchase, and post-purchase touchpoints. Then add noncustomer interactions like annual reports, office buildings, supplier invoices, and other corporate touchpoints. This tack, though, requires you to double-list touchpoints that serve more than one function since customers' purchase journeys have become less linear and the influences on their purchase decisions, less discrete. For example, customers might interact with a mobile app during the prepurchase stage while they are considering buying the product, during the purchase stage when they place the product they want to buy in the cart and check out, and during the postpurchase while they leave a customer review of the product or need to find the customer service number. The "mobile app" brand touchpoint, therefore, would need to be listed in several of the purchase journey stages.
- Organize your touchpoints into three groups: objects (e.g., advertising or packaging), people (e.g., call centers or salespeople), and interactions or experiences (e.g., social media or websites).
- Group touchpoints according to those the company controls or owns (e.g., service request forms, coupons, and employee interactions with customers), those it shares responsibility for (e.g., delivery service and sponsorships), and those that it merely influences (e.g., review sites and employee word of mouth).

Whatever organizing logic you use, remember to include your products themselves, since they usually have the greatest impact on brand perceptions and yet are often overlooked as brand touchpoints in this kind of exercise.

Step three, map. For each touchpoint, list the internal departments, groups, or people who develop or deliver it, and identify the processes or practices they use to do so. Then map out the areas where you find commonalities or overlaps so you can group them together into layers of people or processes.

For example, your company might use product project teams to manage the pricing, packaging, distribution, and marketing of a product and all the touchpoints in each of those areas, so you might locate those touchpoints next to each other on your wheel and add a "product team" layer inside the wheel that spans across them. Or your sales process might include touchpoints from product brochures to references and invoices, so you'd want to group those together under a "sales process" layer.

As you work through this step, resist the natural inclination to create layers by internal departments only and instead consider how people from different departments might work with each other to influence the touchpoints. Doing so will produce a tool that not only clearly identifies who and what is involved with each touchpoint, but also helps break down organizational silos by illuminating where cross-functional collaboration is imperative. In the sales process example above, the marketing department might be responsible for the product brochures, the sales department for the references, and the accounting department for the invoices. By grouping all three touchpoints under one layer, you draw attention to the coordination that is needed between all three groups during the sales process.

Step four, arrange: Arrange the touchpoints, people, and processes into a visual wheel, with your brand in the center, all of the touchpoints on the rim, and the different groups or processes from step three as spokes radiating out to them. (See figure 4.1. Go to the *FUSION* website, **http://deniseleeyohn.com/fusion**, to download a worksheet and wheel example to help you create a Brand Touchpoint Wheel for your organization.)

Analyze, Prioritize, and Optimize Your Brand Touchpoints

Once you have a visual representation of all your brand touchpoints, assess how well each touchpoint reflects your desired brand identity. Use customer research, self-assessments, and industry reports to help you analyze how important each touchpoint is in shaping people's perceptions of your brand. Next, prioritize the touchpoints that are most critical to revisit by considering the size of the gap between how well you're delivering on them today and how well you should be—and the cost and time required to close the gap.

Finally, once you've designated a touchpoint as a priority, you can determine if you need to change your organizational design or your operations or perhaps both to bring it to its optimal state. In the sales process example, you might discover that adding a new position like Southwest Airlines' boundary spanners would facilitate the sharing of best practices across business units, leading to better sales pitches and to your desired culture of collaboration. Or you might find that instituting a clearer invoicing process would reduce redundant efforts and support your core value of transparency.

Working on brand touchpoints by going through the process of visualizing, assessing, prioritizing, and optimizing them in this way is particularly useful in your efforts to create brand-culture fusion because it connects the dots between what you do inside your organization and how you're perceived on the outside. If you can better align these processes and practices with your desired culture, then your touchpoints will create the clear, cohesive identity you desire for your brand. By engaging your colleagues and employees in the process of developing a Brand Touchpoint Wheel and tackling the necessary improvements to your operations that it reveals are needed, you enroll your entire organization in your transformation effort.

CULTURE IS NOT "SOFT STUFF"

Culture-change efforts often fail because culture is considered only an input to operations. That is, leaders believe—mistakenly—that if they had a better culture, then their organization would run like a well-oiled machine. While it's true that a good culture can influence the effectiveness of your organization—for example, by bridging organizational silos and overcoming disconnects in company operations—culture is also an *outcome* of your organizational design and operational functions, processes, and practices.

In an article for the *Harvard Business Review*, organizational behavior expert Jay W. Lorsch and his colleague Emily McTague explain that "culture isn't something you 'fix.' " They believe "cultural change is what you get after you've put new processes or structures in place to tackle tough business challenges like reworking an outdated strategy or business model."[32]

Organizational guru Jon Katzenbach adds, "Trying to change a culture purely through top-down messaging, training and development programs, and identifiable cues seldom changes people's beliefs or behaviors."[33] His point makes sense. Research in neuroscience suggests that people are more likely to *act* their way into believing something than they are to *think* their way into acting. Therefore, set up your company to *act* differently by changing your organizational design and operations.

For too long culture has been considered the "soft stuff" of business, downplayed in favor of hard strategies and metrics or relegated to feel-good efforts. It's no wonder only 19 percent of culture changes are successful.[34] But leaders who employ a more integral approach to designing and running their businesses to cultivate their desired culture end up succeeding—and over time they achieve brand-culture fusion.

Once you have the large structural and operational pieces of your desired culture puzzle in place, you can move on to imbuing it into your employee experience. The next chapter shows you how.

Key Takeaways from This Chapter:

- You must operationalize culture through organizational design—the units, hierarchy, and roles in your organization—and operations—your business functions and day-to-day processes and practices.

- Use the three primary elements of organization design—structure, standards, and roles—to design or redesign an organization that's aligned with your desired culture.

- Oftentimes, your operational processes and practices prohibit employees from executing on your core values.

- You can align your operations with your culture to any degree—either more tactically by tackling specific processes or practices, or more strategically by launching broad initiatives that align or improve processes and practices across the organization.

- Working on brand touchpoints helps you connect the dots between what you do inside your organization and how you're perceived on the outside.

CHAPTER 5

CREATE CULTURE-CHANGING EMPLOYEE EXPERIENCES

Read this chapter to learn:

- How employee experience involves far more than traditional human resource efforts and produces far greater results too
- How to deliberately design your employee experience so that it advances your desired culture
- Why employee experience and customer experience must be inextricably linked

When the overarching purpose of your company is "to help create a world where you can belong anywhere," your employees ought to feel they belong in your organization. At least that's what the leaders of Airbnb, the lodging rental and hospitality company, believe. And this belief explains why they place so much importance on employee experience (EX).

In fact, EX is the critical strategy that Airbnb—which has reached a $31 billion valuation in less than ten years—relies on to build its brand and pursue its purpose. In 2016, the company adopted the slogan "Belong Anywhere" to express its brand identity and launched the "#belonganywhere" brand campaign. But its leaders believed these efforts needed to represent more than an external idea—the concept of belonging needed to apply inside the company as well. Mark Levy, who was Airbnb's global head of employee experience, explained to me, "We need to create a place where our employees feel they belong," he says. "Belonging starts here. We have to figure out internal belonging first, then we can break down the walls [with customers]."[1]

The fact that Levy's role even existed at the company is a testament to its commitment to aligning employees' everyday experiences with its purpose and values. Before Levy's arrival, the talent department was a small team doing traditional HR work, and the recruiting department was a larger team tasked with growing the employee base to meet the needs of the business, while a group called "Ground Control," which was responsible for bringing the company's culture to life through its workspace environment, internal communications, employee events, celebrations, and recognition programs, reported into a different unit. Realizing that these functions and others in the company could address the end-to-end employee experience if they were combined, Levy and the company's founders asked themselves how they could bring together all the different ways they help employees be successful and feel that they belong.[2]

Taking a cue from their customer experience (CX) department, they created an "Employee Experience" group by:

- Combining the previously disjointed HR and company culture efforts
- Adding or joining facilities, safety, security, food, global citizenship/social impact, diversity, and belonging functions
- Developing the specialist areas of total rewards, learning, talent design, and talent systems—"everything in the whole journey of an employee's experience," as Levy describes it

The EX team works across functional silos to "create a seamless service delivery model or support for employees," he explains. "Running across everything is a focus on mission, values, and culture—that's the glue that holds everything together."[3]

EX at Airbnb starts well before an employee officially joins the company. Since Airbnb has far more interested applicants than positions to fill (in 2016, it received 180,000 resumes for 900 positions), its hiring process primarily involves weeding people out, not attracting them, as is the case for some companies. To do that, Airbnb interviews candidates to make sure they are a good fit not only with the position they are interviewing for but also with the company's culture. Candidates are asked to participate in two interviews reserved exclusively to assess their fit with Airbnb's core values. The founders select the employees who conduct these "core values" interviews— and although they work outside of the function for which a candidate is interviewing, they have final say in whether or not a candidate gets offered the job.[4]

This rigorous interview process serves another function as well: It offers candidates their first experience with Airbnb's unique culture, Levy explained. By taking the time to learn about the candidate as a person and their values, the interviewers live out and model one of Airbnb's core value: "Be a Host: Care for others and make them feel like they belong."[5]

The company's overarching purpose and core values are also at the heart of its week-long on-boarding experience, which introduces new hires to Airbnb's purpose and core values, its business strategies and functions, and ways of working. Part of the experience includes shadowing a support specialist to give new employees firsthand exposure to the challenges guests and hosts face and how Airbnb supports them. By going through the on-boarding process with other new hires, Levy told me, Airbnb also inspires a sense of belonging among them, enabling them to form cohorts that hopefully stay together throughout their careers.[6]

Once employees begin their jobs, their daily experiences—where and how they work—continue to be directly informed by the company's brand identity, purpose, and values. The food served in their café, for example, is inspired by a different travel destination every day. Hosts are celebrated everywhere: Each conference room is designed to match an actual host property, and giant portraits of hosts line the hallways.

Airbnb also designs its offices to help employees feel at home, a place where they belong. Included are a kitchen, a library, and places to meditate, practice yoga, or write on the walls. A green atrium that stretches up to three floors high evokes the feelings of being in a home garden. The company provides "landing stations" where employees can charge their devices and store their stuff, but it doesn't confine them to assigned desks, so they can work wherever they feel most comfortable.

The "Ground Control" team continuously shapes the employees' experiences in ways that reinforce belonging. By staging pop-up celebrations and themed events based on holidays in the communities around the globe where Airbnb does business, the team creates an environment that not only supports employees' sense of belonging to a worldwide community but also encourages them to create belonging experiences for customers. Airbnb sees employees as brand ambassadors who can increase the brand's awareness and reduce one of the company's biggest brand challenges, which is confusion about what it does and how it works. If employees personally experience the company's purpose and feel they belong, Levy explained, they can help clarify Airbnb's brand proposition to others.[7]

These are some of the many ways that Airbnb infuses its EX with its unique core values. It's no coincidence that the company is producing sustained growth (with profits projected to increase by 3,400 percent in four short years),[8] enjoys the strongest advocates of any brand according to YouGov BrandIndex,[9] and is one of the best companies to work for according to jobs site Glassdoor.[10]

WHAT IS EX?

Airbnb is only one of a growing number of companies discovering the importance of EX and its power to positively impact business performance in many areas—not only employee satisfaction, productivity, and retention, but also brand equity, competitive advantage, and sustainable growth. EX, they've found, produces these far-ranging results by planting the seeds that grow into a strong and definitive culture. No wonder "creating a compelling employee experience" was named by *Forbes* as the No. 1 HR trend in 2017[11] and 70 percent of executives around the world surveyed by Deloitte's Human Capital Group said EX was an important or very important trend.[12]

But there's a lot of confusion and misunderstanding about what EX actually entails. Is it new-and-improved HR? Does it simply involve making employment more fun and enjoyable? Is it is about relating to employees as if they're customers?

In some ways, it's helpful to understand EX by describing what it's *not*. EX is not "employer branding," which is about developing a distinctive external reputation to help you build your corporate image and recruiting efforts. If your efforts are geared exclusively toward people outside your company, not only will they fall short of engaging your existing employees, but also they will fail to cultivate the employee mindset and behaviors that are needed to support your desired brand identity.

THE RULES OF EX

Some of the old and new rules of EX, according to consulting firm Deloitte[13]:

	Old Rules	New Rules
EX Definition	Defined by annual engagement surveys	Defined as a holistic view of life at work, requiring constant feedback, action, and monitoring
EX Management	A series of HR leaders working on recruiting, rewards, engagement, and other HR programs	Someone responsible for the complete employee experience, focused on employee journeys, experiences, engagement, and culture
Employee Wellness	Wellness and health programs focused on safety and managing insurance costs	An integrated program for employee well-being focused on the employee, her family, and her entire experience at life and work
Rewards	Designed to cover salary, overtime, bonus, benefits, and stock options	Also include nonfinancial rewards: meals, leaves, vacation policy, fitness, and wellness programs

Figure 5.1

EX is also not about giving employees perks simply to make them feel good. Nor is EX the same as employee engagement, although the two are closely related:* great experiences produce engaged employees. For years, companies have studied the end result—employee engagement—without understanding how to produce it—employee experience.

Finally EX is not about engaging employees as you would customers. Employees and customers differ in significant ways. But CX does provide a model for defining and understanding EX. Since CX is the sum of all interactions a customer has with a company, then EX is everything an employee experiences throughout his or her connection to the organization—every employee interaction, from the first contact as a potential recruit to the last interaction after the end of employment.

Jeanne Meister, founding partner of HR advisory and research firm Future Workplace, refers to the helpful phrase "workplace as an experience" to explain EX: "The essence of the 'workplace as an experience' is where all the elements of work—the physical, the emotional, the intellectual, the virtual, and the aspirational—are carefully orchestrated to inspire employees."[14] Perhaps Airbnb's Levy says it best: "Anything that sets employees up for success or improves our culture should be a part of EX."[15]

If you want your EX to be as effective as Airbnb's, then you must deliberately, clearly, and carefully design it to support your overarching

---

* There is enough confusion between EX and employee engagement that even two experts seem to offer conflicting perspectives. Bruce Temkin, managing partner of the customer experience firm Temkin Group, says organizations should focus on employee engagement. "Employee experience deals with how employees enjoy their job or environment. It deals with making things fun and enjoyable. Employee engagement deals with how committed employees are to the mission of their organization." But Jacob Morgan, author of *The Employee Experience Advantage*, believes that "engagement has been all about the short-term cosmetic changes that organizations have been trying to make to improve how they work." He writes, "If employee engagement is the short-term adrenaline shot, then EX is the long-term redesign of the organization. It's focus is on the engine, not the paint and upholstery." (Sources: Temkin, Bruce. 2017. "Focus on Employee Engagement, Not Employee Experience." *Experience Matters*, April 4, 2017. https://experiencematters. blog/2017/04/20/focus-on-employee-engagement-not-employee-experience. Morgan, Jacob. 2017. The Employee Experience Advantage: How to Win the War for Talent by Giving Employees the Workspaces They Want, the Tools They Need, and a Culture They Can Celebrate. New York: Wiley. Page 6.)

purpose and express your core values. The rest of this chapter will show you how. I will take you inside many companies that have developed EX programs and share their approaches to designing them effectively so you can learn what they know:

- How to design EX to advance your desired culture with a four-step process of segmenting employees, prioritizing inter-actions, adopting a design model, and designing experiences to support your desired culture
- How to involve employees in EX design
- Why EX should be integrated with CX to produce better out-comes for employees and customers and greater brand-culture fusion

The companies I highlight in this chapter excel through EX because they elevate it to a top priority. Leaders at these organizations don't regard EX as merely an initiative to be delegated to HR managers—they consider it a critical way to run their business and they channel the necessary resources and attention to it accordingly. You should too.

MAKE EX A PRIORITY

The research group Bersin by Deloitte reports that organizations currently spend over $1 billion annually to improve employee engagement.[16] And yet the Gallup organization has found only 13 percent of employees working for an organization are engaged and has declared a "worldwide employee engagement crisis."[17]

According to Jacob Morgan, author of *The Employee Experience Advantage*, this disconnect is the direct result of the short-term thinking that leaders often revert to when it comes to their employees. Most companies rely on a system of carrots and sticks to try to motivate and engage people. Instead, Morgan argues you should focus on how employees experience your organization day by day and redesign your workplace and practice around them.[18]

His research shows that organizations that invested most heavily in EX were not only included 11.5 times as often in Glassdoor's Best Places to Work and 4.4 times as often in LinkedIn's list of North America's Most In-Demand Employers, but they were also 28 times more often listed among *Fast Company*'s Most Innovative Companies, 2.1 times as often on the *Forbes* list of the World's Most Innovative Companies, and twice as often in the American Customer Satisfaction Index. Most important, he finds that "experiential organizations had more than four times the average profit and more than two times the average revenue. They were also almost 25 percent smaller, which suggests higher levels of productivity and innovation."[19]

These findings make a clear case for adopting EX as a top priority for your company. How? By allocating resources—human, financial, technological, etc.—to EX. For some companies, investing in EX may require incremental spending, but you can often achieve EX excellence simply by using existing resources in new ways. Plus, if you determine that benefits like childcare or an on-campus gym are critical to providing an EX aligned with your core values (not just to make you a trendy employer) but can't afford to provide them, you can still offer these benefits by acting as a middle man between employees and services they pay for. Morgan notes that most experiential companies are only in "the concierge and convenience business.... They coordinate with service providers for a price break and then make those services available and convenient for their employees."[20]

Above all, you'll need to think differently—you'll need to understand that a new "implicit social contract between employers and employees," as a research report from Deloitte calls it, is emerging. The stability that once characterized the best employee-employer relationships is being disrupted by employees' tendency to change jobs more frequently and other factors. Therefore, "employers must provide development more quickly, move people more regularly, provide continuous cycles of promotion, and give employees more tools to manage their own careers," the report by Deloitte concludes. Your efforts, they say, must be oriented around the different needs and expectations that today's employees have.[21]

In my work with companies that want to transform themselves, I've found that they're only able to do so if their core values are woven into the fabric of their EX at every point in an employee's journey with the company. You must imbue the core values of your desired culture in the daily experiences you create for your employees so that they can soak them in and reflect them back with their behaviors and attitudes. As the company's core values come to life for employees, a better culture and stronger brand identity emerge.

DESIGN YOUR EX IN FOUR STEPS

You can apply the same methods and tools that produce successful CX to the design of your EX. There are four main steps to follow:

1. Segment employees into discrete groups.
2. Identify the employee interactions that you should explicitly design.
3. Adopt a design model.
4. Design experiences so they support your desired culture.

Step 1: Segment Your Employees

Marketing and operations teams start CX design by segmenting customers into discrete groups because different people have different wants and needs. To design great experiences for their customers, companies must first identify these differences. Fast food chains, for example, usually differentiate between customers who are primarily motivated by low prices vs. customers who seek out new products or those who just want a convenient meal. Different customers also represent different value to companies. A large organization that needs a sophisticated telecommunications system is probably more valuable to a telecom provider than is a small firm that needs little more than a basic phone system. Segmentation enables companies to understand and prioritize their customers.

Like customers, different employees have different needs and desires and contribute different value to the organization. These differences don't always manifest themselves by role, level, or department, so sometimes you need to use a segmentation approach that enables you to see beyond groups in your organizational chart. Your objective should be to identify meaningful distinctions within your employee base and define clearly discrete segments of employees.

There are several ways to identify and profile the most relevant employee segments in your organization. Here are four particularly helpful ones:

By the role that work plays in employees' lives. A *Harvard Business Review* article suggests grouping your employees in the following six role-based segments:

1. Expressive legacy—work for these employees is about creating something of value that lasts.
2. Secure progress—work is about improving one's station in life and progressing along a predictable path.
3. Individual expertise and team success—work is about being a valuable part of a successful team.
4. Risk and reward—work is one of many ways to live a life full of change and excitement.
5. Flexible support—work is a source of livelihood but not a priority.
6. Low obligation or easy income—work is a source of immediate financial gain.

By using this segmentation approach, you can design EX to address employees' different personal values.[22]

By the value that employees contribute to the organization. Researchers from the University of Glasgow recommend factoring how your people contribute beyond their costs, their employment mode (employee vs. contractor), and how much they identify with the organization. They identify four potential segments:

1. Core knowledge employees—e.g., senior managers, financial analysts and fund managers, senior design engineers, senior medical staff, etc.
2. Compulsory, traditional human capital—e.g., maintenance workers, technicians, software engineers, mid- to low-level managers, administrators, etc.
3. "Idiosyncratic" human capital or business partners—e.g., consultants, project managers, academic researchers, etc.
4. Ancillary human capital/contract workers—e.g., call center staff, low-level HR specialists, etc.[23]

Although the terms the researchers use to describe each group might lack nuance, they convey meaningful differences in the level and nature of employees' contributions and therefore the amount or kind of investment you should make in each.

By how aligned employees are with the company's strategy and goals. Dr. Leslie de Chernatony uses an assessment of employees' alignment with the company on two dimensions: "intellectual buy-in," the extent to which people are aware and aligned with their organization's strategy and understand how they can contribute to it, and "emotional buy-in," their commitment to achieving the company's goals. Laying them out on a two-by-two matrix, four segments emerge:

1. Weak links—low intellectual and low emotional
2. Bystanders—high intellectual and low emotional
3. Loose cannons—low intellectual and high emotional
4. Champions—high intellectual and high emotional[24]

This segmentation approach allows you to prioritize champions in your EX and then devise specific EXs to try to convert the others into champions.

By the degree to which employees adopt strategic change. For some of my clients, I segment employees by their position on an "adoption curve," that is, by their willingness and ability to change their attitudes and behaviors and adopt new ones. By differentiating among "doubters," "observers," "supporters," "participants," and "drivers," you can tailor your strategies and communications to move people along the adoption curve and achieve the desired change.

Rather than come up with an employee segmentation to use throughout your entire EX, you might also consider segmenting employees specifically for the design of a particular EX interaction. NCR (formerly National Cash Register), the maker of transaction systems, adopted a segmentation specifically for its on-boarding interaction. NCR takes its core values extremely seriously, especially its value of "customer dedication: We genuinely care about the success of our internal and external customers. We partner with them to understand their businesses and develop solutions that deliver the highest levels of quality, service and value."[25] When designing a new global on-boarding program, NCR's human resources managers leaned on this core value to guide their employee segmentation: How could they serve their internal customers best and develop high-value solutions for their specific needs? They decided to group new hires not just by their roles, like software engineers and executives, but also based on their professional background or experience, such as recent graduates and veterans who might need help transitioning into the corporate world. They then tailored their on-boarding portal by segment, creating, for example, unique curriculum for recent graduates with lessons to help them better navigate their first professional experience after college.[26]

Whatever segmentation approach you choose, you will find it makes your EX design work more manageable and your EX efforts overall more successful.

Step 2: Identify Priority Employee Interactions

Once you've identified your employee segments, you are ready to pinpoint the employee interactions that you should prioritize. It's impossible to provide an excellent experience for every employee and for every interaction he or she has with the company—nor is it necessary. Instead, you should focus on designing experiences that address the needs and wants of employees who represent the most value to your organization and those interactions that have the most potential to advance your desired culture.

To identify those priorities, you can borrow another tool from CX: experience architecture. Architectures, such as brand architectures or information architectures, are used by companies to bring focus and structure to planning in much the same way they are used by architects and contractors when building a house. An employee experience architecture helps you identify and prioritize the specific interactions that should comprise your EX.

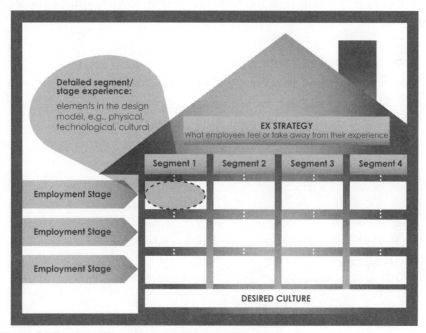

Figure 5.1 Employee Experience Architecture Template

To create an Employee Experience Architecture, start by drafting short statements that define the foundation of your "house"—your desired culture, the culture that corresponds to your brand identity—and the roof—your overall EX strategy, the feeling or takeaway employees should glean from their entire experience with your organization. Your foundation and roof should be closely related and explicitly articulated. For example, at Airbnb, its foundation—its desired

culture—can be summarized by its purpose, "belonging," and its core
values, which include "own the mission" and "be a host." Its roof—
Airbnb's overall EX strategy—is the feeling that "employees belong
anywhere and help people belong wherever they go." (See figure 5.1.
Go to the *FUSION* website, **http://deniseleeyohn.com/fusion**, to
download a worksheet and architecture template to help you create an
Employee Experience Architecture for your organization.)

The rooms in the architecture in between your foundation and roof
are the specific interactions that comprise your overall EX. Create a
grid with your employee segments as columns and interactions as rows.
For example, a client of mine identified the following ten interactions
(but you may have more or fewer of them):

1. Sourcing and recruiting
2. Pre-boarding (after the job offer is accepted but before work
   begins)
3. On-boarding (orientation and initial training)
4. Compensation and benefits
5. Ongoing learning and development
6. Ongoing engagement, communication, and community involvement
7. Rewards and recognition
8. Performance planning, feedback, and review
9. Advancement
10. Retirement, termination, or resignation

Once you've listed the interactions, then prioritize the intersection
of each segment and interaction in the grid. Assign a value to each
based on factors such as:

- Its potential impact on your culture. For example, in Chapter 3, I
  explained that hiring employees who fit your culture and values
  is critical, so you should prioritize the recruiting interaction for
  most, if not all, your segments. Identify other interactions that
  are particularly important in your organization and influential to
  your specific desired culture.

- The importance of the employee segment. While all employees are important, your focus should be on interactions for segments who contribute the most irreplaceable value to your organization and those who wield the most influence on customers and other employees.
- The size of the gap between what an interaction currently delivers to employees and what employees feel the interaction should deliver to actually address their needs. Use employee research to help you identify the biggest gaps from your employees' point of view. For example, if core knowledge workers express a desire to know more about the company's business strategy before they begin working, then you should prioritize that as part of their recruiting and on-boarding interactions. Generally speaking, the bigger the gap, the more you should prioritize the interaction.

As you prioritize, look for synergies between the intersections of segments and interactions—a focus on one intersection might yield improved results in another. The resources you put into on-boarding training for one segment may be easily extended into ongoing learning and development for it and others, for example.

With your Employee Experience Architecture complete, there is one more step before you begin designing specific EXs.

Step 3: Adopt an EX Design Model

Once you know the interactions you should prioritize, determine the categories of elements you will include in each experience. I recommend a three-category design model:

1. Environment—elements of the physical workplace plus everything else that employees see, hear, touch, taste, or smell; for example, posters in the hallways, flowers or other decorative items, and food and drinks
2. Tools—technology and other instruments or materials that employees use, such as software applications, reference guides, and office supplies

3. Intangibles—elements that impact the way employees think and feel, including communications, leadership styles, and policies

Rabobank Nederland, a large financial services provider in the Netherlands, used a similar model when it began developing an EX to support a new, more self-directed work culture. The new EX, which it called "Rabo Unplugged," was designed to enable "the organisation to better respond to all needs of customers, while at the same time giving more freedom and responsibility to the employees," writes Josee Lamers in a Cornell University case study.[27]

The Rabo Unplugged design team delineated three categories of EX elements: mental (which they defined as "personal responsibility and freedom of choice for the employee"), virtual (information and communication technology infrastructure, tools, and equipment), and physical (design of offices). By dividing elements of the experience into these three categories, they could easily assign managers from the company's functional groups to lead changes in each (e.g., the virtual elements were spearheaded by someone from the information technology group) as well as articulate the key requirements for each (e.g., standardization and a user-driven approach for the virtual elements).[28]

A different model might make sense for your organization, but be sure to explicitly set the categories of elements that you want to include in your EX. This simplifies and organizes the actual design work, which is the next and final step.

Step 4: Design Experiences that Support Your Desired Culture

Now apply the design model to each priority employee segment/ interaction intersection that you identified in Step 2 and determine the experience you should design and deliver. To start, focus on creating an experience for a single high-priority interaction and designate it a "signature experience." A signature experience is the most "visible, distinctive" experience of an organization's overall EX, explain Tamara Erickson and Lynda Gratton in the *Harvard Business Review* article

"What It Means to Work Here." They recommend designing a signature experience to serve as "a powerful and constant symbol of your organization's culture and values."[29]

Let's say you've prioritized designing a new recruiting experience for the segment of employees who engage with customers face-to-face on a daily basis. Using the three-category design model (environment, tools, and intangibles), determine the elements of the experience for each of those categories.

First, decide the "environment" elements of the recruiting interaction, such as where to conduct the interviews, the design of the room or space where the interview will take place, and leave-behinds such as a company brochure or thank-you gift. Then consider the "tools" of the experience, like the online application, personality tests, and other elements used during the process. Finally identify the "intangible" elements that shape the recruiting experience, such as the tone and manner of the invitation to interview, of the interview itself, and of the follow-up to the interview.

Imbue each element with the core values and other unique aspects of your desired culture. For example, if your culture is performance-oriented, consider incorporating tests and assignments into the interview process to reinforce the core value of achievement. If one of your core values is transparency, consider laying out the screening process for candidates or giving them information about their status as a prospective employee.

Don't limit yourself to commonly-accepted practices and don't be afraid to design an experience that might be very attractive to some people and a complete turnoff to others. Instead of sending a standard email thanking potential candidates for submitting their resume, for example, use the tone and manner of the message to reflect your company's unique core values and brand personality. If your company's desired culture is casual, sending a funny and friendly electronic greeting card that expresses your sincere gratitude for their submission would be enough to attract potential candidates that fit your laid-back culture. But this approach will probably turn off employees who are more serious and earnest and expect a formal message outlining when they will hear back from you and how.

"Companies—even very large ones—don't need to be all things to all people. In fact, they shouldn't try to be," Erickson and Gratton advise. Your signature experience should not only serve as a tool to express to everyone what makes you unique, but also specifically to ensure you attract and retain people who fit into your organization more easily and enthusiastically.[30]

Once you've designed your signature experience, move on to the rest of the interactions you identified as priorities in Step 2. For each interaction, consider what experience is in place currently in your organization and whether it should continue as is, be fine-tuned, or be stopped and redesigned entirely.

Most important, as you go through this design process, remember your objective is to cultivate your desired culture. Ground your EX designs in the desired culture that you articulated as the foundation of your architecture. And once you have an initial architecture draft complete, inspect your whole "house" and ensure your design supports its roof—your overall EX strategy. You might have to go back to the drawing board several times before you get it right. Later on in this chapter I'll discuss why and how to involve your employees in that process.

CRAFT AN EX THAT IS RIGHT FOR *YOU*

Just as great houses don't pop out of the ground on their own, great employee experiences don't just happen. You must work through each step described above deliberately—taking shortcuts will likely increase the complexity of the process. You also need the discipline to design EX to your desired culture. Think carefully about what behaviors and mindsets you want to reinforce and reject any ideas for experiences that don't align, no matter how creative they might be.

It might be helpful to find inspiration in the successes others have had with their EX. Since EX design and management has only recently emerged as a business priority, there are only a few organizations that have implemented comprehensive and integrated EX programs like Airbnb. But many organizations have designed isolated employee experiences that can serve as fodder for your efforts. The following are some of the best ones that I use to inspire and instruct my clients.

Recruiting experience: One of the five attributes HubSpot, an inbound marketing software company, values in prospective candidates is "adaptability." HubSpot looks for "constantly-changing people who are life-long learners."[31] Culture leader Katie Burke says she and her team re-did the company's job descriptions to "make it abundantly clear that if you're a lifelong learner, open to challenging us, open to challenging the status quo and an interesting dynamic, you would be a great fit here." Note that she doesn't say they want people to "fit *in*." In fact, they avoid using acronyms in the descriptions, which they found not only confused candidates but also sent the message that they were expected to adapt and conform to the company's "language" and processes rather than bring their own (and new) perspective to them.[32]

On-boarding experience: One of the core values at church staffing company Vanderbloemen Search Group is "Wow-Making Excellence," so it puts books about operational excellence such as *The Nordstrom Way* and *The New Gold Standard* (about the Ritz-Carlton Hotel Company) on a reading list it gives to new employees. This is only one of the small company's unique approaches to on-boarding, and it shows that you don't have to be a large company with deep pockets to design an influential EX. You just need to be as convinced of its importance as CEO William Vanderbloemen is. Achieving "total buy-in from new hires" is the best way to preserve his company's culture, he writes. "Each hire can make an impact on your culture, so from day one, make sure you're teaching your new employees about your culture."[33]

Training experience: Clio, a provider of legal practice management software, expects its employees to know not only what the company's purpose is—"to help our customers succeed and realize the full value of our product"—but also how they contribute to bringing it about. In his book *The Service Culture Handbook*, customer service expert Jeff Toister describes how Clio goes beyond training its customer service agents on how to answer customers' questions and fix their problems efficiently and effectively. It also helps them develop the specific skills required to fulfill the company's purpose, like rapport building, active listening, and empathizing. For example, they learn how to engage in a constructive, helpful dialogue with customers regarding their unique needs and how Clio might fulfill them, so customers are more likely to be delighted with the solution presented and less likely to discontinue their accounts.[34]

Engagement experience: San Diego–based nonprofit Plant With Purpose seeks to reverse deforestation and poverty through its work with over 500 rural communities in places like Haiti and Burundi. Because its leaders believe that employees best understand and embrace the purpose of the organization when they experience it firsthand, the nonprofit arranges for all employees, regardless of role, to spend time working at one of their field locations. Executive director Scott Sabin explains that, although providing this employee experience consumes time and money (both in low supply at this twenty-person, $3.5 million organization), it is critical because "we believe that this work flows from the heart." The experience of working alongside the local farmers helps employees, Sabin told me, "feel the connection between what we are doing here and the lives we are impacting elsewhere."[35]

Performance Review experience: As part of its efforts to create a more customer-oriented culture, Adobe redesigned specific EX experiences, including eliminating annual performance reviews. In place of a system that was out of sync with the fast pace that a customer-oriented company requires, Adobe instituted regular check-ins where managers and employees meet for informal discussions at least once a quarter. EX/CX head Donna Morris describes check-ins as "an ongoing mechanism for ensuring that all our employees are aligned with the overall goals of the organization" and lists it as one of the critical ways the company has changed its culture.[36]

Compensation experience: Valve, the creator of video game platform Steam, promotes a culture of creativity and democracy. These values enable it to attract and motivate the kind of self-directed employees who produce the constant stream of innovations by which the brand is identified. To reinforce its culture, Valve applies a unique approach to compensation decisions in which project teams evaluate their own members on their contribution to the group and the product as well as on their technical ability and outputs. By using a peer-ranking system and factoring in a range of ways that employees contribute value, Valve's leaders "gain insight into who's providing the most value at the company and thereby adjust each person's compensation to be commensurate with his or her actual value." Its handbook explains the goal is "to get your compensation to be 'correct...'—paying someone what they're worth."[37]

Office Hours experience: Lifestyle brand Tower made a dramatic change to its office hours—employees only work 8:00 A.M. to 1:00 P.M. Monday through Friday. Its founder and CEO, Stephan Aarstol, explains in his book *The Five-Hour Workday* why he decided to move his company to a shorter work schedule. Tower sells stand-up paddleboards and other gear for the "beach lifestyle," and one day while reflecting on his business, Aarstol realized he needed to make his brand values a part of his company's "fabric." "We're telling customers to take life by the horns," he writes. "To live more extraordinarily. To live differently. To play more. But were we really doing this ourselves?" He had previously researched the benefits of a reduced work schedule, and in that moment, he decided to implement a five-hour workday for his employees. "Leaving work at 1:00 P.M. every day would be an unavoidable daily reminder of the exact brand we aspired to be," Aarstol explains. "We would be different from everyone else."[38]

Workplace Environment experience: Chinese Internet giant Tencent designed its new headquarters in Shenzhen to echo and reinforce its cultural emphasis on innovation. The company wanted to heighten the sense of community among its employees, increase their "social well-being," and encourage "serendipitous interactions" between teams to spark collaboration and new ideas. In an interview with *Architectural Digest*, architect Jonathan Ward explained that he designed a series of sky-bridges as a "critical solution" to meet these objectives. Each bridge incorporates a theme such as health, culture, or education "to help Tencent employees think and work differently than they had before." He clarifies that the bridges aren't just "visual aesthetics": "The design draws employees together more frequently and in new ways. . . . They also house most of the common areas for employees to interact."[39]

I've provided these examples to give you a sense of the range of experiences you might consider as you design EX at your company. But keep in mind, your approach should not be to copy any one of these tactics exactly or to try to achieve the "cool" factor that some of these companies seem to have. Instead, you should design your EX to uniquely express and embody your unique desired culture.

Ultimately, your goal should be to implement a cohesive, comprehensive approach to EX across all employee interactions—not to come up with a couple of disjointed experiences. Of course, you have to start somewhere, but continue to build your EX over time. In this way, EX is more a mindset than an initiative. Companies that use EX to achieve their business and brand goals view it as an ongoing effort, and they constantly seek out new ways to support and advance their desired culture through it.

GET EMPLOYEES INVOLVED

Just as leading CX companies have reaped the benefits of involving their customers in the CX design and development process, your EX will be more successful if you involve your employees in your design efforts. By seeking input from your employees, you'll design experiences that not only better address their needs, but that are uniquely suited for your company. HubSpot's Burke observes, "Even the most humble, involved, and on-the-floor executives do not see and experience the same challenges as employees on the frontline, making feedback from the frontline critical, not just to understand what's going on in your business, but to actually fix it."[40]

Involving employees in EX design also increases their involvement in cultivating your culture in general. Airbnb's Levy, for example, told me that inviting employees to design the company's conference rooms "democratized" the culture at the company and increased employees' feelings of ownership of it.[41] And when a company involves its employees in EX, it affirms their value to the organization and generates goodwill. *The Employee Experience Advantage* author Morgan says, "Successful organizations don't create things *for* employees, they create things *with* employees."[42]

There are many ways to effectively solicit input and collect feedback from your employees. You can collect this info via informal group check-ins, employee focus groups, formal employee engagement surveys, and "pulse" surveys. In addition, you can gather valuable and candid feedback on your company's EX from departing employees during exit interviews and even from prospective employees by fielding recruitment surveys. The key to gathering employee input, Morgan says, is to remember that "communication, collaboration, and feedback need to happen in real time." Although data collected through an annual or semi-annual employee engagement survey is valuable because it is quantifiable and trackable, consider collecting employees' feedback at various intervals and continuously.[43]

As important as it is to use the right methods for collecting employee input and feedback, you must also ensure your organization has the right mindset to act on the input it receives. You need "managers who are open to asking for and receiving feedback, a culture that embraces transparency as default mode, and an organization as a whole that is prepared to take action based on the learning," advises Morgan.[44] Nothing will alienate your employees and destroy your EX faster than to ask for their opinions and then ignore them.

However, you can—and should—set expectations for how you will use employees' input. When HubSpot's chief revenue officer Mark

Roberge redesigned the compensation plan for his company's sales reps, he sought input from members of the sales team by holding town hall meetings and opening up the floor for brainstorming sessions. After each meeting, he created a page on the company's internal website to describe some of the ideas that had emerged and to invite comments. But, throughout the process, he clarified who would ultimately make the final decision. "I was very explicit that the commission plan design was not a democratic process," he explains. "It was critical that the salespeople did not confuse transparency and involvement with an invitation to selfishly design the plan around their own needs." He found that most people appreciated being involved, even if the change ended up not being favorable to them.[45]

INTEGRATE YOUR EX WITH YOUR CX

One of the most efficient ways to move your organization closer to brand-culture fusion is to directly and explicitly integrate your EX with your CX. When people have an experience as employees that is clearly and distinctively on-brand, they're more likely to deliver an experience for customers that is as well. As they experience the benefits of the brand themselves, they gain not only the motivation to deliver them to customers, but also the knowledge of what it takes to do so. And if they see a gap between their actions or capabilities and what it takes to deliver excellent CX, they usually develop interest in closing that gap by learning new skills and working with others on new ways to do so. Ultimately, they feel more ownership for delivering on your company's brand promise.

Directly connecting employees to customers helps companies integrate EX and CX. Annette Franz, author of the popular CX blog, *CX Journey*, calls this giving employees "a clear line of sight" to customers. Often, though, organizations only make sure employees at the front line have a clear line of sight to the customer. But, Franz writes, "The customer experience isn't just created at the frontline." You should use your purpose, core values, and most of all, communications, to ensure that "everyone has their sights set on the right target." [46]

USAA, a company that provides insurance and financial services to millions of military members and their families, creates an EX to help employees feel directly connected with their customers' lives. To begin their training, employees receive "deployment letters" that real soldiers get. They are told, "Get your affairs in order and report to the personnel processing facility." During training, they often eat MREs (meals ready to eat), which gives them a literal "taste" of a soldier's life, and they are expected to walk around with sixty-five-pound back-packs. They are asked to read actual letters that soldiers in the field have written to their families back home. These experiences help employees cultivate empathy for their customers and develop new products and innovative solutions that customers love—such as a mobile service for deployed customers to receive account balance updates by texting USAA, and biometric authentication technology that provides extra security for customers' mobile devices.[47]

At Airbnb, EX and CX are so intertwined it's somewhat difficult to separate them. Employees stay in Airbnb locations whenever they travel for business, and each employee is given $2,000 a year to spend on staying with Airbnb hosts while on vacation. Since the company also considers hosts as customers, it strongly encourages employees to serve as hosts—and when the company invites hosts to attend meetings at its offices, it expects employees to host them in their homes.[48]

What's more, every year, hundreds of Airbnb employees attend a three-day event alongside hosts. They discuss the successes and challenges of the past year and have the opportunity to learn from one another. Desirree Madison-Biggs, Airbnb's CX program leader, says EX and CX at Airbnb parallel and reinforce one another. "We are the customers, the customers are us."[49] The result? Employees and hosts develop empathy for each other, experience belonging together, and ultimately create better experiences for each other.

In addition to creating opportunities for your employees to interact directly with customers, you should also give them the tools and insights to understand how they and their teams are performing on CX. Customer feedback empowers employees to understand how their day-to-day actions impact customers and to take ownership for those actions, which leads to improved CX and EX. Adrian Walkling, vice president of insights at Medallia, a customer experience management platform, explains, "Getting customer feedback into the hands of your employees and empowering them to act on it actually drives significant employee engagement."[50]

FUEL FUSION WITH EX

EX is just now emerging as a discipline that many companies are exploring. If you want to lead the field and ward off competitive threats, the time to invest in it is now. And the way to get the most out of your investment is to design EX specifically to develop your desired culture.

EX excellence by itself may increase your competitive advantage as an employer, but putting EX at the center of your efforts to align and integrate your brand and culture will give you an edge as a business. Your employees won't simply be more productive, they will produce the right results. They won't just stay at your company because they have a good experience, they will want to be a part of creating a great experience for your customers. And they won't just be motivated because they feel valued, they will feel connected to your purpose and be driven to help fulfill it. These results are what brand-culture fusion—the integration of brand and culture—is all about.

This chapter has covered why EX is important, how to design it, how different companies use it, and how to integrate it with CX. The next strategy advances EX by weaving your desired culture into the daily details of your organization. Read on to learn how to make a big impact by thinking small.

Key Takeaways from This Chapter

• Companies that invest in EX are recognized as better employers and produce better business results.

• To achieve your desired culture, you must express and demonstrate it in the daily experiences you create for your employees.

• There are four main steps in EX design: segment your employees, prioritize interactions, adopt a design model, and design experiences that support your desired culture.

• Your EX will be more successful if you involve your employees in your EX efforts.

• To move your organization closer to brand-culture fusion, directly and explicitly integrate your EX with your CX.

CHAPTER 6

SWEAT THE SMALL STUFF

Read this chapter to learn:

- What rituals and artifacts are and how to use them as subtle but powerful cues about your desired culture
- How to use your company's policies and procedures to communicate and reinforce your desired culture
- How to ensure your policies and procedures don't just sit on a shelf in a manual

Recently while attending a business conference, something unusual caught my eye: monks. After maneuvering my way toward the front of the room so I could get a good seat for the keynote presentation, I saw a group of about twenty or so Buddhist monks with their shaved heads and flowing yellow robes sitting in the next section over. It was a strange sight at a technology conference, and I wondered if they had possibly wandered into the wrong venue and would soon be surprised when a businessperson and not a spiritual leader took the stage.

A few moments later, the lights were dimmed and a man decked out in traditional Hawaiian garb appeared in the far corner and started blowing a conch shell. As the long baritone notes resonated through the room, I began to think that perhaps *I* was in the wrong place. This was not the typical start to a presentation by the CEO of an $8.5 billion company.[1] But eventually I came to realize there is nothing typical about Marc Benioff or his company, Salesforce.

Benioff started Salesforce at a time when software-as-a-service and cloud-based software was a new technology, but in less than twenty years, he's been able to turn what was then a novel idea—that enterprise software could be delivered over the Internet and as a subscription service—into the standard of the industry. Salesforce now counts GE, Toyota, and Facebook[2] among its 150,000 customers.[3] It has been named by *Forbes* as one of the World's Most Innovative companies six years in a row. *Fortune* has listed it as one of the World's Most Admired Companies and Best Companies to Work For, and Benioff has been heralded one of the Most Respected CEOs in the World by *Barron's*.[4]

As noteworthy as these accomplishments may be, what stands out most about Salesforce is its organizational culture. Unlike the culture of most technology companies, which emphasize innovation or performance above all else, Salesforce's culture is built around the spirit of *Ohana*, the Hawaiian concept of family and the strong, supportive bonds that form within families.

Ohana explains why Salesforce not only begins its annual customer "Dreamforce" conference with a traditional Hawaiian blessing, but also why it is attended by the monks and nuns from the Plum Village Monastery, who lead meditation sessions and encourage mindfulness throughout the conference. These are just a few of the manifestations of the *Ohana* culture at Salesforce.

Dreamforce is an annual ritual through which Salesforce shares its organizational culture with external customers and third parties. But employees experience many rituals and artifacts that cultivate *Ohana* among them as well on a day-to-day basis at the company. Like other great organizations, Salesforce regularly expresses and cultivates its desired culture through ceremonies, symbols, and other similar small gestures.

Another company that couldn't seem more different from Salesforce but similarly recognizes the value of infusing even the smallest details of organizational life and employee behavior with its culture is Zingerman's, a specialty food business. How to clean a knife, double-check an order, and run a meeting may seem like procedures that don't need to be explained to employees, but Zingerman's seventy-two-page "Staff Guide" includes detailed instructions for these and myriad others.[5]

Started as a single deli over thirty-five years ago in Ann Arbor, Michigan, today Zingerman's is a $64 million "Community of Businesses"[6] that spans fourteen operating specialty food units.[7] *Inc.* magazine has called it "The Coolest Small Company in America"[8] and it counts the editors of *Bon Appetit,* Alton Brown from the Food Network, and even Oprah among its fans.[9] Well-known for its playful, down-to-earth brand identity (its catalogs and website feature hand-drawn images and folksy language), Zingerman's infuses its fun and funky brand and culture into every aspect of its business, including its Staff Guide. Besides offering specific details on procedures like knife cleaning, the guide, of course, includes the company's policies on harassment, disabilities, and other legally-required subjects. But even those are written in such plain and clear language and presented in such a visually-attractive manner that any employee who takes the time to read them might actually understand and value these policies.

So far in this book I've shared how to cultivate your desired culture by changing strategic aspects of your organization—how it is structured, how it is run, how employees experience working at it. But to nurture your desired culture, you also must focus on the smaller, tactical but equally significant aspects of your organization: (1) rituals and artifacts—things your organization regularly does or creates to commemorate or symbolize what's important to it; and (2) employee policies and procedures—the codes of conduct, rules of engagement, and other instructions that set the tone and guidelines for working at the organization. Although these aspects of the organization are part of your employee experience (EX), I'm covering them in this separate chapter because they are often overlooked. I recognize that they may seem too commonplace to be significant or warrant attention, but they wield more power to facilitate your desired culture than you might realize.

In this chapter I share how companies including Salesforce and Zingerman's have leveraged seemingly insignificant but absolutely critical aspects of their organization to integrate and align their brands and cultures. I also provide ideas for rituals and artifacts and an inventory of common organizational policies and procedures that you can adapt to better express and align with your core values. My goal is to inspire you to brainstorm ways—big and small—that make your organization more on-brand in the details of the day-to-day.

GIVE YOUR CULTURE LIFE THROUGH RITUALS

The *Ohana* spirit that I experienced firsthand at the Salesforce conference is intricately woven into the fabric of the company's organizational culture—in everyday practices that individually might seem small but collectively bind employees together.

One way in which the *Ohana* culture comes alive at Salesforce is through its rituals—meaningful, recurring activities or events that mark a milestone. Every time an employee at Salesforce greets someone with "*Aloha*" or signs off an email with "*Mahalo*," he or she is engaging in a daily ritual that expresses the company's unique family-oriented culture.

Similarly, some employees wear Hawaiian shirts on Fridays, as a reminder of the *Ohana* spirit that Benioff started the company with. Sam, a business development representative at the company, explains on the company blog that when employees wear the shirts, they are "remembering the early days of Salesforce.com when the company was just a few people and a bunch of servers in an apartment. We're reminding our teammates that even today, it's possible to work hard and have fun at the same time." He admits, "They're just shirts—but the shirts represent a history that I'm proud to support."[10] Today, those who have been with Salesforce for over ten years are inducted into the "Koa Club" and treated to a memorable Hawaiian-themed appreciation dinner to mark the special event in the employee's journey with the company.[11]

Jason Martin, head of public services at Stetson University, explains that the value of rituals such as these is more than the expression of a fun theme. Rituals, he writes, serve purposes that are both manifest and latent. "The manifest purpose of the ritual generally contributes to the workings of the organization and helps the organization achieve its mission and accomplish its daily tasks. The latent purpose is where the celebration of the sacred occurs. Rituals…can be used to both instill new values into the culture and change the organization's culture."[12] In the case of Salesforce, the Hawaiian-inspired rituals remind employees regularly of the values of *Ohana*: "being genuine, inclusive, caring, and compassionate, enjoying a healthy dose of fun, and treating those around you like family."[13]

Martin also explains that rituals have particularly powerful impact on culture because "they require active participation by the organization's members." When employees participate in a ritual, he says, "they are united emotionally and their energy is focused upon that which is sacred: the values the organization and its culture embrace and hold dear." He explains this is how rituals create community within an organization. "Through the order, community, meaning, and inspiration created by rites and rituals, transformation occurs."[14] In other words, it wouldn't be nearly as effective for Salesforce executives to give talks about *Ohana* or for the company to distribute a guide that promotes its culture. By regularly and personally engaging in company-specific rituals, employees experience *Ohana* and contribute to cultivating it.

To identify appropriate rituals for your organization, start with your core values and determine which ones need to be promoted or reinforced the most. Then think about shared experiences that you could create around them or identify special events or dates that you could turn into celebrations of these values. Look at the rituals in societal cultures of various ethnic, geographic, or other groups to see if they offer helpful parallels to your organization and its values. Invite employees to brainstorm with you.

Consider important moments at your organization such as critical customer presentations or other high-stakes meetings. How might you use rituals to prepare your people to take on these challenges? SDA Bocconi School of Management Professor Paolo Guenzi explains that rituals are used in sports to stimulate athletes' emotions and reduce their anxiety when they're preparing to compete. When the New Zealand rugby team performs the *haka*—a legendary Maori posture dance—before their matches, Guenzi writes, it triggers "feelings of connectivity, timelessness, and meaning, which stimulate mental flow states. These, in turn, reduce anxiety and increase energy and focus."[15] You can achieve the same results with your rituals.

In fact, you can influence your culture simply by adding an element of ritual to a regular occurrence. An executive at a media company—who was the designated leader of the remote location that housed the division she headed as well as other divisions of the parent company—used the first few minutes of every all-hands meeting to reinforce a sense of unity among everyone who worked under the same roof. In a ritual that became known as "I'm excited about...," she would kick off the meetings by saying, "I'm excited about" and then she would announce a recent success or initiative that had recently been launched, or progress on a challenge or problem that her people had been grappling with in her division.

Then people from all divisions would follow suit: they would raise their hands and share what they were excited about, always prefacing their remark with "I'm excited about...." Sometimes they were excited about the launch of a program or a new product, or the fact that a new employee was joining the group, or someone was back from leave. Most employees, regardless of role, felt comfortable sharing. Even the office manager would share milestones about upgrades to the facility that were eagerly anticipated by everyone. After each announcement, everyone would clap. With this simple ritual, this leader effectively cultivated a collaborative culture that enabled disparate parts of the organization to come together and learn about each other and what success looked like for them.

As you think about how you might use rituals to cultivate your desired culture, don't be afraid to imbue even the most routine practices with significance. In the book *Corporate Cultures*, organization consultants Terrence Deal and Allan Kennedy say, "In strong culture companies, nothing is too trivial. Any event that occurs in a work context is an event to be managed."[16]

In setting up a ritual, your greatest challenge will be to identify one that feels organic and meaningful to employees. Sometimes it's best to observe the ways employees already interact with each other and see if an existing behavior or practice can be imbued with cultural meaning by explicitly linking it to an aspect of your desired culture. For example, if you want to cultivate a stronger culture of recognition and you notice that your employees often send congratulatory messages to their colleagues after a job well done, you could ask them to share their messages with you, and then every Friday you could send a thank-you note to each of the people who deserve to be recognized.

Michael Kerr, author of *The Humor Advantage*, provides a good list of opportunities for rituals, including:

- A start-of-the-day or -week ritual that jump-starts people's attitudes or reminds them of the biggest priority of that day or week
- End-of-the-day or -week ritual that celebrates the top successes of that day or week
- A different ritual for each day of the week
- A ritual to kick off each quarter or to celebrate the end of the fiscal year
- Rituals around welcoming new employees and making them feel part of the team
- A ritual that kicks off or ends every meeting
- A ritual that celebrates the founding date of your company
- Rituals to celebrate every big sale over a certain amount, each time your organization takes on a new major client, or when your company hits a certain monetary milestone or number of customers
- Rituals that celebrate "smart failures" and setbacks in fun ways[17]

There are so many possibilities, but take care not to waste these opportunities by implementing widespread, meaningless, or random rituals. Every company can—and probably should—celebrate people's birthdays to affirm its commitment to employees. But your goal should be to develop rituals that are more unique to your organization; rituals that help you cultivate the specific culture that corresponds to your brand type.

As you develop these rituals, be thoughtful about the subtle messages that they send and their long-term implications. Matthew Prince, CEO and cofounder of Cloudflare, a cybersecurity firm, told Adam Bryant in the *New York Times'* "Corner Office" column how he thought carefully about his company's growth when considering a proposed ritual. In the company's early days, a young engineer suggested that they start a tradition of going out every Friday after work to get to know each other and talk about the week. When Prince and his partner vetoed the idea, they initially got a lot of flak for their decision. But they explained to their people that they wanted the company to be able to hire a diverse group of employees and going out for drinks after work might not fit into the lifestyles of future employees. "If they can't feel like they're part of the team, then they're not going to come work for us," he said. "We wanted to make Cloudflare a place where, no matter who you were, you could come here and work, and you'd be judged on that work. We weren't trying to re-create college."[18]

Here are some examples of other companies' rituals that may inspire you or provide a thought-starter:

- Chevron employees reinforce the company's core value of safety by opening each meeting with a "safety moment," whether to report on an accident that was avoided due to safety procedures or to simply encourage people to use handrails in the stairways.[19]
- When BELAY, a company that provides virtual assistants to companies, has a milestone or success to celebrate or announce, its leaders call an impromptu late-afternoon meeting. But since every employee works remotely (BELAY doesn't even have a corporate office), everyone dials in from their location through Zoom, a video conferencing system, with beers in hand to participate in a virtual toast. Founder Bryan Miles credits this ritual as well as the company's annual summits and regular community service days with maintaining a strong culture within his remote workforce.[20]

- At moving company Gentle Giants, every new hire is required to run the stairs at Harvard Stadium. More than a rite of passage, the ritual is considered an integral part of training. The company believes that only once someone has run up and down the 3,441 steps of the venerable venue is he or she prepared for the "inevitable stress of moving day," so it uses the ritual to ensure its people are "always ready with both a powerful body and calm mind."[21]
- A different kind of moving company uses an entirely different ritual for an entirely different purpose. At 11:11 A.M. every day (an easy time to remember), College Hunks Hauling Junk holds a football-inspired meeting in which selected staff kick field goals for rewards. Doing so enables the company to make what could be hard, menial work fun and to differentiate its culture from competitors. Nick Friedman, one of the company's cofounders, explains, "I think what sets us apart is that while we're serious about quality service, we also know how to have fun. When our team members have a good time, they make the experience more enjoyable for clients."[22]

As with all aspects of your culture, your rituals should be unique to your organization. What works at your company might feel totally out of place or be misunderstood at someone else's. The key is to identify those routines and activities that interpret and reinforce the specific elements of your desired culture. Developing a ritual is a seemingly small act that over time can produce big advances in your culture-building.*

---

* In addition to their powerful culture-building impact, rituals provide an additional benefit to an organization's leaders. Employee participation in them provides a gauge of the culture. In *Leading Teams*, Guenzi and his coauthor describe how Italian football manager Luigi Delneri uses a pregame ritual as a "thermometer" to measure his team's motivation level. "Before the game begins we hold hands and shout 'All for one and one for all,' " Delneri says. "Even the way the players shout tells you whether they are properly focused." (Source: Hackman, J. Richard. 2002. *Leading Teams: Setting the Stage for Great Performances*. Brighton, Massachusetts. Page 196.)

MAKE YOUR CULTURE VISIBLE
THROUGH ARTIFACTS

Artifacts—symbolic objects or other physical items that either make the organizational culture visible or that commemorate a milestone—can play a similar role as rituals in cultivating your desired culture. At Salesforce, the *Ohana* culture is reinforced by artifacts such as the names of the company's conference rooms (e.g., Maka Launa and Hala Kahiki) and the glass surfboard awards that are distributed to acknowledge employees' years of service. The Hawaiian-themed artifacts subtly remind employees of the company's not-business-as-usual culture and provide them with a means of identification with the Salesforce family.

Companies often use artifacts externally to reinforce their brand identity. In *Entrepreneur's Guide to the Lean Brand*, Brant Cooper and Jeremiah Gardner explain how packaging, uniforms, and logos serve as "memory triggers" for customers. "The goal in building brand artifacts," they write, "is to create a strong, distinct memory structure, by which your audience navigates a crowded marketplace to find its way to the value you are providing." By turning abstract ideas into clear cues (sights, sounds, touches, tastes, and smells), artifacts allow consumers "to better identify with who you are, your story, and ultimately what value you offer to them," they write.[23]

Artifacts can also serve as memory triggers and play explanatory roles inside an organization. Organizational psychologist Amy Bucher says, "Cultural artifacts are symbols that help both insiders and outsiders understand what it means to belong to that group." In addition, artifacts engage employees the same way that rituals do: By using, receiving, or otherwise interacting with artifacts, they personally and directly experience the culture—even if it's in the smallest way. "For group members, artifacts can also help solidify commitments and guide daily behaviors," Bucher explains.[24]

To determine how to use artifacts to solidify your employees' commitment to your culture and guide their daily behavior, ask yourself, "What are the crucial memories or associations that we need to trigger internally?" Then consider how to link those memories and associations to tangible

objects including elements of your physical environment, the language
your organization uses, technology and tools, artistic creations, expressions
of style (e.g., dress code or uniforms), and communications and publications. As with rituals, even the smallest item can symbolize a big idea.

The key is to be deliberate in your choices. "Cultural artifacts can
subtly but surely impact the way an organization feels and functions,"
Bucher explains.[25] David Burkus, author of *The Myths of Creativity*
and *Under New Management*, expounds on the point, writing that an
organization's core values are the "plumb line" to which artifacts must
align in order to be meaningful and productive. For example, he writes,
"There is nothing magical about a free food program, but a free food
program in a culture with basic assumptions about the value of collaboration and sharing can enhance the creative output of the entire organization by providing meals over which to share ideas."[26]

You might select very obvious artifacts like these companies have:

- Amazon hands out "Door Desk Awards" to acknowledge
  employees who develop an idea that creates significant cost
  savings for the company, enabling it to charge customers lower
  prices. Early on, the company used to save money by hammer-
  ing legs onto doors to build desks. Since then, the door desk has
  become a symbol of the company's frugal, pragmatic culture.[27]
- City Year, a nonprofit organization that places young Americorps
  members in urban schools to help students stay in school and on
  track to graduate, is known for the iconic red and yellow jackets
  that the members—the organization's employees—are required
  to wear during their year of service. CEO and cofounder Michael
  Brown says the jackets are a symbol of the members' "idealism
  and commitment to give a year and change the world."[28] Gillian
  Smith, former chief marketing officer, explained to me that the
  jackets are more instrumental than a simple uniform would be.
  They instill "a sense of unity and pride" among the members.
  The jackets also serve as a powerful identifier and inspiration for
  the school's students. "Students know that if they see someone
  in our red jacket that person is someone who can help them and
  who they can look up to," Smith says.[29]

Other companies use artifacts that are more subtle:

- When Chip Conley was CEO of the boutique hotel chain Joie de Vivre, which he founded, he would show employees his appreciation by giving them copies of the children's book *The Little Engine that Could* when one of them displayed a "can-do" attitude. The book, he writes in *PEAK: How Great Companies Get Their Mojo from Maslow*, helped "define the Joie de Vivre spirit.... Although simple and somewhat sentimental, the book's optimistic and resourceful message resonates well with Joie de Vivre's history and reputation as a David struggling among the Goliaths of the hospitality industry."[30]
- At Siebel Systems, the CRM software company, customer satisfaction is a core value. To subtly reinforce it, all the artwork on the walls comes from customers' annual reports, and all the conference rooms are named after customers.[31]

USE RITUALS AND ARTIFACTS TO ENGAGE EXTERNAL STAKEHOLDERS

If your organization has external stakeholders such as investors, franchisees, agencies, etc., who play an integral role in shaping your brand identity, you can use rituals and artifacts to extend your culture-building efforts to them. City Year, for example, uses its red jackets to engage its key donors. Donors who meet a certain threshold of giving are inducted into the "Red Jacket Society" in a special ceremony where they are given a red jacket just like the ones worn by the organization's employees. During the ceremony, donors join City Year leaders and employees in a tight huddle so that everyone can talk about what the jacket means to them. The ceremony (the ritual) and the jacket (the artifact) not only bond together employees and key external stakeholders, but also cultivate the organization's core value of inclusivity by welcoming into the organization's fold those external stakeholders.[32]

These are just a few examples of company artifacts. The possibilities of artifacts that you can create are only limited by your imagination. Be careful, though, not to create artifacts that are simply gimmicky memory-triggering devices that employees will find little value in, and don't default to the standard tchotchkes and swag that most every company has doled out at some point. Your employees don't need another random T-shirt or wristband; they do need powerful reminders of your desired culture. Along with rituals, artifacts serve as the glue that binds your people together and the scissors that carve out the virtual shape of your organization.

PROMOTE YOUR CULTURE THROUGH POLICIES AND PROCEDURES

From the beginning, Zingerman's founders Paul Saginaw and Ari Weinzweig have operated their company thoughtfully and deliberately. Early on, they established "12 Guiding Principles" for the organization, including "Strong Relationships" and "A Place to Learn," and adopted "3 Bottom Lines"—great food, great service, and great finance—to convey their goals.

Today, the culture at Zingerman's is distinguished by a strong, almost palpable passion for food, service, and results. Everyone there loves food and is committed to making and selling flavorful, high-quality, authentic products. They don't just strive to meet customers' expectations, they aim to exceed them. They try to give customers, as their Staff Guide notes, "a sense of wonderment at how we have gone out of our way to make their experience at Zingerman's a rewarding one." The organization's leaders cultivate creativity, hard work, and commitment among employees so they will deliver this brand of service. And they believe profits are the "lifeblood" of their business, so they enroll as many of their people as practical in operating and improving the company.[33]

To support these foundational values, Zingerman's emphasizes employees' growth and development and seeks to empower them through education. Its leaders state: "Learning keeps us going, keeps us challenged, and keeps us on track." They educate employees about the food they sell because "the more we learn about food...the more effectively and profitably the business will operate." And they educate them about the workings of the business because "the more we understand about the business, the more productive we will be."[34] Zingerman's commitment to education and empowerment is so strong that one of its businesses, ZingTrain, offers public seminars, private trainings, and a host of resources to executives around the world, including a series of books written by Weinzweig, *Zingerman's Guide to Good Leading*, which explain what his company does and why and how they do it.[35]

Given their focus on educating employees in all aspects of the business, it shouldn't come as a surprise that the founders have developed a detailed guide of company policies and procedures, as I described earlier in this chapter. What may be surprising, though, is that their employees actually read and refer to it. That may have something to do with the guide's tone and manner. Zingerman's Staff Guide used to be like so many other companies': a dry manual that gathered dust on the shelf. But when Weinzweig and his colleagues asked themselves why their product catalogs and other external communications were "colorful, engaging, and informing" but their internal materials weren't, they decided to "apply what we do for the consumer to the staff."[36]

Today, the Staff Guide is designed in the same creative style as the company's external communications. Its content is also more engaging than most. Alongside explanations of the company's systems, measurements of success, "5 Key Areas that Make Us Different," and information on its extensive training and education offerings are puzzles, pithy quips, and humorous anecdotes. These additions draw employees into the guide and facilitate their personal experience with it.[37]

But perhaps the best explanation for why the Staff Guide is actually used by employees comes from Weinzweig. He explained to me how, in keeping with the organization's culture of empowerment, the information in the guide is differentiated between standard operating procedures (SOPs) and what he calls "recipes"—general guidelines for how Zingerman's leadership wants an employee to do something. "An SOP tells people the way you do something; there's no creative application," Weinzweig said. "But recipes require creativity." Their "Service Recipe," for example, outlines three ingredients: (1) find out what the guest wants; (2) get it for them accurately, politely, and enthusiastically; and (3) go the extra mile—that is, "do something that's small but blows the customer's mind." It's up to the individual employee, Weinzweig explained, to figure out what that something extra should be—even if they have to do it on their very first day of work.[38]

These recipes are so powerful that many employees cite them as one of the reasons why they like working for the company. Recipes assume employees are capable of using their judgment and creativity to do things in keeping with the company's culture—and with the intent of delivering on the brand promise. Employees, in turn, appreciate being trusted to contribute in their unique way. "You treated me like I was smart from the beginning," employees have told Weinzweig. For him, recipes are a way to "honor people's integrity, intelligence, and creative ability and require them to put them to use."[39]

"A handbook is one of the top materials a leader can develop," he says. "It's an essential communications tool."[40] The Zingerman's Staff Guide is specific and prescriptive when it needs to be, but otherwise it is a collection of culture-building information, insights, inspiration, and examples that help employees understand what the company is all about.

Zingerman's serves as a terrific model for how all companies should leverage their policies and procedures to cultivate their desired culture. Here are the steps involved:

Step 1: Establish Policies and Procedures that Align with Your Culture

First, establish policies (decisions and behavioral norms and guidelines) and procedures (plans of action required to carry out or implement policies) that are right for your organization and that reflect the uniqueness of your culture. As always, start with the overarching purpose of your organization. What strategies have you set to pursue it? And which of the company's core values would support those strategies? Once you've identified these strategies, you can create guidelines and procedures to achieve them and support your values.

For example, Google's original purpose ("to organize the world's information and make it universally useful and accessible to everyone"[41]) and business strategies (pioneering new offerings that attract audiences to use its search engine more often) required a highly empowered workforce and core values that promote innovation. As a result, the company instituted a policy allowing employees to use 20 percent of their time to work on what they think will most benefit the company.[42]

For each policy you establish, Nancy Flynn of the ePolicy Institute recommends asking yourself a series of questions:

- Who is the intended audience for this policy?
- Why does this particular situation or behavior merit a formal rule?
- What do we hope to accomplish with this policy?
- What benefits will this policy deliver to our organization and our employees?
- Are employees likely to respond positively or negatively to this policy?[43]

Craft each policy by answering these questions in a way that conveys and cultivates your desired culture. And remember to articulate each policy so that it is clear, relevant, and accessible to employees.

The following are some of the policies and procedures you should consider establishing or revamping:

- Employee benefits (beyond holidays and insurance)
- Attendance and working days/hours/locations
- Pay periods, days, methods
- Paid time off: vacation, sabbaticals, sick days, and other personal days
- Family and medical leave
- Use of supplies, technology, equipment, and vehicles

- Dress code
- Approvals of budgets, expenses, people decisions, etc.
- Customer service standards
- Training and education
- Office visitors
- Recycling and other sustainability practices
- Use of social media
- Communications
- Office decor
- Discipline and termination
- Health and wellness
- Performance planning and reviews

As you look through these, remember that many policies and procedures must be in place for legal or regulatory reasons and they often must follow specific laws—they're an important and necessary part or organizational life. But your company policies and procedures should serve a purpose beyond legal compliance. If you develop your employee handbook for legal reasons only, you will likely set a tone of defensiveness and give the appearance that the company considers employees variables that need to be controlled rather than partners in creating something special.

But if you think of your policies and procedures as the foundation for the relationship between your employees and your organization, you can use them to express its unique core values, show employees how to work together to fulfill its overarching purpose, and convey its distinctive personality. Consider the following examples:

- A policy at Joie de Vivre asks every employee to spend a night each quarter in one of the company's hotels other than the one where they work (at the company's expense, of course). The policy is designed to help employees see the guest experience with fresh eyes, which in turn supports one of the company's culture goals: encouraging employees to define their work by Joie de Vivre's purpose (delivering a great guest experience), not by the specific tasks assigned to them that might or might not involve contact with a customer.[44]

- San Francisco–based advertising agency Traction has "The Burning Man Policy," which refers to the notoriously wild, weeklong art and self-expression festival that takes place every year in the Nevada desert. The policy states that the company "will prioritize requests for time-off—even if employees have no vacation time left—to attend events that inspire or enhance professional and/or creative development such as Burning Man or SxSW." CEO Adam Kleinberg explains that he and his colleagues created the policy to ensure employees would be able to attend events that "inspire creativity, innovation, and original thought." As a creative agency, Traction sees these events as "rare opportunities to light the fire of creative energy that fuels this business," so it doesn't shy away from encouraging employees to participate in them even if other companies would be concerned about the nudity, drug use, and sex that some, like Burning Man, might involve.[45]

- Motley Fool, the company behind the investment advice website, says one of its core values is "Honest. Make us proud." In that spirit, its "Fool Rules" guide tells employees it's okay to send and receive personal emails at work and that no one at the company monitors emails or checks employees' computers. By allowing employees to use their computers at their own discretion, the company conveys that it trusts them to use their time honestly.[46]

Step 2: Design a Compelling Employee Handbook or Guide

The next step is to codify your policies and procedures into a guide or handbook that is designed as if it were a communications piece for an external audience. If your guide is high-quality and designed to engage, employees will be more likely to read and regularly refer to it. Be sure the tone and manner of the guide or handbook aligns with your brand. Your brand identity and culture should be mutually reinforcing, even in the styles used to communicate your policies and procedures.

Step 3: Engage Employees with Your Guide

Developing and publishing your policies and procedures is only the beginning. You must then disseminate the guide and train employees on the policies and procedures in it. Engage new employees with your guide right from the beginning during their on-boarding process. At Zingerman's, Weinzweig and Saginaw personally conduct orientations for all new employees even though the company has grown to over 500 employees. In these "Welcome to Zingerman's Community of Businesses" classes, they convey "the intellectual, emotional, historical, and ethical story of Zingerman's, and some of the key ways we work to make it all happen," Weinzweig writes in his latest book.[47] They review material from the Staff Guide in the class, but he believes offering both the class and the guide are important because different people learn in different ways.

When new employees experience the company's founders' personal involvement with the guide, they sense the importance of the policies and procedures outlined in it—and are more likely to absorb and use them. Weinzweig considers teaching the class so critical to the company's culture-building efforts that, he writes, doing so is "one of the last things we'll give up in the steady and sustainable march of our organizational progress."[48]

You should also engage your employees with your guide by keeping it up-to-date. University of Massachusetts Dartmouth Professor Michael Griffin says an employee guide should be a "'living document'—very much dynamic—subject to change." He explains, "Existing policies need to be expanded, supplemented, and revised as business conditions change, as business process reengineering takes place, as an organization downsizes, and as quality improvement initiatives are implemented."[49] Whenever you make policy changes, use the occasion to renew employees' attention to your guide.

DESIGN EVERY DETAIL

In my previous book, *What Great Brands Do: The Seven Brand-Building Principles that Separate the Best from the Rest*, I described how great brands sweat the small stuff in their customer experiences because they know all the little things they do for someone in person are far more influential in shaping brand perceptions than all the big things they promise in their advertising. Great brands design their customer experiences down to the finest details of execution and constantly search for new opportunities for brand expression in every element of what they do.

Great companies apply that level of detail and discipline inside their organizations as well. They cultivate their desired culture through every aspect of the organization from their employee handbook to how they run or open a meeting. They know that even the smallest rituals and artifacts and the most mundane of policies and procedures can communicate and reinforce their overarching purpose, core values, and desired culture. Like Salesforce, Zingerman's, and the other companies described in this chapter, they leverage small and sometimes seemingly inconsequential aspects of the business to make big, significant statements.

In the next chapter, you'll learn how to launch culture changes that lead to brand-culture fusion—including those involving rituals, artifacts, policies, and procedures—through employee brand engagement efforts.

Key Takeaways from This Chapter

- To nurture your desired culture, infuse even the smallest and most ordinary (but still influential) aspects of your organization's daily life with your values and purpose.

- Create rituals that interpret the unique and specific elements of your desired culture and reinforce your most important core values.

- Use artifacts as "memory triggers" of your desired culture and the daily behaviors you expect from employees.

- Include "recipes"—general guidelines for behavior that allow employees to exercise their own judgment and apply their own creativity—in your policies and procedures.

- Draw your employees into your policies and procedures with an engaging handbook that is produced with the same tone and attention to detail as a communication tool created for customers.

CHAPTER 7

IGNITE YOUR TRANSFORMATION

Read this chapter to learn:

- Why brand-culture fusion depends on employee brand engagement
- How to launch the fusion process through brand engagement experiences and integrated communications campaigns
- How to use brand toolkits to facilitate employees' ongoing engagement with your desired culture and brand

If your company employed over 77,000 people in over twenty-seven locations and needed to execute a company-wide, comprehensive training program, no one would fault you for hiring an outside company or using an e-learning platform to execute it. But the leadership at MGM Resorts considered neither an adequate option when in 2010 they set out to train their workforce as part of a wholesale brand and culture transformation. They believed it was imperative to meet with every single employee in person to truly engage them and to achieve the high degree of consistency in the desired brand and culture it wanted across all its properties. Their ambitious training and engagement agenda reflected the magnitude of the transformation they set out to accomplish.

MGM Resorts had adopted a strategy to reposition itself from merely a casino company to a worldwide resort and entertainment company. It was a bold move that involved leveraging its brand and expertise to develop entertainment venues and hotels that were not gaming-centric—such as Bellagio, MGM Grand, and Skylofts—around the world. The change was as much a strategic business investment as it was a brand metamorphosis. Lilian Tomovich, the company's chief experience and marketing officer, explained to me that the company wanted to transform itself into "what we believed was at the core of our DNA: entertainment."[1]

While the company developed and acquired new properties and initiated advertising campaigns to execute the brand repositioning, its executives knew that they couldn't solely direct their efforts externally. Tomovich recalled their thinking at the time: "We can't tell a story to Wall Street and consumers that we can't deliver on and employees can't understand. If we're going to reposition the brand, we're going to have to transform the way we do our work and attack our culture to become more consumer-centric."[2]

Moreover, as a hospitality company, MGM Resorts realized that its employees must be engaged in a culture that is aligned and integrated with the company's brand so they are equipped and empowered to constantly provide excellent customer service that delivers on the brand promise. "MGM is in the experience business," she noted. "We work very hard to ensure we deliver amazing experiences, but sometimes we miss, and that's when we need an incredibly strong culture and backbone to recover and win back consumers."[3]

As a result, Tomovich and her team initiated an internal culture change effort that they called "We Are the Show." The goal was to engage employees—even by the name of the initiative—with the idea that they played a role in delivering a "show" to guests. Using the metaphor of a show not only reinforced the company's desired brand identity as an entertainment brand but also helped seed the "SHOW" acronym that summarized its desired culture: S for smile and greet the guest; H for hear their story; O for own the experience; and W for "Wow" the guest.[4]

Tomovich and her team kicked off the culture transformation initiative with a summit for the company's top 7,000 leaders, where they explained why they were embarking on the transformation and what it would take to accomplish it. They also showed them how to train their direct reports, cascading the desired culture throughout the organization, so that after eight months, all 77,000 employees would be trained personally by their managers. In these sessions, employees went through a custom curriculum that engaged them with the attitudes and behaviors that were consistent with the new desired culture. For example, leaders used "Skillbuilder" templates to take their employees through property- and department-specific guidelines and expectations, such as "Be visible and accessible to guests with open body language and friendly facial expression."[5]

Tomovich and her team also developed an internal communications campaign that they launched in conjunction with the initiative. The campaign included posters that showed employees at work under the headline "This Is My Stage," regular news updates to leaders and "daily team update" emails to generate enthusiasm across the board, and signage specifically for display in "back of house" areas. These communication efforts reached all employees from all angles, thus creating "360 degree integration" and contributing to the company's culture transformation.[6]

As part of their training, leaders were given a leadership playbook and an "engagement calendar" to help them plan the content and timing of their initial training sessions with their employees, as well as regular follow-up discussions. Tomovich's team also gave leaders an engagement toolkit that included teaching aids, such as "SHOW cards" they could use to facilitate discussions on the different elements of the SHOW acronym and to reinforce their training on a continuous basis. Even as I write this book, her team continues to cultivate the desired culture by sending leaders reminders of questions and topics they can review with their employees.[7]

The all-encompassing approach to transforming the company's culture and brand was fueled, as Tomovich explains, by the company's "remarkable passion and interest in changing the focus of employees." MGM Resorts has achieved its desired culture because it "continues to have the same conversation; it's not an afterthought," Tomovich clarifies. The leaders' conviction in the brand-culture connection, she believes, was the reason why the company accomplished a successful internal transformation.[8] The company has also realized financial gains from its efforts, reporting increased revenues, REVPAR (a hospitality industry key metric), and net income in 2016.[9]

To change your brand and culture, you must engage your employees just as rigorously as MGM Resorts has. You must kick off your cultural and brand transformation efforts and communicate them clearly and creatively—and you must continuously keep these efforts alive thereafter. The key to launching these efforts and to keeping the momentum going is employee brand engagement—that is engaging your employees with your brand deeply and completely. In this chapter I will lay out three tactics for doing so, starting with launching your journey to brand-culture fusion with employee brand engagement experiences, continuing the effort with internal communications campaigns, and developing toolkits to facilitate ongoing employee engagement with your desired culture and brand.

But first, what *is* employee brand engagement?

EMPLOYEE BRAND ENGAGEMENT CREATES CULTURE CHANGE

Employee brand engagement is the process of immersing your employees in your brand—what it stands for; why it's important; what it entails; and how they are to nurture, reinforce, and interpret it—so that they form a meaningful connection with it. As I explained in Chapter 2, employee brand engagement involves personal and emotional engagement with your brand (e.g., employees' sense of personal connection to your overarching purpose), engagement with your brand in the day-to-day (e.g., their belief that they are responsible for building your brand), and engagement in your brand strategy (e.g., their understanding of your brand's target audiences and their primary wants and needs). Essentially, employee brand engagement involves engaging employees with their emotions, actions, and intellect.

To be clear, employee brand engagement is different from "employer branding" or "employment branding," terms that refer to an organization's efforts to enhance its image to attract and retain talented employees. It's also more than "internal marketing" or "invertising," which describes when an organization promotes its brand to employees as it would to customers and expects them to "buy" the message its leaders or marketing department are trying to "sell" to them. Having an image as a good employer and trying to make employees feel good about your brand is important, but these alone won't cultivate the mindset and behaviors that contribute to your desired culture.

Your employees must internalize your brand. They must understand what your brand strategy is and why it's important as well as how their work impacts brand perceptions and, therefore, what is expected of them. That's what employee brand engagement is all about.

When you engage your employees with your brand deeply and completely, you cultivate a culture that is so intertwined with your brand that they become inseparable. In their research on employee relationships, Dr. Lucy Gill-Simmen and Professor Andreas Eisingerich at Imperial College Business School in London found that employees who show a strong relationship with the brand and strong brand attachment are more likely to exhibit on-brand behaviors than those who don't. "The employee brand relationship is an extremely complex process but one which mirrors consumers' relationships with the brand," Gill-Simmen told me. "When you can get your employees to form a relationship with your brand through the benefits it provides, you are onto a winner, since these employees do extraordinary things for the brand in return."[10]

But achieving employee brand engagement at this level is pretty rare. A *Journal of Brand Management* paper shows that four in ten employees struggle to describe their organization's brand or how they think customers feel their organization is different from competitors.[11] Brand consultancy Tenet Partners reports that only 28 percent of employees strongly agree that they know their company's brand values, and only one in five employees strongly agree that company leaders communicate how employees should live their company's brand values.[12]

Even if your employees know your brand strategy, it is not enough. As Gregg Lederman explains in *Achieve Brand Integrity*, employees shouldn't just *understand* your brand and the behaviors required to deliver on it. They must be *committed* to doing them, and then they must actually *do* them. To get employees to "buy in," he writes, "you need to ensure that employees know how to take action and are able to actually do it."[13] That's where brand engagement and the three tactics I describe in this chapter—brand engagement experiences, internal communications campaigns, and toolkits—come into play.

STAGE GREAT EMPLOYEE BRAND ENGAGEMENT EXPERIENCES

Benjamin Franklin once said, "Tell me and I forget. Teach me and I remember. Involve me and I learn." Learning and engagement are, indeed, most effectively accomplished when you involve people experientially. That's why staging experiences for your employees to engage personally and interactively with your brand is crucial.

Employee brand engagement experiences are vibrant, thoughtfully designed programs and initiatives created either to launch a cultural or brand initiative or to reinvigorate it after a period of time. When launching brand-culture transformation efforts within your company, these experiences can help you explain to all employees where you're taking the organization, why, and what role they play in that transformation. Like the cascading training sessions at MGM Resorts, which immersed all 77,000 employees in the company's new brand strategy and what would be required of everyone to deliver on that new brand, employee brand engagement experiences can activate the attitude and behaviors that characterize your desired culture.

Organizations with large numbers of frontline employees who interact daily with customers are not the only ones who benefit from employee brand engagement experiences. Even companies where the majority of employees don't interface directly with customers can leverage these experiences to fuel their cultural transformation.

San Diego–based Mitchell International, a $300 million automotive insurance software company, designed a remarkable brand engagement program to involve its employees with "The Mitchell Way"—the company's mission, vision, brand promise, and brand beliefs (core values). An explanation of The Mitchell Way had been published and distributed to all employees, but the company needed to "get it into everyone's hearts and minds," Jennifer Forman, the company's marketing leader, told me. "We needed to educate them, to show how we all work together to deliver on The Mitchell Way." So Forman and her team created "The Mitchell Way Day" to inspire and galvanize Mitchell employees.[14]

The Mitchell Way Day, as its name suggests, was a one-day event that included all sorts of activities dedicated to engaging employees in the company's desired culture and brand. One of the most successful activities of The Mitchell Way Day was the department exhibits. A few weeks prior to the event, Forman's group asked all department leaders to enlist their people in creating science-fair-type exhibits showing how their department had been inspired by the company's core values to positively impact customers. Even after arming them with arts and crafts supplies and issuing a call to be as creative as possible, Forman was still unsure if the exercise would be effective at engaging the engineers and developers who make up the majority of Mitchell's 1,700-person workforce.

But on The Mitchell Way Day, when the groups revealed their exhibits, she was "blown away" by their ingenuity and creativity. The exhibits were colorful, fun, and innovative—some even incorporated mechanical features to create motion and interactivity. But most important, they delivered on the assignment. One department's exhibit used a golf swing metaphor to exemplify how it implemented a streamlined process for customers that aligned with the company's "simplicity" core value; another employed a foosball game design to show the value "passion for delivering results" (the employees' department was represented by the foosball team persistently moving the ball toward a sales goal). Forman observed, "People really do get engaged when you create opportunities to celebrate what we do."[15]

The Mitchell Way Day event also featured interactive installations, some focusing on the core values, others reinforcing other elements of The Mitchell Way. One installation, for instance, allowed employees to adopt a customer persona and listen to a day-in-the-life narrative of that customer—a powerful way for employees to understand their customers better and discover how to fulfill the company purpose of empowering them. A fun-house mirror display reminded employees about the importance of customer perceptions—even potentially distorted ones—of the Mitchell brand. And coffee stations that encouraged employees to customize their drinks were set up to remind everyone of the company's core value of being "personal" in the way they interacted with customers and each other.

Forman and her team also distributed kits to remote offices to help them set up their own installations, sent packages to employees who worked out of their home offices, and set up a live stream for everyone to tune into the CEO's presentation at the event.[16]

While The Mitchell Way Day was a fun and energizing experience, Forman made sure it was first and foremost a learning one. To stage an experience that gets employees involved with brand and culture, she explained, "You have to begin with what you want people to walk away with and then start framing the event." While developing the event, she and her team repeatedly asked themselves what elements of the desired culture they wanted to cultivate and carefully designed each activity and installation to be a learning opportunity. "We were not just having an event to have an event," she said. They were moving people along what she called "brand-culture indoctrination phases," from simply being aware of The Mitchell Way to being ready to defend and promote it, and eventually to becoming a passionate advocate for it.[17]

Follow-up surveys showed that Forman and her team achieved the learning objective they set for The Mitchell Way Day. The company has seen a marked increase in employees' belief that the company is delivering on its core values and in their understanding of what delivering on the company's brand promise means.[18]

How to Create Multi-Dimensional Brand Engagement Experiences

When launching a cultural transformation, you should stage an employee brand engagement experience for every single employee, either by bringing all employees together in one venue for a single event or by holding sessions for separate regions, departments, or groups over a period of time. Either way, the experience should be multi-dimensional and experiential and include a mixture of elements, such as a presentation by company leadership, hands-on exercises, facilitated discussions, distribution of tools and instructions, and department- or role-specific content.

Hands-on exercises and facilitated discussions are best conducted in small groups of eight to twenty people. If you're gathering a large group, consider setting up different "stations" for different activities that employees rotate through in smaller clusters, just as Mitchell did with its installations.

The experiences should also be designed to meet your specific learning objectives. As such, you might stage different activities with different groups of employees. Here are just a few examples of the activities I use for my clients and the objectives I usually use them for:

Sprechen Sie brand? *This exercise is helpful in increasing understanding of what a brand is and why it's important in general. It's particularly useful for engaging employees who don't see how they influence customers' brand perceptions.* Ask each participant to name their favorite brand and explain why they like it. Write down everyone's contribution, share the list with all participants, and facilitate a discussion about how these brands are liked because of what they do for customers, such as producing quality products, providing excellent customer service, or enabling them to do something they hadn't been able to before. You might want to point out that rarely does someone like a brand because of its logo or tagline. Ask participants which attitudes and actions of the people inside those companies they think might have resulted in the brand being so well-liked or successful.

After this discussion about brands in general, you can then transition to talking about your brand and what employees in various roles can do to inspire your customers to consider it their favorite brand.

Brand identity collage. *This experience increases your employees' understanding of your brand identity.* Launch a photo scavenger hunt in which groups of employees take pictures or look through magazines to find images that embody the company's brand identity—not just pictures of products or the logo, but also of employees, customers, artifacts, tools, physical spaces, etc. Instruct each group to assemble a collage of the images and to use captions and headlines to explain its interpretations of the brand to the other groups. Then, to create one common understanding of your brand among all groups, facilitate a discussion of the collages to clarify what ideas and images align best with your brand and why.

Funeral and birth. *This experience helps to break ties with your previous brand or culture and increase adoption of the new one.* Stage a mock funeral in which you put your previous brand identity and/or core values into a grave. Ask people to give brief eulogies about what everyone should remember about them and why they need to change. Then stage a mock baby shower in which you celebrate the arrival of your new brand identity and/or core values. Ask people to give toasts to celebrate what they like about them and how they expect them to develop.

Customer listening booth. *This experience helps to develop customer empathy and disperse knowledge of how customers perceive your brand.* Set up phone-booth-like stations where employees listen to prerecorded interviews with customers about their experiences with the brand. After employees have visited the booths, facilitate a discussion about their learnings and conduct a brainstorming session to develop ideas for how to improve the brand experience.

Game show. *This experience helps to increase knowledge of your brand strategy and target customers.* Hold a game-show-like contest in which teams or individuals compete for prizes based on their speed and accuracy of answering questions about the elements of your brand strategy and target customer profiles.

If it's not possible to stage in-person experiences, today's technologies provide the capabilities for you to provide brand engagement experiences that are just as immersive and instructive—and sometimes even more. Consider how Telenor, the Norwegian telecom company, relies on "The Visionary," an e-learning program, to successfully accomplish its engagement goals. The program, as Nicholas Ind describes in *Living the Brand*, was designed to develop individual employees' understanding of Telenor's brand vision and core values, "not just to inform employees about the values, but rather to see the applicability of the values."[19]

The Visionary is a modular program comprising video sequences that present various scenarios and choices for employees to select from. With each selection, employees demonstrate how they would change their behavior and communications in each situation to align with the company's core values. Once they complete the program, their selections are scored to show what impact they would have on the brand and customers. "Not only does this wrong way/right way approach encourage the user to learn how to use a value in a specific instance," Ind explains, "but it makes the more generalizable point that seemingly non-brand events have clear brand implications."[20]

With a little creativity, you can create your own live or digital experiences to launch your cultural transformation and help employees connect with your brand, overarching purpose, and core values in relevant and memorable ways. You can also stage these experiences at different points on your journey to refocus your people and reinvigorate your cultural transformation efforts. Whenever they need inspiration, your people become participants in your company's journey to brand-culture fusion through these experiences.

Whether you are designing your employee brand engagement experience to launch your cultural transformation or to reignite it, the goal should be the same: to get your employees excited about your brand and to help them identify the attitudes, decisions, and behaviors they need to adopt to support your desired brand identity. A great employee brand engagement experience is by definition a discrete event, though, whereas cultural transformation requires a sustained effort. To engage your employees over a period of time, you should also put together a communications campaign that convincingly supports and continues your transformation.

CAREFULLY CRAFT COMMUNICATIONS CAMPAIGNS

In 2013, O2, a telecommunications business that is part of Madrid-based Telefónica, was in the midst of transforming from a mobile service provider to a digital telecommunications brand. Like the leaders at MGM Resorts, O2's management knew that repositioning the company's brand required changing the customer experience, and that, in turn, required changing their culture and engaging their employees in the change. But they found that their employees weren't exactly clear on what being a digital telecommunications brand entailed. So the company launched an integrated employee brand engagement communications campaign to increase employees' understanding of digital telecom and O2's motivation for undertaking the transformation.[21]

The "Rally Cry" campaign, as O2 labeled it, centered on the colloquialism "going for a 10 out of 10" with customers. The campaign was kicked off with a high-energy event at 10:10 on April 10, 2014, which had been preceded by a series of fun 10-themed videos featuring Telefónica's board members. At the lively event, which featured music and games for the employees, more videos were shown to communicate the brand vision and its targets. Afterwards, the company released a Rally Cry special internal TV program of "sofa chats" with senior leaders who discussed the company's digital telecom strategy and its results.[22]

The Rally Cry campaign also included a comprehensive set of communications to continue momentum over time. To allow employees to communicate with senior leaders as well as with each other about the rebranding efforts, the team behind the campaign created a company-wide social networking group on Yammer. It also produced notice boards that were put up in the back of its retail stores that showed actual store performance numbers in relationship to the company's digital telecom goals. And it published a dashboard on an ongoing basis that summarized activities related to the rebranding initiative, and reported the results from the campaign in weekly leadership team presentations.[23]

The communication efforts were an integral part of the Rally Cry campaign, which succeeded in helping employees understand what a digital telecom company is and why and how O2 set out to become one. In a postcampaign survey, 92 percent of employees said they fully understood the company strategy. The Rally Cry campaign communications also increased engagement, with 88 percent of employees reporting feeling more engaged with the business.[24]

These improved attitudes among employees sparked innovations that advanced the company's new digital telecom brand identity. Across the company, employees were "vying to create new ways to enable and engage our customers with our digital assets," according to an O2 report submitted for the 2016 Marketing Society Excellence Awards. Employees at one store, for instance, introduced a near-field communication-enabled kiosk for mobile customers that allowed them to upload O2 apps on their phones as soon as they bought them. "Rally Cry has been a major success," the O2 report concludes. "Our people were fully engaged with the programme, and their actions enabled us to exceed our targets 2 years running, leading to increased customer engagement and customer retention."[25]

O2's brand transformation was not only successful because it effectively engaged employees with a big event—an experience—but also because it was supported and extended through a comprehensive and continuous communications campaign. In addition, the campaign was carefully orchestrated with the same level of detail and forethought as external communication campaigns are. This thoughtful approach to employee communications, however, is not common in most organizations.

If you're honest, your organization probably has a different—lower—standard for its internal communications than it does for communications created for external audiences. Most do. *PR Week* observes, "Employee communications has never been viewed as a particularly glamorous part of the communications industry. Staff are often sidelined as an HR concern, in favour of customers, investors or the media."[26] Colin Mitchell, a former executive at advertising agency Ogilvy & Mather, says that most companies' approach to the task of communicating with employees is "so generic, so removed from the business's frontline realities, and, frankly, so dull."[27]

But as the success of O2's Rally Cry campaign demonstrates, the same standards you use to communicate with customers should apply to your employee communications. After all, your goals—to get people's attention, appeal to and engage them, and prompt them to action—are the same for both groups. If you're trying to cultivate employee brand engagement, upholding the same high standards for your internal communications as your external ones is even more important, since these employee communications give you the chance to reinforce your brand message by embodying your brand attributes and personality.

Your employee brand engagement communications should conform to the basics of all good external communication:

- **Be clear**. Convey the information you want employees to know and what you expect them to do as a result without any jargon or nuance, which are often confusing.
- **Be explicit, even prescriptive**. Don't assume people will interpret information in the same way.
- **Be creative**. Like customers, employees are human beings, emotional creatures, so communications must touch them emotionally. Design your communications to inspire as well as teach.

Develop your employee brand engagement communications as if you were running a marketing communications campaign, as O2 did. First, target discrete segments with discrete messages based on their needs and your desired outcomes (e.g., managers might require a level of detail about certain aspects of the initiative, the business, or the results expected from these efforts that wouldn't be appropriate for other employees). Then, plan to reach each audience and trigger desired actions at the right times in the engagement process. For example, when you kick off your cultural transformation initiative, you might simply want to generate awareness and run communications that preview your efforts, explain why you are moving toward your desired culture, and what that will entail. With later communications, you might drive employees to specific actions like attending an event, signing up for a class, or accessing a tool.

Different people learn in different ways, so use multiple communications methods and channels to engage more people more effectively. Use videos to share stories, as O2 did with the 10-themed videos featuring board members. Rely on emails to convey instructions (e.g., how to download a tool or sign up to participate in a special event). Produce high-quality banners, posters, and other large-format signage to broadcast short messages about your brand or to inspire employees to engage in the rebranding efforts, like the employee posters at MGM Resorts. And leverage any intranet or internal collaboration platforms to communicate more informally about your brand and culture and to encourage conversations, as O2 did with its dedicated Rally Cry Yammer group.

Above all, employee brand engagement communications should motivate employees at a personal level. In *Brand from the Inside,* Libby Sartain and Mark Schumann observe that companies should adopt a more audience-centric posture when creating employee communications today. "We must move from an emphasis on business saying what it wants to say, to an emphasis on articulating what employees... need to hear—the 'What's in it for me.'"[28] You need to explain why your cultural transformation is important to every employee—how it will help them do their jobs; make their experience better; ensure the viability of the company, which increases their job security; and so on. Connecting the dots explicitly between each employee and your brand is the crux of employee brand engagement—and the key to culture transformation success. Mitchell, the former Ogilvy executive, explains, "Failure to communicate at a personal level can undermine the most sophisticated and expensive rebranding campaign."[29]

• •

YOUR EMPLOYEE BRAND ENGAGEMENT
COMMUNICATIONS SHOULD BE:

- Clear
- Explicit
- Creative
- Targeted
- Multi-channel
- Personal

• •

DEVELOP TOOLKITS FOR
ONGOING ENGAGEMENT

While staging interactive experiences and carefully crafting high-quality employee communications campaigns can draw attention to your cultural and brand transformation at discrete periods of time, developing a "brand engagement toolkit" is a powerful tactic to help your employees connect with your desired brand on an ongoing, longer-term basis.

A brand engagement toolkit is a collection of materials and tools that employees can access—likely through an intranet portal or dedicated social networking site—and that help them connect with the brand on three different levels: their heads, hearts, and hands and feet.

To engage employees' heads, for example, a toolkit might contain flash cards or quizzes employees can self-administer to test their own knowledge or use with others. Or they might include "case studies" about situations employees might encounter, including questions for them to answer or discuss with their managers, or downloadable reports (updated on a regular basis) with hard data and insights about the brand, the brand strategy, and its related business goals.

To engage employees' hearts, a toolkit might contain videos featuring customer stories or letters from customers along with corresponding worksheets for employees to note how the videos or letters inspire them to change their attitudes and behaviors to improve the customer experience. Or you might provide journals containing quotes and brand- or customer-related images to encourage employees to jot down their personal reflections of your company's culture or add their own quotes and images.

To engage employees' hands and feet—their actions, that is—a toolkit might contain decision guides, process flowcharts, workbooks, or mobile apps containing role-playing exercises or other activities that help them easily align their decisions and actions with your desired culture.

The possibilities for your toolkit are endless and the tools you include should be based on the specific needs of your organization. But all effective toolkits share a common element: they contain items that your people use to accomplish a task or purpose. Messaging and other one-way communications play a role in employee brand engagement, but they are not tools. Effective employee brand engagement tools are interactive and produce outcomes however big or small.

Here are more examples:

- Workbooks containing quizzes, fill-in-the-blank exercises, and sections for note taking to help employees process information. Example: The leadership playbooks that MGM Resorts distributed during its leadership summit featured areas for people to write in the dates they would train their employees and their own ideas for how to engage them.

- Note cards or other items for employees to communicate or share with other employees. Example: Brand Integrity, a culture consulting and software firm, recommends setting up a system where employees give "I Caught You" cards to coworkers when they exhibit behaviors that are in line with the desired culture or that support the brand identity. When a card is given to an employee, a copy goes to his or her supervisor and recognition is given to both the recipient and the recognizer.

- Digital games, polls, or activities to get employees to interact with content or practice decision-making. Example: Mortgage loan company Quicken Loans deployed an online learning tool comprising electronic flash cards, one for each of its core values, and learning modules that engage users with the flash cards in simple games like fill-in-the-blank and matching terms and definitions.

• Displays or posters that employees use to express their insights or post their progress. Example: When I headed brand and strategy at Sony's electronics business unit, we developed an online bulletin board and encouraged employees to post their insights about and examples of the Sony brand in action. People benefited from both sharing their ideas and reading others'.

These toolkits serve as brand engagement references and resources for employees over time. They can be deployed to leaders and managers in advance of an employee communications campaign or brand engagement experience to preview what's coming, they can be shared with employees during these campaigns or experiences to support them and collect feedback, and they can be used afterward to continue the momentum and build on the learning. The goal is to create a resource that your people refer to regularly. That's why employee brand engagement toolkits should be designed to accommodate changes. You should update the tools in it and add new ones regularly to keep the content fresh and to prompt people to come back to the toolkit often.

A WORTHY INVESTMENT

If employee brand engagement sounds like a significant undertaking, it is. Employee brand engagement experiences, communication campaigns, and toolkits don't have to cost a lot of money*—but they do take time. MGM Resorts' Tomovich told me she and her team had started working on their brand engagement efforts two years prior to its launch and still considered themselves "knee-deep into the journey."[30]

---

* Mitchell's Forman, for example, assured me that she didn't have a big budget for The Mitchell Way Day; her team redirected existing budget to do things "on the cheap." (Source: Mitchell, Jennifer. Interview with Denise Lee Yohn. Telephone interview on July 19, 2017.)

A thorough employee brand engagement program takes time to develop and implement—and to see results.

But the investments are worth it. As Tomovich clearly articulates, "Without aligning your culture to your brand, you have no chance of winning the hearts and minds of consumers. You will just have a hollow brand that can't deliver."[31]

When launching the brand-culture fusion process, consider how all three employee brand engagement tactics—experiences, communications campaigns, and toolkits—can be used in a combined, coordinated effort. But keep in mind, these tactics are the means to an end. The true measure of their effectiveness is when they're no longer needed. "You know it's working when you no longer have playbooks, templates, reminders, etc.," Tomovich explained. When employees start undertaking their own grassroots approaches to support the desired culture, she said, you know people are "on their way."[32]

I have now covered all four strategies for infusing your brand into your culture. If you think of your desired culture as the vehicle that transports you from your existing state to brand-culture fusion, I started Part 2 of this book describing the engine of that vehicle—your organizational design and operations. They are at the core of your efforts and give you power. I then introduced the frame of the vehicle, the main supporting structure for the culture—employee experience. Then I showed how rituals, artifacts, policies, and procedures express your desired culture, essentially forming the design and features of the vehicle—the sometimes small but distinctive aspects of it. And in this chapter, I added the gas—employee brand engagement—to propel your vehicle forward.

These are the essential strategies to nurture your desired culture by aligning and integrating it with your brand identity. They provide the path to achieve brand-culture fusion if your culture is less developed or defined than your brand, as I've found it is at most companies. But if your culture is well established, you may achieve fusion by using it to shape or reshape your brand. The next chapter shows you how.

Key Takeaways from This Chapter

- The key to launching your efforts to infuse your culture with your brand identity—and to keeping the momentum going—is employee brand engagement.

- When you engage your employees with your brand deeply and completely, you cultivate a culture that is so intertwined with your brand that they become inseparable.

- Stage experiences for your employees to engage personally and interactively with your brand and brand strategy.

- To involve employees with your brand, craft internal communications campaigns that are as inspired and coordinated as external ones.

- Use multi-dimensional brand engagement toolkits to keep your employees engaged with your desired culture and brand on an ongoing basis.

- Brand engagement tactics are the means to an end—the true measure of their effectiveness is when they're no longer needed.

CHAPTER 8

BUILD YOUR BRAND FROM THE INSIDE OUT

Read this chapter to learn:

- How to use your overarching purpose to inspire external brand actions that define or redefine your brand
- How to leverage your existing internal values to evolve your brand toward your desired brand identity
- How to use your culture as a brand differentiator

Patagonia's very first catalog didn't look much like a catalog—its first fourteen pages featured a manifesto about "clean climbing," an approach to rock climbing in which climbers avoid permanently damaging rocks by using special techniques and equipment such as hexes and chocks. Yvon Chouinard, Patagonia's founder, felt so strongly about the need for clean climbing that he devoted so much valuable real estate in his first catalog to advocate for it and made chocks the cornerstone of his climbing hardware start-up.[1]

That was back in 1972. In the years since, Chouinard has often expressed his convictions about environmental issues through his company. In the mid-1990s, for example, after learning about the devastating effects of chemicals used in growing cotton, he determined that Patagonia would use only 100 percent organic cotton in its products. Doing so required the company to drop some of its most successful products because there wasn't enough supply of organic cotton. The company also had to rework its entire cotton supply chain, which resulted in the tripling of cotton costs.[2] Also in the mid-2000s, Patagonia started making clothing out of recycled materials, and more recently it expanded its emphasis on recycling with a program through which customers can donate as well as buy used clothing.[3]

Today, Patagonia's commitment to the environment permeates its organizational culture. Its mission statement reads, "Build the best product, cause no unnecessary harm, use business to inspire and implement solutions to the environmental crisis." Most employees share Chouinard's values and are just as passionate about operationalizing them. They've ensured the company's business strategies and operations are informed by its overarching purpose to protect and preserve the environment.[4]

That purpose influences Patagonia's brand identity too. Die-hard Patagonia customers have always known about the company's sustainable business practices. But as the brand has grown to appeal to a more mainstream consumer, the company has intentionally leveraged its core values and purpose to define its brand identity. "Patagonia has long used its catalog and website as an editorial outlet for stories from the outdoors, seeding its environmental agenda amid the colorful, high-end fleece," a 2014 *Fast Company* article reported. "But over the last few years, the brand has stepped up its efforts to draw a clearer line between its goods and its overall mission."[5]

Vice president of global marketing Joy Howard explains that customers usually come to Patagonia for its products. In the past, it would have taken them awhile to learn about the company's environmental consciousness. "As a marketing team," Howard said, "the task is very simple, and that's to make it easy for people to discover what the company is all about, and make sure it's not hidden and tough to access. Because once they do know, they're in. They're with us."[6] To help customers discover Patagonia's purpose, Howard and her team have created a thirty-minute documentary extolling the virtues of long-lasting and used clothing, "DamNation"—a film that urges the U.S. government to tear down what Patagonia calls "deadbeat dams"— and other content marketing pieces.[7] As customers are exposed to Patagonia's environmental efforts and philosophy, they understand the brand the way Chouinard and his employees do.

Patagonia is an example of a company that has leveraged its well-defined, deeply entrenched culture to shape its brand identity. Its purpose and values are crystal clear—and that clarity is expressed in its brand actions and communications, so that how Patagonia works on the inside perfectly mirrors how the brand is perceived in the outside.

If your culture is as deeply rooted as Patagonia's, then trying to change it to align with your desired brand identity—as I've advocated in the previous four chapters—might be a mistake. In most cases, your attempts won't work. They will likely result in only superficial changes that fade away after awhile or are quickly abandoned when pressures from outside forces cause your people to retrench. There is a greater risk of this happening if your organization has entrenched subcultures of people who don't see the need to change. Or your efforts to change might be too much of a stretch for your employees—especially if many of them have been with your company for a very long time—and they just aren't able to adopt the new mindset and behaviors needed to support your brand identity.

In some situations, you're actually better off allowing your culture to lead your brand. If your convictions are so strong that you are more committed to promoting your purpose and values than achieving any particular business or brand goal, then you should prioritize your culture as the driver of your brand identity. Or if you operate in the public sector or yours is an institution such as a science or faith-based organization where a well-defined brand was not needed in the past, you can shape a more authentic brand identity through the inherent values of your people than through an external or contrived aspiration. So long as your culture is not fundamentally toxic or dysfunctional, you can use it to shape your brand. Whatever the case, the goal remains the same—achieve brand-culture fusion by infusing your culture into your brand.

In this chapter I share examples from a handful of great organizations that have produced brand-culture fusion this way, so you learn three strategies for leveraging your culture in your brand: how to use your overarching purpose to inspire external brand actions, how to leverage your existing internal values to evolve your brand toward your desired brand identity, and how to apply your culture as a brand differentiator.

PUT YOUR PURPOSE INTO ACTION

In 2005, GE's former CEO Jeff Immelt pledged to the world to "address challenges such as the need for cleaner, more efficient sources of energy, reduced emissions and abundant sources of clean water." Fulfilling this pledge would involve doubling the company's investment in clean technology R&D, doubling its revenues from products and services that "provide significant and measurable environmental performance advantages to customers," and changing its operations to reduce carbon emissions and become more energy efficient.[8]

Dubbed "Ecomagination," this new business strategy was the company's latest interpretation of its overarching purpose: turning imaginative ideas into leading products and services that help solve some of the world's toughest problems. In fact, the Ecomagination website explains the initiative is a natural expression of GE's culture: "Working to solve some of the world's biggest challenges has inspired our thinking and driven our actions for more than 125 years. And as a technology company, sustainability is embedded in our culture and business strategy."[9] By emphasizing technology solutions as the cornerstone of the strategy, Immelt drew upon the organization's inherent strengths and focus on innovation.

The new strategy required the company to dramatically step up its culture. Joel Makower, chairman and executive editor of *GreenBiz Group*, described how GE "created a set of internal standards for what constituted Ecomagination products and revenue, and a score carding system, audited by outsiders, to measure Ecomagination's energy and environmental improvement claims."

But GE didn't simply stop with culture changes, it also transformed its operations. It introduced a range of new products and services, including hybrid locomotives and steam turbines. It shed many business units, including appliances, media, and financial services, so that the company would be "firmly entrenched in engines, power generation, water systems, and other businesses that sync with Ecomagination's focus on efficiency and emissions reductions. It even reduced its own emissions by installing solar panels and switching to natural-gas fired power instead of oil."[10]

It also strategically used this purpose-driven business strategy to shape external perceptions of the company. Immelt and other executives have met regularly with customers, analysts, and regulators to discuss environmental strategies and to identify new opportunities to produce eco-friendly solutions. GE also initiated the "Ecomagination Innovation Challenge," an open competition that invited people to submit ideas to help "power the grid" and "power the home."[11]

In the first year of the initiative, the company spent $90 million on an Ecomagination public relations and advertising campaign. In addition to broadcast and online ads, it launched a microsite for the initiative that showcased animated vignettes of the company's first seventeen eco-friendly products and created interactive online games to build awareness of eco-products and their benefits, such as saving money. The games, featuring life on a fictitious island named "Geoterra," engage visitors in activities that involve GE products.[12]

These efforts have produced a new brand identity for GE. In the past, the company had been plagued with a reputation as "an environmental dinosaur from the industrial revolution," as Alexander Haldemann, CEO of MetaDesign, wrote in *Huffington Post*. It couldn't shake the bad PR it had generated from reports that claimed the company had polluted the Hudson River for decades and that former CEO Jack Welch refused to clean it up.[13] Today, GE's customer research shows that awareness of its Ecomagination efforts is higher than anything else that GE is currently working on.[14] The company continually receives awards recognizing its environmental contributions, such as the Gold Asian Power Award,[15] and *Fortune* recently named it to its 2016 "Change the World" list.[16]

Haldemann observes, "By making massive, bold changes in how they conducted business, GE reinvented a new brand story rooted in green innovation, thereby shifting how the world perceived them."[17] Deb Frodl, Ecomagination's global executive director, confirmed that the strategy's external appeal was deliberate. "Eco is always so much more than just a traditional sustainability program where we're focused internally," she said. "We are bringing technology to market to help our customers be as productive as they possibly can. That strategy has been key to our success. It allows us to scale and win the hearts and minds of both consumers and our customers."[18] The internal and external success of Ecomagination has produced significant growth for GE. In 2015 the company reported that the initiative had generated up to $160 billion dollars in revenue.[19]

If you find that your overarching purpose—or even a new corporate priority or core strategy that is deeply connected to your purpose—is not well known or valued by your customers, you can use a similar approach to GE's: infuse your brand identity with your culture and purpose. To define or re-define your brand in this way, you must connect the dots between your motivations and your actions clearly for customers and other stakeholders.

While advertising campaigns will help draw attention to your efforts, other communications, such as videos, reports, documentaries, and social media content, are more likely to generate word-of-mouth. When people are talking about your brand, the messages they share with each other about it are usually far more influential than any message your company issues. So enroll customers and engage influencers to help spread the word about what you're doing internally, why, and what difference it makes. Whenever possible, link to actual actions you've taken or tangible outcomes you've produced—results are far more persuasive than promises.

To be clear, I'm not advocating that you promote your corporate social responsibility programs. Too many companies engage in corporate philanthropy, participate in charitable activities, or run cause marketing campaigns that have nothing to do with their overarching purpose. These efforts do little more than generate some short-lived goodwill. The results don't last because they fail to influence customers in a significant and meaningful way. I'm talking about living out your purpose so that it impacts everything in your organization, including its brand identity.

And while the two companies highlighted in this chapter so far have undertaken environmentally-related initiatives, I am not suggesting that aligning and integrating your culture and brand only works with a green-inspired purpose. Any overarching purpose, core values, and culture that are unique can be used to define an equally unique brand identity. Many progressive organizations of all kinds, in fact, are living out their purposes through substantive actions. By doing so, they are defining their brands clearly and distinctively. Consider, for example, how Starbucks' purpose, to "inspire and nurture the human spirit— one person, one cup, and one neighborhood at a time," has influenced its brand identity by inspiring a unique customer experience.

From the company's inception, former CEO Howard Schultz emphasized cultivating and preserving an organizational culture that would fulfill the company's purpose—one characterized by core values such as "creating a culture of warmth and belonging, where everyone is welcome," and "being present, connecting with transparency, dignity, and respect."[20] The company has designed a unique experience for its employees (including offering them stock options, comprehensive health insurance, reimbursement for education, and other generous benefits) so they feel the purpose and values personally. Starbucks even calls employees "partners" to signal the human, personal relationship that it aims to develop with them—a relationship in line with its purpose.

This purposeful culture has produced a differentiated customer experience. "The feel of Starbucks stores isn't created merely by the layout and the décor," explain consultants from Strategy&. "It exists because the people behind the counter understand how their work fits into a common purpose, and recognize how to accomplish great things together without needing to follow a script." Culture and strategy are so tightly woven at Starbucks that culture is what most strongly influences how customers experience the brand, they observe.[21]

Both GE and Starbucks are distinguished from other companies because their external brand identity is the result, at least in part, of actions motivated by an internal drive.

LEVERAGE YOUR VALUES TO
REDEFINE YOUR BRAND

There are many types of organizations that naturally have a stronger organizational culture than brand identity. Think of organizations in industrial, scientific, or other sectors like education and non-profits, where brand power has not historically been a driver of customer choice or business performance. Conglomerates with a portfolio of brands also sometimes develop a unified corporate culture, but not a cohesive corporate brand identity. And small businesses are often more concerned with their internal operations than their external identity.

These organizations, however, would greatly benefit from a clear and unique brand identity that helps them stand out from competitors and clarify their value to customers and other stakeholders. If any of the above describe your situation, then you too can use your core values to develop a compelling brand identity.

In Chapter 2, I laid out a process for determining your desired culture by pinpointing your brand type and then identifying the core values that correspond to it. But you can do the opposite: you can use the core values of your organization to identify the brand type(s) that would be most compatible with them.

The following are twenty-seven common organizational values that I described earlier in the book, along with the general brand type that each typically corresponds to. Find the top three values that characterize your culture:

Core Value	Description	Corresponding Brand Type
Accessibility	People at your company make themselves easy to understand and engage with, regardless of rank or role.	Value
Achievement	People at your company focus on the successful attainment of goals typically by effort, courage, or skill.	Performance
Caring	People at your company consistently display kindness and concern for others.	Service
Competition	People at your company strive to win or be more successful than others.	Disruptive
Consistency	People at your company adhere steadfastly to the same principles, course, or form.	Performance
Continuous Improvement	People at your company engage in ongoing efforts to improve products, services, or processes.	Innovation
Creativity	People at your company rely on imagination or foster original ideas.	Style
Design	People at your company focus on the look, style, or fashion of everything they do or produce.	Style
Discernment	People at your company emphasize using acute judgment and discretion.	Style
Distinction	People at your company like to set it apart from the competition clearly and deliberately.	Luxury
Empathy	People at your company try to put themselves in other people's shoes—especially those of other employees and customers.	Service
Enjoyment	People at your company go out of their way to have fun and seek out delight.	Experience
Entertainment	People at your company emphasize amusement or celebration.	Experience
Excellence	People at your company try to be outstanding or to meet the highest standards.	Performance
Experimentation	People at your company experiment with new methods and approaches, knowing some will fail.	Innovation
Fairness	People at your company go out of their way to act without bias or partiality.	Value

Core Value	Description	Corresponding Brand Type
High Commitment	People at your company believe in acting with intense and ironclad dedication to a purpose.	Conscious
Humility	People at your company believe in adopting a modest or low view of one's own importance.	Service
Inventiveness	People at your company like to create new things with imagination.	Innovation
Originality	People at your company champion independence, creativity, and fresh perspectives.	Experience
Pragmatism	People at your company deal with things sensibly and realistically and try to find the most practical way to do things.	Value
Purposefulness	People at your company pursue its goals with intention and determination.	Conscious
Risk-taking	People at your company engage in activities that involve danger or risk in order to achieve a goal.	Disruptive
Sophistication	People at your company rely on social or esthetic standards to discriminate between options.	Luxury
Standing Out	People at your company attract attention to it by being particularly noticeable or different.	Disruptive
Status	People at your company care about the relative social standing of someone or something.	Luxury
Transparency	People at your company do things openly and in a straightforward way.	Conscious

As I explained previously, these are fairly broad and common values, so the list probably doesn't include the precise core values of your organization. But your values probably fit into some of these general ones.

Once you identify the brand type that corresponds to your existing core values, use it as a springboard to develop a unique and definitive brand identity. For example, a university might determine its core values are represented by achievement and excellence. Those values correspond to the performance brand type, so it might consider developing a brand identity based on dependable results. A different university might recognize its core values are more about continuously improving its curriculum and experimenting with new teaching methods. Those values—continuous improvement and experimentation—are associated with the innovation brand type, so it might develop a brand identity as an organization that is on the cutting edge.

DEVELOPING YOUR BRAND IDENTITY

Since your core values may point you only to a general brand type, you must develop a specific and unique brand identity. As you do so, keep in mind that a strong brand is:

Meaningful—Your brand identity should be relevant and compelling to a valuable customer target.

Differentiating—Your brand identity should be distinct from others in a way that customers perceive is important.

Believable—Your brand identity should be grounded in the natural and inherent strengths of your product or service so that customers believe you can deliver on it.

Transcendent—Your brand identity should convey value beyond a specific product or service.

Sustainable—Your brand identity should be based on an enduring purpose that enables you to resonate with customers and compete now and in the future.

In some cases, one or more of your core values might lead you to the precise brand identity that is compelling and valuable to your customers. This is the case at Argentinian credit card provider Tarjeta Naranja. Its number one core value is "happiness at work," and the company truly tries hard to help employees feel happy. Its employee experience, which it calls "Joy for Your Day," involves activities and celebrations that promote the company's culture of happiness. It's only natural that the company has adopted a brand identity of happiness and promises happiness in its customer service. Naranja president Alejandro Asrin explains, "The essence of Naranja, our DNA, is reflected in the joy of teamwork, with clear motivating goals, so that employees are happy and, as a consequence, they are able to provide services for people to be happy."[22]

Unilever, the consumer goods company behind household brands Dove, Lipton, and Surf, among others, shows how some corporations look to their core values to sharpen their corporate-wide brand identity. Responsibility is deeply embedded in Unilever's culture.[23] William Lever, who founded the company in the late nineteenth century, had emphasized this core value by taking responsibility for the well-being and security of his employees, building housing for them adjacent to the company factory and offering them fixed workweeks, paid holidays, and a health and safety program (an unusual benefit at that time.)[24] Shareholders eventually pressured Lever to scale back some of his social ambitions, but the company continued to live out its values of responsibility, respect, and pioneering in various ways through the years, such as establishing sustainable fisheries and working with Greenpeace to remove HFC refrigerants from its ice-cream freezers.

When CEO Paul Polman arrived at the company in 2009, he brought with him the conviction that "the real purpose of business has always been to come up with solutions that are relevant to society, to make society better."[25] He restored social and environmental responsibility as a company priority and launched the "Unilever Sustainable Living Plan" (USLP). The plan has three primary goals: "to improve the health and well-being of more than one billion people around the world; reduce the company's environmental impact by half; and enhance the livelihood of millions of people while doubling revenues from $40 to $80 billion."[26]

As a part of the USLP, Unilever reduced the amount of saturated fat in its Flora and Becel margarine brands and then used those brands to encourage customers to be proactive about their heart health. It built its Lifebuoy soap brand into a platform for teaching millions of people across the globe how to stop the spread of disease simply by washing their hands effectively. And it promotes the development of young girls' confidence through the Dove Self-Esteem Fund, reinforcing that brand's identity as an advocate for women and their individual potential for being and feeling beautiful.[27]

The core values that underpin the USLP guide the strategy and tactics of Unilever products like Flora, Becel, Dove, and more in a consistent and cohesive way, sharpening Unilever's corporate brand identity. During the past few years, Unilever has even started to promote the Unilever brand along with its product brands. Television ads for some Unilever products close with motion graphics of other Unilever product brand logos flying in to form the U in the Unilever logo. The goal is for the U to become the "trust mark of sustainable living," explains chief marketing and communications officer Keith Weed in a *Fast Company* article. "The USLP is of course a way of doing business, but it's also the reason to believe, the differentiator ultimately of the Unilever brand."[28]

Unilever's efforts appear to be working. "Since 2010," the *Fast Company* article reports, "the Unilever brand has gone from being known mainly to discrete groups, such as financial analysts, to being seen worldwide as a leader in sustainable business."[29] Unilever's corporate and product brands are now perceived as forces for good. They "inspire social innovation, encourage more sustainable behaviors, and improve the lives of people loyal to those brands," observes *Sustainable Brands*.[30] Through the USLP, Unilever has leveraged its core values to evolve its brand identities.

If you want to elevate your core values to drivers of your brand identity as Unilever has done, you must make them salient to customers and other stakeholders. You must focus on and perhaps increase your communications about your values. You must show customers and stakeholders clear proof that you are operating by your core values, whether that's retooling factories and making costly product formulations, as Unilever has had to do, or making smaller but similarly visible and tangible changes. And you must ensure these values translate into benefits for your customers—either directly through improvements to the customer experience or more transcendentally through alignment with their personal values.

Doing so is not always easy. "If you believe in something, you have to fight for that and have the courage to take the tougher decisions that come with it," Polman argues. But he also believes there's a good reason to take this tack: "Brands with a purpose and that are values-led over time are going to be by definition more successful."[31]

SHOWCASE YOUR CULTURE TO DIFFERENTIATE YOUR BRAND

Companies in categories that are highly commoditized, like airlines and fast food chains, or where it's hard to discern the difference between products offered by different brands, such as professional service firms or banks, may find that their organizational culture is more distinct or meaningful than their brand. If that's the case at your company, you can use your culture to differentiate your brand. You can show customers that your purpose and values are worthy of their support when they're choosing between seemingly similar brands and that your culture helps you make a better product or provide better service. Because people increasingly care about the companies that make the products and services they buy, doing so can be an effective way to stand out in a sea of sameness or to connect with customers on a different level.

You can also leverage your culture to improve perceptions of your brand if you believe that your external image or identity is not accurate or complete—that is, your product or company has more to offer than how it's perceived in the market. REI, the outdoor retailer, felt this way about its brand. Although REI has become a popular purveyor of outdoor apparel and gear by providing a great customer experience, the company's compelling culture (which is rooted in its founders' love of the outdoors and its co-op business model, which pays out annual dividends to employees and customers) was not widely known until 2015.

At that time, the company found itself looking for sustainable ways to differentiate its brand as it faced tough competition from Amazon and other specialty retailers. In an interview for *The Atlantic*, company president and CEO Jerry Stritzke explained, "There was an explicit decision that we needed to do a better job telling people what we believed, what we're about."[32] The company did just that when it decided to close its doors on Black Friday, the U.S. retail industry's biggest sale day. With this decision, the company risked losing significant revenues and alienating shoppers, but the move firmly reinforced its culture. Chief creative officer Ben Steele explained he and his colleagues believe "success is first and foremost about our 12,139 employees." So they decided, "We are going to pay them to spend the day outside rather than pay them to spend time indoors. That's the truest expression of us as a co-op."[33]

The company turned its decision to close on Black Friday into the "#OptOutside" brand campaign, in which it also encouraged customers to get out into the outdoors instead of shopping indoors. Stritzke explained in the company's announcement, "Black Friday is a perfect time to remind ourselves of the essential truth that life is richer, more connected, and complete when you choose to spend it outside. We're closing our doors, paying our employees to get out there, and inviting America to Opt Outside with us because we love great gear, but we are even more passionate about the experiences it unlocks."[34] The move worked: by REI's estimate, it got 1.4 million people to enjoy the outdoors instead of going shopping that day.[35]

Now an annual tradition, closing on Black Friday and running the Opt Outside campaign has clearly established a differentiated position for REI, not just among other retailers and sporting goods companies but also among lifestyle brands in general. The effort increased the brand's social media impressions 7,000 percent; produced spikes in REI sales, memberships, and employee applications[36]; and sparked a movement of encouraging outdoor activity that is supported by over 400 organizations, including state and regional parks, nonprofits and community organizations such as Nature Conservancy and Meetup, and companies including Clif Bar and Sanuk.[37]

REI provides a powerful example of how launching a campaign with a bold message rooted in your culture can bring attention to your brand and set it apart. Oakley, the maker of optics and other products popular among athletes and extreme sports participants, faced a similar brand challenge—increased pressure from new competitors—to what REI did. But Oakley leveraged its culture in a different approach: While REI *promoted* its organizational culture through a campaign to differentiate its brand from others, Oakley *explained* its culture and linked it to its products.

From its start, Oakley has operated with a "culture is brand; brand is culture" mentality. The "Oakley Five," the company's five core values—performance-obsessed, authentic, innovative, humble, and passionate—have been expressed in employees' attitudes and their working style as much as in the products they've made and commercialized. In fact, the Oakley brand book states, "Oakley isn't where we work, it's who we are," and, "We are on the outside what we are on the inside."[38]

Because Oakley founder Jim Jannard and the company's other early leaders believed "Oakley is an idea," as the brand book says, they didn't want to define the brand beyond its core values.[39] Brian Takumi, who has served as the brand's creative director and head of product creative, explained to me, "They didn't want the brand to be limited to what the brand participated in.... They wanted license to do what we wanted in an Oakley way." As a result, the brand was always "a moving target."[40]

Despite its lack of definition, Oakley became a hugely successful brand because the people who designed its products were also users of them, so the products and experiences they developed were highly relevant and appealing to customers. "People from marketing, R&D, engineering, manufacturing, sales—they all participated [in sports]," Takumi says, so Oakley's products "made customers feel like we understood them."[41]

From challenging industry-standard motorcycle grips to producing eyeglass frames made with titanium, which had previously been thought impossible, the company's designers and engineers had an insatiable desire to make their products better for athletes—and a passion for taking unconventional approaches. Even the sales and marketing departments held themselves to doing things the way no other company would. They once staged a triathlon for owners and employees of their retail accounts to participate in alongside the company's sponsored athletes so they could experience the products and brand firsthand. This disruptive approach earned Oakley the respect and loyalty of professional and amateur athletes alike.[42]

Oakley's open-ended approach to its brand served the company well for many years, but as the brand started to expand its appeal and the company grew its retail presence, the lack of brand definition turned out to be a problem. Oakley needed to be clearer about how it was different from other sports lifestyle brands like Nike and Red Bull (which had started selling sunglasses in 2015), especially for the new generation of younger customers who didn't have years of experience with the Oakley brand to draw upon to appreciate it. Oakley also needed to change the way it presented itself to customers, Takumi added. Previously it had stoked "a cloak of mysteriousness" about the company, but the market shifted and customers wanted brands to relate with them, not just talk to them. "It was the first time we had to take a step toward creating relationships and talking more about what we're about, not just about the product and technology," Takumi explained.[43]

To address these challenges, the company launched a campaign entitled "Disruptive by Design" to tell the story of the brand's culture. Tom Cartmale, global brand communications director at the time, told *Adweek*, "Disruption has always been core to our DNA, and for the first time, we are giving insight into our practices. It's time for our brand point of view to be better known."[44] Takumi described the campaign as an opportunity to talk about the company "being disruptive for a purpose, being authentic, and getting back to the company's brand-culture connection."[45] He and his colleagues wanted to show that the company's willingness to break from convention and develop products that shook up the industry was not just a publicity-seeking ploy; rather, being disruptive was why the company was founded in the first place and at the root of the company's culture—and of its superior products.

The ads highlighted Jannard and the company's iconic bunker-style headquarters in Southern California. New retail displays included interactive videos that showed how the craftsmanship of Oakley's products distinguished them from competitors'.[46] And a partnership with *Wired* magazine featured multimedia content that traced the company's history back to when Jannard started it, through its invention of the eyeshade that revolutionized the sunglass industry, and culminating in the 1,000 utility and design patents it held at the time.[47] The campaign used Oakley's culture of disruption to clarify its brand differentiation and establish the basis for increased differentiation in the future.

Both promoting your culture as REI did with its #OptOutside campaign and explaining it as Oakley did with its Disruption by Design campaign are effective strategies for successfully advancing the perceived differentiation of your brand.* But for these strategies to work, of course, your culture must be unique and remarkable in the first place.

TRANSFORM YOUR BRAND AND CULTURE TOGETHER

It's very difficult to redefine a brand—that's why so many attempts don't work. The best way to set up your brand transformation efforts for success is to root them in a truth about your organization—your overarching purpose, core values, or culture in general. This chapter has shown you how some companies have successfully prompted a reconsideration of their brands by doing so.

Infusing your culture into your brand takes time because customer perceptions are usually harder to change than employees'. It will also likely require you to invest heavily in communications, marketing programs, and customer experiences to draw attention to your internal efforts and convince naturally skeptical customers that your culture actually produces benefits that are real and valuable to them. That's why most of this book has focused on achieving brand-culture fusion by infusing your brand into your culture.

---

* There are other ways to leverage your culture to differentiate your brand. UPS promoted the color brown in its advertising as a symbolic differentiator of its brand because the color's lack of flashiness aptly represented the company's culture of reliability and humility. And Zappos showcased the generous and humorous attitude that characterizes its culture by running ads using recordings of actual customer service calls with its representatives gracefully handling unusual customer demands.

But the two strategies aren't as mutually exclusive as they appear to be. As you work on cultivating your desired culture, you can also leverage that culture externally. And as you seek to re-define your brand, you can also build a stronger brand-led culture internally. Your culture- and brand-building efforts can and should be mutually reinforcing. Brand-culture fusion is produced through the seamless integration of the two, and that integration is really an ongoing process.

Key Takeaways from This Chapter

- If your culture is well established, you can use it to successfully define, or re-define, your brand identity.

- To define your brand distinctively, live out your overarching purpose through substantive actions and clearly connect for customers and other stakeholders the dots between your motivations and your actions.

- If you want to leverage your core values to position or strengthen your brand, you must be firmly committed to them and demonstrate to consumers how your organization is operating by them.

- You can strengthen the differentiation of your brand by explicitly promoting or explaining your culture to customers.

CONCLUSION

THE JOURNEY TO BRAND-CULTURE FUSION

In the early days of writing this manuscript, I met with a friend for breakfast. When our conversation turned to organizational culture, he told me, "You know, people want to think their organizations are special and unique, but they're really not. Most cultures ladder up to the same basic things: purpose, teamwork, and execution. As long as you are working toward those, that's what's important."

His comment shocked me so much, I almost choked on my donut. Could this guy, whom I admired and respected in large part because he had run hugely successful, nationally-recognized culture initiatives at two different organizations, be telling me that a good, generic culture was enough? "Don't you think organizations should be the same on the inside as they are on the outside?" I asked him. "And if their brands are distinct, then shouldn't their cultures be too?"

He paused for a moment. "You know what?" he then said. "I think I'm just setting a low bar because most workplaces are so decidedly un-human today. Maybe organizations need to operate first as a *human* culture before they can be a *distinct* culture. And, right now, human is distinct."

Now I understood his point.

For some organizations, a *distinct* culture that is fully aligned with their brand may seem far out of reach. If you find yourself in this situation, then it's true you must first right your ship before you can get it to sail. But to set your sights on merely having a *decent* culture seems the surest way to end up with only that. And most of the leaders I know want more than to be good—they want to be great. Most leaders tell me they work too hard and care too much to settle for leading an organization where people put in a decent day's work, make a decent product, and get a decent paycheck. They want to create an environment where greatness happens. They're trying to make a meaningful, lasting difference in their own lives, in their people's lives, in the world. It's the way they're wired. I'm guessing it's the way you're wired too.

For years, leaders at companies like Southwest, Amazon, and Starbucks have been creating an environment for greatness by doing something differently that's put their organizations at the top of the "most admired companies," "best brands," *and* "great workplaces" lists. But they don't often talk about that "something" specifically in terms of brand-culture fusion—that is, aligning and integrating their brands and cultures. Sure, Southwest's Herb Kelleher credits the people at Southwest Airlines for its success, but he doesn't talk about the role that integrating EX and CX has played in that success. Jeff Bezos at Amazon says his organization is "customer-obsessed," but he doesn't necessarily extol the unifying power of Amazon's overarching purpose and core values. Even when Howard Schultz of Starbucks talks about how the most powerful and enduring brands are built with the strength of the human spirit, he doesn't describe how he fused the Starbucks brand and culture together.

In fact, leaders of companies that excel at aligning and integrating their brands and cultures might not even be aware they're doing so. It's simply the way they lead their organizations. When I asked Mark Levy at Airbnb what advice he would give leaders who want to fuse together their brands and cultures, he struggled to answer. He told me, "We don't talk about it a lot, it just works. It's very natural, not forced. It's just the amorphic, informal way we work together."[1] In many of the interviews I conducted, other leaders expressed similar sentiments. Brand-culture fusion was so essential at their companies, it came naturally. Ardine Williams told me brand and culture were "inseparable" at Amazon.[2] Lilian Tomovich at MGM Resorts explained how "culture and brand became one synonymous conversation because it was very clear at the most senior levels of the organization that the two went hand in hand."[3] Ari Weinzweig at Zingerman's described it as a matter of fact: "Your brand really is your culture."[4]

But the fact that these leaders don't talk about brand-culture fusion explicitly in the terms I've outlined in this book doesn't mean their companies don't work hard at it. Many described how they purposefully and explicitly wove their brands and cultures together by taking deliberate actions and adopting specific strategies—the very strategies that I describe in this book. They are clearly intent on powering their organizations by combining their brands and cultures. They aren't taking it for granted.

Neither should you. My hope is that *FUSION* has provided the language and insight for understanding what brand-culture fusion is and how to achieve it. And now that you know what it is, do it. There's no reason why you shouldn't. No organization has a culture so strong that its leaders don't need to continue to build it. No brand has such market power that makes it immune to competitive threats.

Culture and brand are only going to increase in importance. As savvy employers increasingly use data and analytics to pinpoint the skilled workers needed in their organization, the war for talent is only going to escalate. More companies will then have to offer more distinct and sustainable cultures to attract and retain in-demand talent. The need to unify and align diverse and dispersed employees with a singular purpose and values is only going to grow as companies continue to globalize, workforces continue to diversify, and the pace of business continues to accelerate. Brand power is only going to become more important in the fight against commoditizing product categories, shrinking attention spans, and consolidating channels. And customers are only going to demand more from the companies they do business with.

These trends suggest that culture and brand are going to become even more critical than they already are today—and if individually they are so vital, how much stronger might they be if they are fused together? Get out in front of these trends and your competitors by embarking on your journey to brand-culture fusion today.

It is indeed a journey. As I've shown you in this book, you start your journey to brand-culture fusion by laying the foundation with an overarching purpose and core values that set your destination and guide your organization. After assessing your current state of fusion and where you need to focus to achieve your desired state, you take up the charge to lead your organization through this journey by communicating clearly, walking the talk, and making people decisions that align with your purpose and values.

You are then ready to put into motion the five strategies that cultivate your desired culture, brand, or both:

- Organize your company and operate it on-brand—implement an organizational design, optimize your core operations, and work on brand touchpoints to *operationalize* your desired culture.
- Create culture-changing employee experiences—design employee experience (EX), involve your employees in EX design, and integrate EX and customer experience.
- Build culture through rituals, artifacts, policies, and procedures— cultivate your desired culture in the small, yet significant aspects of organizational life.
- Kick-start your cultural transformation and keep the momentum going through employee brand engagement—stage brand engagement experiences, run carefully crafted communications campaigns, and develop and deploy brand engagement toolkits.
- Define or redefine your brand by leveraging your culture—put your purpose into action, use your core values to shape your brand identity, and differentiate your brand through your culture.

As you work toward brand-culture fusion, you'll need to be patient, focused, relentless, and disciplined. You will be addressing the fundamental drivers of brand and culture, not their superficial appearances, so it's hard work. Garry Ridge, CEO of the WD-40 Company told me, "Building culture is not simple or easy. Time is not your friend. It depends on continuous, relentless, passionate execution."[5] Plus, you're never really finished. "Culture takes budgeting, resources, and time all year long. Culture is not something that's seasonal. It is not something you can ever stop," says Cheryl Hughey, managing director for culture at Southwest.[6] Any culture change requires ongoing leadership because culture depends on people and people change, forget, veer, and turn over. Brand-culture fusion requires an even-longer-standing commitment because as the market, your competitors, and your customers' needs and wants change, so do the requirements for your brand and therefore your culture. If you want to fully integrate and align your brand and culture, you will need to constantly evolve both.

But the commitment is worth it. Whether you are starting with a thriving culture or a broken one, whether your brand is already strong or needs to become more powerful, whether brand-culture fusion makes intuitive sense or is a new concept for you, ask yourself if you aspire to greatness. Do you want to align your organization with a single goal so that it is not just productive and efficient but operates with excellence? Do you want to future-proof your company by creating value that is sustainable and inimitable? Do you want to have a truly authentic brand? Do you want to galvanize your people and move toward your vision?

If your answer is yes, then seize the opportunity to become great. Engage the power of brand-culture fusion.

ENDNOTES

Introduction

1 Market Watch. "Annual Financials for Amazon.com Inc." Accessed August 22, 2017. http://www.marketwatch.com/investing/stock/amzn/financials.

2 Roth, Daniel. "LinkedIn Top Companies 2017: Where the World Wants to Work Now." LinkedIn, May 18, 2017. https://www.linkedin.com/pulse/linkedin-top -companies-2017-where-us-wants-work-now-daniel-roth.

3 Goode, Lauren. "Amazon Hired 100,000 People Last Year, and It's Hiring 100,000 More." *The Verge*, February 3, 2017. https://www.theverge.com/2017/2/3/14504526/ amazon-job-growth-2016-new-employees-hires-shipping.

4 Kantor, Jodi, and David Streitfeld. "Inside Amazon: Wrestling Big Ideas in a Bruising Workplace." *New York Times*, August 15, 2015. https://www.nytimes .com/2015/08/16/technology/inside-amazon-wrestling-big-ideas-in-a-bruising -workplace.html.

5 Byrd, Aaron, and Emily B. Hager. "Depiction of Amazon Stirs a Debate about Work Culture." *New York Times,* August 18, 2015. https://www.nytimes.com/ 2015/08/19/technology/amazon-workplace-reactions-comments.html?_r=0.

6 Blattberg, Eric. "Inside Amazon's 'Gladiator Culture.'" *Venture Beat*, October 13, 2013. https://venturebeat.com/2013/10/10/inside-amazons-gladiator-culture/.

7 Braun, Eduardo. *People First Leadership: How the Best Leaders Use Culture and Emotion to Drive Unprecedented Results.* Columbus: McGraw-Hill Education, 458. Kindle.

8 Ibid., 365.

9 Guinto, Joseph. "A Look at Southwest Airlines 50 Years Later." *D Magazine,* May 2017.　https://www.dmagazine.com/publications/d-ceo/2017/may/southwest -airlines-50-year-anniversary-love-field-dallas/.

10 Great Place to Work. "About Us." Accessed August 22, 2017. https://www .greatplacetowork.com/about-us.

11 Gallup. "State of the American Workplace." Accessed August 22, 2017. http:// www.gallup.com/services/178514/state-american-workplace.aspx.

12 Lederman, Gregg. *Achieve Brand Integrity: Ten Truths You Must Know to Enhance Employee Performance and Increase Company Profits.* Rochester: B@W Press, 2007. 128.

13 Gascoigne, Joel. "Tough News: We've Made 10 Layoffs. How We Got Here, the Financial Details and How We're Moving Forward." *Buffer,* June 16, 2016. https://open.buffer.com/layoffs-and-moving-forward/.

14 Michelman, Paul. "The End of Corporate Culture as We Know It." *MIT Sloan Management Review,* April 12, 2017. http://sloanreview.mit.edu/article/theend ofcorporatecultureasweknowit/.

15 Amazon. "2015 Letter to Shareholders." Accessed August 22, 2017. https://www .sec.gov/Archives/edgar/data/1018724/000119312516530910/d168744dex991 .htm.

16 Mosley, Richard W. "Customer Experience, Organisational Culture and the Employer Brand." *Journal of Brand Management* 15, no. 2 (November 2007): 123–134.

17 Norman, Laura. "A Founder's Perspective: Why Culture Is Insanely Important for Your Startup." Salesforce Blog, April 10, 2017. https://www.salesforce.com/ blog/2017/04/why-culture-is-important-for-startups.html.

Chapter 1

1 Knight, Phil. *Shoe Dog: A Memoir by the Creator of Nike.* New York: Scribner, 2016. 792. Kindle.

2 Conlon, Jerome. "The Brand Brief Behind Nike's Just Do It Campaign." *Branding Strategy Insider,* August 6, 2015. https://www.brandingstrategyinsider .com/2015/08/behind-nikes-campaign.html.

3 Farfan, Barbara. "Nike's Mission Statement." *The Balance,* May 11, 2017. https://www.thebalance.com/nike-mission-statement-and-maxims-4138115.

4 McGirt, Ellen. "Read Nike CEO's Heartbreaking Letter to Employees about Race and Violence." *Fortune,* July 15, 2016, http://fortune.com/2016/07/15/ nike-ceo-letter-race-police/.

5 Woolf, Jake. "Meet the Mastermind Who Designed Your Favorite Nikes." *GQ,* March 26, 2016. http://www.gq.com/story/tinker-hatfield-interview-steph-curry -nike.

6 Willigan, Geraldine E. "High-Performance Marketing: An Interview with Nike's Phil Knight." *Harvard Business Review,* July-August 2002. https://hbr .org/1992/07/high-performance-marketing-an-interview-with-nikes-phil-knight.

7 Everson, Kate. "Nike's Andre Martin: Just Learn It." *CLO Media,* July 17, 2015. http://www.clomedia.com/2015/07/17/nikes-andre-martin-just-learn-it/.

8 Scholer, Kristen. "Nike Passes $100 Billion Market Cap for First Time Ever."

Wall Street Journal, September 25, 2015. https://blogs.wsj.com/moneybeat/ 2015/09/25/nike-passes-100-billion-market-cap-for-first-time-ever/.

9 Ozanian, Mike. "Forbes Fab 40: The World's Most Valuable Sports Brands." *Forbes,* October 24, 2016. https://www.forbes.com/sites/mikeozanian/2016/10/24/forbes -fab-40-the-worlds-most-valuable-sports-brands.

10 Deloitte. "The Deloitte Millennial Survey 2017." Accessed August 22, 2017. http://www2.deloitte.com/global/en/pages/about-deloitte/articles/millennial survey.html.

11 Becker, Jan. "What Makes Autodesk a Best Place to Work." *In the Fold,* March 5, 2015. http://inthefold.autodesk.com/in_the_fold/2015/03/what-makes-autodesk -a-best-place-to-work.html.

12 Branson, Richard. "You Can't Fake Personality, Passion or Purpose." LinkedIn, August 31, 2015. https://www.linkedin.com/pulse/how-i-hire-you-cant-fake -personality-passion-purpose-richard-branson.

13 Safian, Robert. "Facebook, Airbnb, Uber, and the Struggle to Do the Right Thing." *Fast Company,* April 11, 2017. https://www.fastcompany.com/40397294/face book-airbnb-uber-and-the-struggle-to-do-the-right-thing.

14 Amazon. "Biography." Accessed August 22, 2017. http://phx.corporate-ir.net/ phoenix.zhtml?c=97664&p=irol-govBio&ID=69376.

15 Des Jardins, Jeff. "The Extraordinary Size of Amazon in One Chart." *Visual Capitalist,* December 30, 2016. http://www.visualcapitalist.com/extraordinary -size-amazon-one-chart/.

16 Starbucks. "Mission Statement." Accessed August 22, 2017. https://www.star bucks.com/about-us/company-information/mission-statement.

17 Johnson & Johnson. "Our Values." Accessed August 22, 2017. http://www.jnj .ch/en/our-values/mission.html.

18 Rookie Investor. "Johnson & Johnson vs. the S&P 500." *Seeking Alpha,* August 29, 2016. https://seekingalpha.com/article/4002758-johnson-and-johnson-vs-s -and-p-500.

19 Zuckerberg, Mark. "Founder's Letter, 2012." Facebook, February 1, 2017. https:// www.facebook.com/notes/mark-zuckerberg/founders-letter/1015450041 2571634.

20 Heller, Steven. "The Job Jobs Did." *New York Times,* August 25, 2011. http:// tmagazine.blogs.nytimes.com/2011/08/25/the-job-jobs-did/?_r=0.

21 Collins, Jim, and Jerry I. Porras. "Building Your Company's Vision." *Harvard Business Review,* September 1996. https://hbr.org/1996/09/building-your-com panys-vision.

22 Ibid.

23 Collins, Jim, and Jerry I. Porras. *Built to Last: Successful Habits of Visionary Companies.* New York: Harper Collins, 1994. 78.

24 Zappos. "Our Higher Purpose." Accessed August 22, 2017. https://www.zap posinsights.com/about/zappos/higher-purpose.

25 Sony Electronics Inc. Intranet site, 2000. "Being Sony."

26 Hindle, Tim. "Mission Statement." *The Economist,* July 2, 2009. http://www .economist.com/node/13766375.

27 YScouts. "Top 10 Core Values at the Top 10 Medium Sized Workplaces." *YScouts Blog,* May 15, 2015. http://yscouts.com/culture-2/top-10-core-values -medium-workplaces/.

28 Goldberge, Itzik. "Becoming a Vision Driven Organization (VDO)." *Aviv Partners,* May 28, 2013. https://itzikg1.wordpress.com/2013/05/28/becoming-a-vision -driven-organization-vdo-4th-post-vision-implementation-part-2/.

29 YScouts, "Top 10 Core Values."

30 Collins and Porras, *Built to Last, 76.*

31 Barbour, Hilton. "HR versus Marketing—The Next C-Suite Confrontation." LinkedIn, May 11, 2017. https://www.linkedin.com/pulse/hr-versus-marketing -next-c-suite-confrontation-hilton-barbour.

32 De Chernatony, Leslie. *From Brand Vision to Brand Evaluation.* Oxford: Butterworth Heinemann, 2001. 99.

33 Di Somma, Mark. "Developing a Powerful Brand Purpose." *Branding Strategy Insider,* April 3, 2015. https://www.brandingstrategyinsider.com/2015/04/ developing-powerful-purpose.html.

34 Morris, Steven. *Brand Love & Loyalty.* San Diego: Mth Degree, 2017. 23.

35 Zuckerberg, Mark. Post on Facebook. June 16, 2016. https://www.facebook.com/ zuck/posts/10154944663901634.

36 Van Lee, Reggie, Lisa Fabish, and Nancy McGaw. "The Value of Corporate Values." *strategy+business,* May 23, 2005. https://www.strategy-business.com/ article/05206?gko=9c265.

37 Yates, Darin. Interview by Denise Lee Yohn. July 18, 2017.

38 Peiken, Matt. "Crossroads Church and the Phenomenon of Its Annual Christmas Show, 'Awaited.'" *Matt Peiken Blog,* December 11, 2014. https://mattpeiken .com/features/crossroads-church-and-the-phenomenon-of-its-annual-christ mas-show-awaited/.

39 Crossroads Church. "Culture Guide." January 2016.

40 Peiken, "Crossroads Church."

41 Van Lee, Reggie, Lisa Fabish, and Nancy McGaw. "The Value of Corporate Values." *strategy+business,* May 23, 2005. https://www.strategy-business.com/ article/05206?gko=9c265.

42 Rhoades, Anne. *Built on Values: Creating an Enviable Culture that Outperforms the Competition.* New York: Jossey-Bass, 2011. 44.

43 WD-40 Company. "Our Values." Accessed August 22, 2017. https://www.wd40 company.com/who-we-are/our-values/.

44   Google. "Ten Things We Know to Be True." Accessed August 22, 2017. https://
     www.google.com/intl/en/about/philosophy.html.
45   Illumina. "Illumina Values." Accessed August 22, 2017. http://welcometo.illu
     mina.com/newhire/IlluminaValues.aspx.
46   Gazelles International. "Core Purpose and Values." Accessed August 22, 2017.
     http://gicoaches.com/purpose.
47   Ind, Nicholas. *Living the Brand: How to Transform Every Member of Your
     Organization into a Brand Champion.* London: Kogan Page Limited, 2008. 53.
48   Banco Supervielle. "Values." Translated by Eduardo Braun.
49   Supervielle, Patricio. Interview by Eduardo Braun. July 27, 2017.
50   Lencioni, Patrick M. "Make Your Values Mean Something." *Harvard Business
     Review,* July 2002. https://hbr.org/2002/07/make-your-values-mean-something.
51   De Chernatony, Leslie. *From Brand Vision to Brand Evaluation.* Oxford: But-
     terworth Heinemann, 2001. 104.
52   Vardi, Nathan. "The Best Stocks of 2010." *Forbes,* December 21, 2010. https://
     www.forbes.com/2010/12/20/crocs-netflix-isilon-business-wall-street-best
     -stocks-2010.html.
53   Sandoval, Greg. "Netflix's Lost Year: The Inside Story of the Price-Hike Train
     Wreck." *CNET,* July 11, 2012. https://www.cnet.com/news/netflixs-lost-year
     -the-inside-story-of-the-price-hike-train-wreck/.
54   Netflix. "Netflix Culture: Freedom and Responsibility." Accessed August 22,
     2017. https://www.slideshare.net/reed2001/culture-1798664/2-Netflix_Culture
     Freedom_Responsibility2.
55   Sandoval, "Netflix's Lost Year."
56   de Chernatony, *"Brand Vision."*
57   Jackson, Eric. Interview by Denise Lee Yohn. May 3, 2017.
58   FedEx. "Purple Promise." Accessed August 22, 2017. http://www.fedex.com/
     purplepromise/docs/en/fedex_pp_booklet.pdf.
59   Crunchbase. "LinkedIn Acquisitions." Accessed August 22, 2017. https://www
     .crunchbase.com/organization/linkedin/acquisitions.
60   Leverich, Nicole. Interview by Denise Lee Yohn. July 11, 2017.
61   Williams, Ardine. Interview by Denise Lee Yohn. July 14, 2017.
62   Miles, Bryan. Interview by Denise Lee Yohn. July 20, 2017.
63   Drucker, Peter. *The Five Most Important Questions You Will Ever Ask about
     Your Organization.* New York: Jossey-Bass, 2008. xii.

Chapter 2

1   Branson, Richard. *Screw Business as Usual.* New York: Portfolio, 2011.
2   Steven R. Covey. "Books." Accessed August 22, 2017. https://www.stephen
    covey.com/7habits/7habits-habit2.php.

3   Rossman, John. *The Amazon Way: 14 Leadership Principles Behind the World's Most Disruptive Company.* North Charleston: CreateSpace Independent Publishing Platform, 2014. 87. Kindle.

Chapter 3

1   Marcial, Jean. "Ford Deserves More Respect on Wall Street." *AOL.com,* June 16, 2010. https://www.aol.com/2010/06/16/ford-deserves-more-respect-on-wall -street/.
2   Vlasic, Bill. "Ford Reports a Record $14.6 Billion Loss for 2008." *New York Times,* January 29, 2009. http://www.nytimes.com/2009/01/30/business/ 30ford.html?mcubz=3.
3   Holley, William H., William H. Ross, and Roger S. Wolters. "The Labor Relations Process." Boston: Cengage Learning, 2016. 402.
4   O'Brien, Shauna. "The Complete History of Ford: Income, Price & Dividends." *Dividend.com,* January 19, 2015. http://www.dividend.com/how-to-invest/ the-complete-history-of-ford-f/.
5   Isadore, Chris. "Big Three Automakers Post Big Gains." *CNN Money,* January 4, 2012. http://money.cnn.com/2012/01/04/news/companies/auto_sales/index .htm?iid=EL.
6   Hirsch, Jerry. "Ford Is Expected to Surpass GM in Sales This Month." *Los Angeles Times,* March 25, 2011. http://articles.latimes.com/2011/mar/25/ business/la-fi-ford-20110325.
7   Hoffman, Bryce G. *American Icon: Alan Mulally and the Fight to Save Ford Motor Company.* New York: Crown Business, 2012. 2157. Kindle.
8   Taylor, Alex III. "Can This Car Save Ford?" *Fortune,* April 22, 2008. http:// archive.fortune.com/2008/04/21/news/companies/saving_ford.fortune/index .htm?postversion=2008042205.
9   Ibid.
10 Gray, Tyler. "How a Painting from 1925 Inspired Ford's Customer-Focused Future." *Fast Company,* June 22, 2013. https://www.fastcompany.com/3012809/ how-a-painting-from-1925-inspired-fords-customer-focused-future.
11 Hoffman, *American Icon, 1886.*
12 Taylor, "Can This Car Save Ford?"
13 Ibid.
14 Hoffman, *American Icon, 1940.*
15 Ibid., 6576.
16 Anonymous Source. Interview by Denise Lee Yohn. April 22, 2017.
17 Ewing, Jack, and Graham Bowley. *"The Engineering of Volkswagen's Aggressive Ambition." New York Times,* December 13, 2015. https://www.nytimes

.com/2015/12/14/business/the-engineering-of-volkswagens-aggressive-ambition.html?_r=0.

18 McGee, Patrick, and Robert Wright. "VW Management Back in Scandal Spotlight." *Financial Times,* March 3, 2016. https://www.ft.com/content/ef00293c-e0f1-11e5-8d9b-e88a2a889797?mhq5j=e2.

19 Ellinghorst, Arndt. Interview by Denise Lee Yohn. June 12, 2017.

20 Ibid.

21 Braun, Eduardo. *People First Leadership: How the Best Leaders Use Culture and Emotion to Drive Unprecedented Results.* Columbus: McGraw-Hill Education, 2016. 1318. Kindle.

22 Ibid., 1834.

23 Estes, Ryan. "Winning with Culture: How Leadership Drives Engagement & Performance." Accessed August 22, 2017. http://offers.ryanestis.com/winning-with-culture/.

24 Towers Perrin. "Towers Perrin Survey Finds Almost Half of American Workers Doubt the Credibility of Employer Communications." Accessed August 22, 2017. http://www.csrwire.com/press_releases/20728-Towers-Perrin-Survey-Finds-Almost-Half-of-American-Workers-Doubt-the-Credibility-of-Employer-Communications.

25 Martinez, Michael. "Does Ford have a communications problem?" *Automotive News,* May 16, 2017. http://www.autonews.com/article/20170516/BLOG06/170519830/does-ford-have-a-communications-problem%3F.

26 Daimler, Melissa. "Listening Is an Overlooked Leadership Tool." *Harvard Business Review,* May 25, 2016. https://hbr.org/2016/05/listening-is-an-overlooked-leadership-tool.

27 Braun, *People First Leadership, 1879.*

28 Rhoades, Anne. *Built on Values: Creating an Enviable Culture that Outperforms the Competition.* New York: Jossey-Bass, 2011. 113.

29 Hoffman, Bryce G. *American Icon: Alan Mulally and the Fight to Save Ford Motor Company.* New York: Crown Business, 2012. 2185. Kindle.

30 Ibid., 2169.

31 Ryssdal, Kai, and Daisy Palacios. "How JCPenney Changed When Marvin Ellison Became CEO." *NPR Marketplace,* November 22, 2016. https://www.marketplace.org/2016/11/22/business/corner-office/how-jcpenney-changed-when-marvin-ellison-became-ceo.

32 Wahba, Phil. "The CEO Who's Reinventing J.C. Penney." *Fortune,* February 24, 2016. http://fortune.com/j-c-penney-reinvention/.

33 Aon Hewitt. "The Multiplier Effect: Insights into How Senior Leaders Drive Employee Engagement Higher." Accessed August 22, 2017. http://www.aon.com/attachments/thought-leadership/Aon-Hewitt-White-paper_Engagement.pdf.

34 Serafeim, George, and Claudine Gartenberg. "The Type of Purpose that Makes Companies More Profitable." *Harvard Business Review,* October 21, 2016. https://hbr.org/2016/10/the-type-of-purpose-that-makes-companies-more-profitable.

35 Ton, Zeynep, and Matthew Preble. "Quik Trip." *Harvard Business School Publishing,* June 23, 2011. http://www.supplychainresearch.com/images/quik_trip.pdf.

36 Bendapudi, Neeli, and Venkat Bendapudi. "Creating the Living Brand." *Harvard Business Review,* May 2005. https://hbr.org/2005/05/creating-the-living-brand.

37 Rhoades, *Built on Values, 55.*

38 Welch, Jack, and Suzy Welch. "Goldman Sachs and a Culture-Killing Lesson Being Ignored." *Fortune,* April 12, 2012. http://fortune.com/2012/04/12/goldman-sachs-and-a-culture-killing-lesson-being-ignored/.

39 Ibid.

40 Braun, *People First Leadership,* 293.

Chapter 4

1 Cameron, Nadia. "How Uniting Employee and Customer Experience Is Helping Adobe Disrupt." *CMO,* June 8, 2017. https://www.cmo.com.au/article/620349/how-uniting-people-customer-experience-helping-adobe-disrupt/.

2 Ibid.

3 Ibid.

4 Kane, Gerald C. "Adobe Reinvents Its Customer Experience." *MIT Sloan Management Review,* May 3, 2016. http://sloanreview.mit.edu/article/adobereinventsitscustomerexperience.

5 Korn Ferry. "Korn Ferry Hay Group Global Study: Driving Culture Change Key Leadership Priority." Accessed August 22, 2017. https://www.kornferry.com/press/korn-ferry-hay-group-global-study-driving-culture-change-key-leadership-priority/.

6 Van Lee, Reggie, Lisa Fabish, and Nancy McGaw. "The Value of Corporate Values." *strategy+business,* May 23, 2005. https://www.strategy-business.com/article/05206?gko=9c265.

7 Ibid.

8 Summary of *The Southwest Airlines Way: Using the Power of Relationships to Achieve High Performance,* by Jody Gittell. Summaries.com, 2003. https://www.theclci.com/resources/thesouthwestairlinesway.pdf.

9 Ibid.

10 Corkindale, Gill. "The Importance of Organizational Design and Structure." *Harvard Business Review,* February 11, 2011. https://hbr.org/2011/02/the-importance-of-organization.

11 Neilson, Gary L., Jaime Estupiñán, and Bhushan Sethi. "10 Principles of Orga-

nization Design." *strategy+business,* March 23, 2015. https://www.strategy -business.com/article/00318?gko=c7329.

12   Creswell, Julie. "The Incredible Shrinking Sears." *New York Times,* August 11, 2017. https://www.nytimes.com/2017/08/11/business/the-incredible-shrinking -sears.html?mcubz=3&_r=0.

13   Frei, Frances X. "The Four Things a Service Business Must Get Right." *Harvard Business Review,* April 2008. https://hbr.org/2008/04/the-four-things -a-service-business-must-get-right.

14   Schmidt, Eric, and Jonathan Rosenberg. *How Google Works.* New York: Grand Central Publishing, 2014. 602. Kindle.

15   Morris, Donna. "Experience Matters." *Adobe Blog,* May 17, 2016. https://blogs .adobe.com/conversations/2016/05/experience-matters.html.

16   McQueen, Nina. "InDay: Investing in Our Employees So They Can Invest in Themselves." LinkedIn Blog, July 29, 2015. https://blog.linkedin.com/2015/07/29/ inday-investing-in-our-employees-so-they-can-invest-in-themselves.

17   Leverich, Nicole. Interview by Denise Lee Yohn. July 11, 2017.

18   Lindeman, Jeff. Interview by Denise Lee Yohn. May 4, 2017.

19   Barbour, Hilton. "HR versus Marketing—The Next C-Suite Confrontation." LinkedIn, May 11, 2017. https://www.linkedin.com/pulse/hr-versus-marketing -next-c-suite-confrontation-hilton-barbour.

20   Magee, Tyler Laird. Organizational culture and brand: A grounded theory assessment of employees' enablement to live the brand at a best place to work." *Doctor of Business Administration* (DBA). Paper 8. http://digitalcommons .georgefox.edu/dba/8.

21   Ibid.

22   Banjo, Shelly. "J.C. Penney's New Role Model: Home Depot." *Bloomberg Gadfly,* August 30, 2016. https://www.bloomberg.com/gadfly/articles/2016-08-30/ j-c-penney-turnaround-plan-looks-like-home-depot-s.

23   Howland, Daphne. "J.C. Penney Vows Change After Customer Service Scores Plummet." *Retail Dive,* March 16, 2016. http://www.retaildive.com/news/jc -penney-vows-change-after-customer-service-scores-plummet/415748/.

24   Manfio, Gilson Paulo, Leonardo Garnica, and Daniela Diogenes. "Natura: An Innovative Company Leader in the Brazilian Market of Cosmetics, Fragrances and Toiletries." *Hélice,* 2013. https://www.triplehelixassociation.org/helice/ volume-2-2013/helice-issue-1/natura-innovative-company-leader-brazilian -market-cosmetics-fragrances-toiletries.

25   Ibid.

26   Ibid.

27   Hashiba, Luciana. "Innovation in Well-Being—the Creation of Sustainable Value at Natura." *Management Innovation eXchange*, May 18, 2012. http://www .managementexchange.com/story/innovation-in-well-being.

28　Ibid.

29　Manfio et al., "Natura."

30　Bodine, Kerry, and Paul Hagan. "The Customer Experience Ecosystem." *Forrester,* February 28, 2013. http://www.crmasia.org/wp-content/uploads/2017/01/The-Customer-Experience-Ecosystem.pdf.

31　Ibid.

32　Lorsch, Jay W., and Emily McTague. "Culture Is Not the Culprit." *Harvard Business Review,* April 2016. https://hbr.org/2016/04/culture-is-not-the-culprit. Katzenbach, Jon, Carolin Oelschlegel, and James Thomas. "10 Principles of Organizational Culture." *strategy+business,* February 15, 2016. https://www.strategy-business.com/feature/10-Principles-of-Organizational-Culture.

33　Sartain, Libby, and Brent Daily. *Cracking the Culture Code: The Key to High Performing Organizations.* Boulder: RoundPegg, 2013. 28.

Chapter 5

1　Levy, Mark. Interview by Denise Lee Yohn. July 11, 2017.

2　Morgan, Jacob. "The Global Head of Employee Experience at Airbnb on Why They Got Rid of Human Resources." *Forbes,* February 1, 2016. https://www.forbes.com/sites/jacobmorgan/2016/02/01/global-head-employee-experience-airbnb-rid-of-human-resources.

3　Ibid.

4　Clune, Bronwen. "How Airbnb Is Building Its Culture through Belonging." *CultureAmp.* https://blog.cultureamp.com/how-airbnb-is-building-its-culture-through-belonging.

5　Airbnb. "Careers." Accessed August 22, 2017. https://www.airbnb.com/careers.

6　Clune, "How Airbnb Is Building Its Culture."

7　Levy, interview.

8　Gallagher, Leigh. "Airbnb's Profits to Top $3 Billion by 2020." *Fortune,* February 14, 2017. http://fortune.com/2017/02/15/airbnb-profits/.

9　Roderick, Leonie. "Airbnb Has the Strongest Brand Advocates." *Marketing Week,* December 16, 2016. https://www.marketingweek.com/2016/12/16/airbnb-strongest-brand-advocates/.

10　Chuck, Elizabeth. "Airbnb Rated the Best Place to Work, Dethroning Google." *NBC News,* February 13, 2017. https://www.nbcnews.com/better/careers/airbnb-best-place-work-year-glassdoor-rating-finds.

11　Meister, Jeanne. "The Employee Experience Is the Future of Work: 10 HR Trends For 2017." *Forbes,* January 5, 2017. https://www.forbes.com/sites/jeannemeister/2017/01/05/the-employee-experience-is-the-future-of-work-10-hr-trends-for-2017.

12　Deloitte. "2017 Deloitte Global Human Capital Trends." Accessed July 12, 2017.

https://www2.deloitte.com/us/en/pages/human-capital/articles/introduction
-human-capital-trends.html.

13 Bersin, Josh, Jason Flynn, Art Mazor, and Veronica Melian. "The Employee
    Experience: Culture, Engagement, and Beyond." *Deloitte University Press,* Feb-
    ruary 28, 2017. https://dupress.deloitte.com/dup-us-en/focus/human-capital
    -trends/2017/improving-the-employee-experience-culture-engagement.html.

14 Meister, Jeanne. "The Future of Work: Airbnb CHRO Becomes Chief Employee
    Experience Officer." *Forbes,* July 21, 2015. https://www.forbes.com/sites/
    jeannemeister/2015/07/21/the-future-of-work-airbnb-chro-becomes-chief
    -employee-experinece-officer.

15 Morgan, Jacob. "The Global Head of Employee Experience at Airbnb on
    Why They Got Rid of Human Resources." *Forbes,* February 1, 2016. https://
    www.forbes.com/sites/jacobmorgan/2016/02/01/global-head-employee
    -experience-airbnb-rid-of-human-resources.

16 Bersin, Josh. "A New Market Is Born: Employee Engagement, Feedback, and Cul-
    ture Apps." "Employee Engagement: Market Review, Buyer's Guide and Provider
    Profiles." *Josh Bersin Blog,* October 9, 2017. https://joshbersin.com/2015/09/a
    -new-market-is-born-employee-engagement-feedback-and-culture-apps/.

17 Mann, Annamarie, and Jim Harter. "The Worldwide Employee Engagement
    Crisis." *Gallup,* January 7, 2016. http://www.gallup.com/businessjournal/
    188033/worldwide-employee-engagement-crisis.aspx.

18 Morgan, Jacob. "Why the Millions We Spend on Employee Engagement Buy Us
    So Little." *Harvard Business Review,* March 10, 2017. https://hbr.org/2017/03/
    why-the-millions-we-spend-on-employee-engagement-buy-us-so-little.

19 Ibid.

20 Young, Heike. "Why Employee Experience and Company Culture Matter to
    Your Marketing." *Salesforce Blog,* March 29, 2017. https://www.salesforce
    .com/blog/2017/03/company-culture-matters-to-marketing.html.

21 Deloitte. "Global Human Capital Trends 2016." Accessed June 8, 2017. https://
    www2.deloitte.com/us/en/pages/human-capital/articles/introduction-human
    -capital-trends-2016.html.

22 Erickson, Tamara J., and Lynda Gratton. "What It Means to Work Here."
    Harvard Business Review, March 2007. https://hbr.org/2007/03/what-it
    -means-to-work-here.

23 Martin, Graeme. "Driving Corporate Reputations from the Inside: A Strate-
    gic Role and Strategic Dilemmas for HR?" *Asia Pacific Journal of Human
    Resources,* July 2009. https://www.researchgate.net/publication/44897940.

24 De Chernatony, Leslie. *From Brand Vision to Brand Evaluation.* Oxford: But-
    terworth Heinemann, 2001. 110.

25 NCR. "Our Shared Values." Accessed August 22, 2017. https://www.ncr.com/
    company/company-overview/our-shared-values.

26 Morgan, Jacob. "How This 30,000 Person Company Designs Great Employee Experiences." *Forbes,* October 6, 2015. https://www.forbes.com/sites/jacob morgan/2015/10/06/how-this-30000-person-company-designs-great -employee-experiences/#9ebe4b575e2b.

27 Lamers, Josee. "Work Organisation and Innovation—Case study: Rabobank, Netherlands." European Foundation for the Improvement of Living and Working Conditions. http://digitalcommons.ilr.cornell.edu/intl/252.

28 Ibid.

29 Erickson, Tamara J., and Lynda Gratton. "What It Means to Work Here." *Harvard Business Review,* March 2007. https://hbr.org/2007/03/what-it-means -to-work-here.

30 Ibid.

31 HubSpot. "Culture Code." Accessed August 22, 2017. https://cdn2.hubspot.net/ hub/216938/file-24940534-pdf/docs/culturecode-v7-130320111259-phpapp02 .pdf.

32 Steimer, Sarah. "HubSpot's Katie Burke Cracks the Company Culture Code." *Marketing News,* March 1, 2017. https://www.ama.org/publications/Market ingNews/Pages/hubspots-katie-burke-cracks-the-culture-code.aspx.

33 Vanderbloemen, William. "How to Build Systems to Improve Your Company's Culture." *Forbes,* March 12, 2017. https://www.forbes.com/sites/william vanderbloemen/2017/03/12/how-to-build-systems-to-improve-your -companys-culture.

34 Toister, Jeff. *The Service Culture Handbook: A Step-by-Step Guide to Getting Your Employees Obsessed with Customer Service.* San Diego: Toister Performance Solutions, 2017. 129.

35 Sabin, Scott. Interviews by Denise Lee Yohn. August 31, 2017, and September 6, 2017.

36 Kane, Gerald C. "Adobe Reinvents Its Customer Experience." *MIT Sloan Management Review,* May 3, 2016. http://sloanreview.mit.edu/article/adobe reinventsitscustomerexperience.

37 Valve. "Handbook for New Employees." Accessed August 22, 2017. www .valvesoftware.com/company/Valve_Handbook_LowRes.pdf.

38 Aarstol, Stephan. *The Five-Hour Workday: Live Differently, Unlock Productivity, and Find Happiness.* Austin: Lioncrest Publishing, 2016. 205.

39 Mafi, Nick. "What Went into Designing the Headquarters of Tencent, Asia's Most Valuable Company." *Architectural Digest,* September 20, 2016. http://www.architecturaldigest.com/story/designing-headquarters-tencent -asias-most-valuable-company.

40 Steimer, Sarah. "HubSpot's Katie Burke Cracks the Company Culture Code." *Marketing News,* March 1, 2017. https://www.ama.org/publications/Market ingNews/Pages/hubspots-katie-burke-cracks-the-culture-code.aspx.

41 Levy, Mark. Interview by Denise Lee Yohn. July 11, 2017.

42 Young, Heike. "Why Employee Experience and Company Culture Matter to Your Marketing." *Salesforce Blog,* March 29, 2017. https://www.salesforce.com/blog/2017/03/company-culture-matters-to-marketing.html.

43 Morgan, Jacob. *The Employee Experience Advantage: How to Win the War for Talent by Giving Employees the Workspaces They Want, the Tools They Need, and a Culture They Can Celebrate.* New York: Wiley, 2017. 179.

44 Ibid.

45 Roberge, Mark. "The Right Way to Use Compensation." *Harvard Business Review,* April 2015. https://hbr.org/2015/04/the-right-way-to-use-compensation-2.

46 Gleinicki, Annette Franz. "6 Tools to Create a Clear Line of Sight to Customers." *CX-Journey,* September 4, 2014. http://www.cx-journey.com/2014/09/6-tools-to-create-clear-line-of-sight.html.

47 Taylor, Bill. 2010. "Brand Is Culture, Culture Is Brand." *Harvard Business Review,* September 27, 2010. https://hbr.org/2010/09/brand-is-culture-culture-is-br.

48 Levy, interview.

49 Markish, Julie. "How Airbnb Fosters Empathy for It's Customers." *Medallia.* https://blog.medallia.com/customer-experience/how-airbnb-fosters-empathy-for-its-customers.

50 Walking, Adrian. "Medallia's VP of Insights on the 'Bigger Picture' for Customer Experience." *Argyle Journal,* May 17, 2016. http://www.argylejournal.com/customer-care/medallias-vp-of-insights-on-the-bigger-picture-for-customer-experience/.

Chapter 6

1 Salesforce. "Salesforce Announces Fiscal 2017 Fourth Quarter and Full Year Results." February 28, 2017. http://investor.salesforce.com/about-us/investor/investor-news/investor-news-details/2017/Salesforce-Announces-Fiscal-2017-Fourth-Quarter-and-Full-Year-Results/default.aspx.

2 Salesforce. "Customer Success Stories." Accessed August 22, 2017. https://www.salesforce.com/customer-success-stories/.

3 Salesforce. "Salesforce Named #1 CRM Provider for Fourth Consecutive Year" May 5, 2017. https://www.salesforce.com/company/news-press/press-releases/2017/05/170518.jsp.

4 Salesforce. "Recognition." Accessed August 22, 2017. https://www.salesforce.com/company/awards/company.jsp.

5 Zingerman's. *Zingerman's Staff Guide.* Ann Arbor: Dancing Sandwiches.

6 Ewan, Beth. "Zingerman's Boss Outlines Strategy of 'Sharing Lavishly.'" *Franchise Times,* November 18, 2016. http://www.franchisetimes.com/news/November-2016/Zingermans-Boss-Outlines-Strategy-of-Sharing-Lavishly/.

7 Zingerman's. "Zingerman's Community of Businesses." Accessed August 22, 2017. http://www.zingermanscommunity.com/about-us/our-businesses/.

8 Burlingham, Bo. "The Coolest Small Company in America." *Inc.,* January 1, 2003. https://www.inc.com/magazine/20030101/25036.html.

9 Zingerman's. "About Us." Accessed August 22, 2017. https://www.zingermans.com/AboutUs.aspx.

10 Boutin, Sarah. "Behind the Scenes at Salesforce.com: Our Aloha Spirit." *Salesforce Blog,* July 28, 2014. https://www.salesforce.com/blog/2014/07/behind-the-scenes-at-salesforcecom-our-aloha-spirit.html.

11 Ibid.

12 Martin, Jason. "'That's How We Do Things around Here': Organizational Culture (and Change) in Libraries." *In the Library with the Lead Pipe,* August 22, 2012. http://www.inthelibrarywiththeleadpipe.org/2012/thats-how-we-do-things-around-here/.

13 Boutin, "Behind the Scenes."

14 Martin, "Organizational Culture (and Change)."

15 Guenzi, Paolo. "How Ritual Delivers Performance." *Harvard Business Review,* February 15, 2013. https://hbr.org/2013/02/how-ritual-delivers-performanc.

16 Deal, Terrence, and Allan Kennedy. *Corporate Cultures: The Rites and Rituals of Corporate Life.* New York: Basic Books, 2000. 60.

17 Kerr, Michael. "Workplace Traditions and Rituals Build Culture, Add Fun to the Workplace." *Humor at Work.* Accessed August 22, 2017. http://mikekerr.com/free-articles/humour-in-the-workplace-articles/humor-in-the-workplace-helped-along-through-traditions-and-rituals/.

18 Bryant, Adam. "Matthew Prince of Cloudflare on the Dangers of Fast Growth." 2017. *New York Times,* August 11, 2017. https://www.nytimes.com/2017/08/11/business/corner-office-matthew-prince-cloudflare.html?mcubz=3&_r=0.

19 Chevron. "2010 Annual Meeting Remarks by John S. Watson." May 26, 2010. https://www.chevron.com/stories/2010-annual-stockholders-meeting-remarks-by-john-swatson.

20 Miles, Bryan. Interview by Denise Lee Yohn. July 10, 2017.

21 Martin, Elizabeth. "An Ode to Harvard Stadium." *Gentle Giant Blog,* December 30, 2016. https://www.gentlegiant.com/ode-harvard-stadium/.

22 EO Global. "Flexing the Entrepreneurial Muscle." *Octane Magazine,* December 2013. https://www.eonetwork.org/octane-magazine/december-2013.

23 Gardner, Jeremiah, and Brant Cooper. *Entrepreneur's Guide to the Lean Brand: How Brand Innovation Builds Passion, Transforms Organizations and Creates Value.* San Diego: Market by Numbers, 2014. 1572.

24 Bucher, Amy. "What That Sign Says about Your Corporate Culture." *Amy Bucher Blog,* July 9, 2015. http://www.amybucherphd.com/what-that-sign-says -about-your-corporate-culture/.

25 Ibid.

26 Burkus, David. "How to Tell if Your Company Has a Creative Culture." *Harvard Business Review,* December 2, 2014. https://hbr.org/2014/12/how-to -tell-if-your-company-has-a-creative-culture.

27 Hamilton, Heather. "The Legend of the Amazon Door Desk." *Amazonian Blog,* July 06, 2015. http://www.amazonianblog.com/2015/07/the-legend-of-the-amazon -door-desk.html.

28 City Year. "Welcome to the Red Jacket Society." Accessed September 6, 2017. http://www.redjacketsociety.org/about/.

29 Smith, Gillian. Interview with Denise Lee Yohn. Telephone interview on August 31, 2017.

30 Conley, Chip. *Peak: How Great Companies Get Their Mojo from Maslow.* New York: Jossey-Bass, 2007. 65.

31 Lencioni, Patrick M. "Make Your Values Mean Something." *Harvard Business Review,* July 2002. https://hbr.org/2002/07/make-your-values-mean-something.

32 Smith, Gillian. Interview by Denise Lee Yohn. August 31, 2017.

33 Zingerman's, *Zingerman's Staff Guide*, 9.

34 Ibid., 9.

35 Zingerman's. "Zingerman's Guide to Good Leading, Part 4: A Lapsed Anarchist's Approach to the Power of Beliefs in Business." Accessed August 22, 2017. http://www.zingermanspress.com/our-books/the-power-of-beliefs-in-business.

36 Weinzweig, Ari. Interview by Denise Lee Yohn. July 24, 2017.

37 Zingerman's, *Zingerman's Staff Guide.*

38 Weinzweig, interview.

39 Ibid.

40 Ibid.

41 Google. "Our Company." Accessed August 22, 2017. https://www.google.com/ intl/en/about/.

42 Alphabet. "2004 Founders' IPO Letter." https://abc.xyz/investor/founders -letters/2004/ipo-letter.html.

43 Flynn, Nancy. "Writing Effective Policies Using Written Policy to Manage Behavior, Mitigate Risks, & Maximize Compliance." *Policy Institute,* April 20, 2011. http://www.epolicyinstitute.com/docs/Prevalent~WritingEffectivePolicy ~WPf.pdf.

44 Conley, *Peak, 96.*

45 Kleinberg, Adam. "Why We Have a Burning Man Policy." *Traction Blog,* August 24, 2011. https://www.tractionco.com/words/why-we-have-a-burning -man-policy/.

46 The Motley Fool. "The Fool Rules!" Accessed August 22, 2017. https://inside motleyfool.files.wordpress.com/2012/04/fool-rules-2012.pdf.

47 Weinzweig, Ari. *A Lapsed Anarchist's Approach to the Power of Beliefs in Business, Part 4*. Ann Arbor, Michigan: Zingerman's Press, 2016. 472.

48 Ibid.

49 Griffin, Michael. *How to Write a Policy Manual*. Accessed August 22, 2017. http://www.templatezone.com/download-free-ebook/office-policy-manual -reference-guide.pdf.

Chapter 7

1 Tomovich, Lilian. Interview by Denise Lee Yohn. July 19, 2017.

2 Ibid.

3 Ibid.

4 Ibid.

5 Tomovich, Lilian. "Building of an Iconic Brand from Inside Out." *Medallia Experience Conference*, April 2017.

6 Ibid.

7 Ibid.

8 Tomovich, interview.

9 MGM Resorts International. 2017. "MGM Resorts International Reports Fourth Quarter and Full Year Financial and Operating Results." February 16, 2017. http://mgmresorts.investorroom.com/2017-02-16-MGM-Resorts-International -Reports-Fourth-Quarter-And-Full-Year-Financial-And-Operating-Results -Announces-Quarterly-Dividend.

10 Gill-Simmen, Lucy. Interview by Denise Lee Yohn. September 6, 2017.

11 King, Ceridwyn, and Debra Ann Grace. "Internal Branding: Exploring the Employee's Perspective." Journal of Brand Management 15 (2008): 358–372. https://www.researchgate.net/publication/247478547_Internal_branding _Exploring_the_employee's_perspective.

12 Tenet Partners. "Brand Culture at the Intersection of Brand and HR." March 28, 2017. https://tenetpartners.com/about-us/news/2017-03-07-brand-culture-webinar.html.

13 Ind, Nicholas. *Living the Brand: How to Transform Every Member of Your Organization into a Brand Champion*. London: Kogan Page Limited, 2008. 152.

14 Forman, Jennifer. Interview by Denise Lee Yohn. July 19, 2017.

15 Ibid.

16 Ibid.

17 Ibid.

18 Mitchell International. "Internal Survey Results." 2017.

19 Ind, *Living the Brand,* 120.

20 Ibid., 120.

21 Marketing Society Excellence Awards. "Mobilising the Organisation: Employee Engagement." February 5, 2016. https://www.marketingsociety.com/sites/default/files/thelibrary/Telefonica%20O2%20-%20Rally%20Cry_Redacted.pdf.

22 Ibid.

23 Ibid.

24 Ibid.

25 Ibid.

26 Magee, Kate. "Why Employees Are More Important than the CEO for a Company's Reputation." *PR Week,* April 26, 2012. http://www.prweek.com/article/1128641/why-employees-important-ceo-companys-reputation.

27 Mitchell, Colin. "Selling the Brand Inside." *Harvard Business Review,* January 2002. https://hbr.org/2002/01/selling-the-brand-inside.

28 Sartain, Libby, and Mark Schumann. *Brand from the Inside: Eight Essentials to Emotionally Connect Your Employees to Your Business.* New York: Jossey-Bass, 2006. 197.

29 Mitchell, "Selling the Brand Inside."

30 Tomovich, Lilian. Interview by Denise Lee Yohn. July 19, 2017.

31 Ibid.

32 Ibid.

Chapter 8

1 Chouinard, Yvon. *Let My People Go Surfing: The Education of a Reluctant Businessman.* New York: Penguin Group, 2005. 31.

2 Patagonia. "Supply Chain: The Footprint Chronicles®." Accessed August 22, 2017. http://www.patagonia.com/20-years-of-organic-cotton.html.

3 Patagonia. "Introducing the Common Threads Initiative—Reduce, Repair, Reuse, Recycle, Reimagine." September 7, 2011. https://www.patagonia.com/blog/2011/09/introducing-the-common-threads-initiative/.

4 Patagonia. "Patagonia's Mission Statement." Accessed August 22, 2017. http://www.patagonia.com/company-info.html.

5 Beer, Jeff. "The Purpose-Driven Marketer: How Patagonia Uses Storytelling to Turn Consumers into Activists." *Fast Company,* November 19, 2014. https://www.fastcompany.com/3038557/the-purpose-driven-marketer-how-patagonia-uses-storytelling-to-turn-consume.

6 Ibid.

7 Ibid.

8 GE. "GE Launches Ecomagination to Develop Environmental Technologies; Company-Wide Focus on Addressing Pressing Challenges." May 9, 2005.

http://www.businesswire.com/news/home/20050509005663/en/GE-Launches
-Ecomagination-Develop-Environmental-Technologies-Company-Wide.

9   GE. Ecomagination. Accessed August 22, 2017. https://www.ge.com/about-us/
ecomagination.

10 Makower, Joel. "Ecomagination at 10: A Status Report." *GreenBiz,* May 11,
2015. https://www.greenbiz.com/article/ecomagination-10-status-report.

11 Walsh, Bryan. "GE Picks Up the Slack on Green Tech." *Time*, June 24, 2011.
http://science.time.com/2011/06/24/ge-picks-up-the-slack-on-green-tech/.

12 Khan, Mickey Alam. "GE Glows Green for Ecomagination Campaign." *DM
News*, July 15, 2005. http://www.dmnews.com/dataanalytics/ge-glows-green
-for-ecomagination-campaign/article/88080/.

13 Haldemann, Alex. "GE's Ecomagination Turns 10: How a Brand Can Be a
Driver for Change." *Huffington Post,* September 16, 2016. http://www.huff
ingtonpost.com/dr-alexander-haldemann/startup-slideshow-test_b_7181672
.html.

14 Ibid.

15 GE. "GE Wins EPC of the Year Award for Malakoff Corporation's 1,000-Megawatt
Tanjung Bin Energy Power Plant." September 22, 2016. http://www.genews
room.com/press-releases/ge-wins-epc-year-award-malakoff-corporation
%E2%80%99s-1000-megawatt-tanjung-bin-energy-power.

16 Scherer, Jasper. "How GE Is Changing the World." *Fortune,* August 19, 206.
http://fortune.com/2016/08/19/general-electric-change-world/.

17 Haldemann, "Ecomagination Turns 10."

18 Makower, "Ecomagination at 10."

19 Hower, Mike. "GE Renews Ecomagination Initiative, Commits $25B to
CleanTech R&D by 2020." March 4, 2014. http://www.sustainablebrands
.com/news_and_views/cleantech/mike_hower/ge_renews_ecomagination
_initiative_commits_25_b_clean_tech_rd_20.

20 Starbucks. Mission Statement. Accessed August 22, 2017. https://www.star
bucks.com/about-us/company-information/mission-statement.

21 Leinwand, Paul, and Varya Davidson. "How Starbucks's Culture Brings Its
Strategy to Life." *Harvard Business Review,* December 30, 2016. https://hbr
.org/2016/12/how-starbuckss-culture-brings-its-strategy-to-life.

22 Asrin, Alejandro. Interview by Eduardo Braun. August 25, 2017.

23 Confino, Joe. "Paul Polman: 'The Power Is in the Hands of the Consumers.'" *The Guardian,* November 21, 2011. https://www.theguardian.com/
sustainable-business/unilever-ceo-paul-polman-interview.

24 Kaye, Leon. "Unilever: Profile of a Sustainable Brand Leader, Part One." *Sustainable Brands*, November 19, 2012. http://www.sustainablebrands.com/
news_and_views/articles/unilever-profile-sustainable-brand-leader-part-one.

25 Walt, Vivienne. "Unilever CEO Paul Polman's Plan to Save the World." *Fortune,*

February 16, 2017. http://fortune.com/2017/02/17/unilever-paul-polman-respons ibility-growth/.

26 Unilever. "Sustainable Living." Accessed August 22, 2017. https://www.unilever .com/sustainable-living/.

27 Unilever. "Unilever Sustainable Living Plan." Progress Report 2011. Accessed August 22, 2017. https://www.unilever.com/Images/uslp-unilever_sustainable _living_plan_progress_report_2011_tcm13-387588_tcm244-409863_en.pdf.

28 Jack, Louise. "Why Unilever Is Betting Big on Sustainability." *Fast Company,* October 2, 2015. https://www.fastcompany.com/3051498/why-unilever-is-betting -big-on-sustainability.

29 Ibid.

30 Kaye, "Unilever."

31 Confino, " 'The Power Is in the Hands of the Consumers.' "

32 Lam, Bourree. "How REI's Co-op Retail Model Helps Its Bottom Line." *The Atlantic,* March 21, 2017. https://www.theatlantic.com/business/archive/2017/03/ rei-jerry-stritzke-interview/520278/.

33 Mark, Jason. "Get Out There: The Backstory of REI's #OptOutside Campaign." *Sierra,* November 22, 2016. http://www.sierraclub.org/sierra/green-life/get-out -there-backstory-rei-s-optoutside-campaign.

34 REI. "REI Closing Its Doors on Black Friday—Invites Nation to OptOutside." November 27, 2015. http://newsroom.rei.com/news/corporate/rei-closing-its -doors-on-black-friday-invites-nation-to-optoutside.htm.

35 Diaz, Ann-Christine. "REI's '#OptOutside' Returns for 2016 with Aims to Become a New American Tradition." *AdAge*, October 24, 2016. http://adage .com/article/advertising/rei-s-optoutside-2016-american-tradition/306431/.

36 Beer, Jeff. "How Values and Purpose Made REI's #OptOutside a Big Winner at Cannes." *Fast Company,* June 27, 2016. https://www.fastcompany.com/3061312/ how-values-and-purpose-made-reis-optoutside-a-big-winner-at-cannes.

37 REI. 2015. "Thank You for Choosing to #OPTOUTSIDE with Us." Accessed August 22, 2017. https://www.rei.com/blog/hike/thanks-for-choosing-to-optout side-with-us.

38 Oakley. "OakleyFive."

39 Ibid.

40 Takumi, Brian. Interview by Denise Lee Yohn. July 19, 2017.

41 Ibid.

42 Oakley. "OakleyFive."

43 Takumi, interview.

44 Voigt, Joan. "Oakley Flaunts Its Culture in New Branding Effort." *Adweek,* February 28, 2014. http://www.adweek.com/brand-marketing/oakley-flaunts-its-cul ture-new-branding-effort-156014/.

45 Takumi, interview.

46 Voigt, "Oakley Flaunts Its Culture"

47 VisionMonday staff. "Oakley Launches 'Disruptive by Design' Campaign." *Vision Monday,* February 27, 2014. http://www.visionmonday.com/business/suppliers/article/oakley-launches-disruptive-by-design-campaign-outlines-future-focus-1/.

Conclusion

1 Levy, Mark. Interview by Denise Lee Yohn. July 11, 2017.

2 Williams, Ardine. Interview by Denise Lee Yohn. July 14, 2017.

3 Tomovich, Lilian. Interview by Denise Lee Yohn. July 19, 2017.

4 Weinzweig, Ari. Interview by Denise Lee Yohn. July 24, 2017.

5 Ridge, Garry. Interview by Denise Lee Yohn. May 18, 2017.

6 Guinto, Joseph. "A Look at Southwest Airlines 50 Years Later." *D Magazine,* May 2017. https://www.dmagazine.com/publications/d-ceo/2017/may/southwest-airlines-50-year-anniversary-love-field-dallas/.

ABOUT THE AUTHOR

Denise Lee Yohn is the go-to expert on brand-building for national media outlets, an in-demand speaker and consultant, and an influential writer.

A student of great brands and enduring organizations, Denise is the author of the best-selling book *What Great Brands Do: The Seven Brand-Building Principles that Separate the Best from the Rest* and the e-book *Extraordinary Experiences: What Great Retail and Restaurant Brands Do.*

News media including FOX Business TV, CNBC, *The Wall Street Journal,* and NPR call on Denise when they want an expert point of view on hot business issues. With her expertise and inspiring approach, Denise has become an in-demand keynote speaker, and she has addressed business leaders around the world.

Denise challenges readers to think differently in her regular contributions to *Harvard Business Review* and *Forbes*, and she has been a sought-after writer for publications including *Fast Company, Entrepreneur, Knowledge@Wharton*, and *Seeking Alpha,* among others.

Denise initially cultivated her brand-building approaches through several high-level positions in advertising and client-side marketing. She served as lead strategist at advertising agencies for Burger King and Land Rover and as the marketing leader and analyst for Jack in the Box restaurants and Spiegel catalogs. Denise went on to head Sony Electronics Inc.'s first brand office, where she was the vice president/general manager of brand and strategy and garnered major corporate awards. Consulting clients have included Target, Oakley, Dunkin' Donuts, and other leading companies.

Contact Denise at http://deniseleeyohn.com.

INDEX

A

Aarstol, Stephan, 115
accessibility, 42, 171
achievement, 42, 171
action inconsistency, 22
Adobe, 75–76
Airbnb, 183
  "#belonganywhere" brand campaign,
    95–96
  design of offices, 97–98
  employee's experience at, 96–100, 108, 112
  "Ground Control" team of, 96, 98
  purpose and core values, 97
  talent department, 96
Amazon, 53, 132
  market value, 8
  Web Services, 26
  workplace culture, xi–xiii
American Express, 33
American Management Association and
    Institute for Corporate Productivity, 64
Andersson, Jörgen, 19
Apple, 11
artifacts, xxii, 41, 131–134
Aspen Institute's Business and Society
    Program, 14, 17, 77
Asrin, Alejandro, 174
assessment of brand-culture fusion
  brand type, 30–37
  culture audit 39–41
  current state of brand-culture fusion, 45–50
  uniqueness, 52–53

values, 37–45
Audacity Group, 12
Autodesk, 6

B

Banco Supervielle, 20
Barbour, Hilton, 12, 84
B2B (business-to-business) companies, xxiv
Becker, Jan, 6
BELAY, 27, 129
Bellagio, 144
Benioff, Marc, 123
Bezos, Jeff, xii–xiii, xx, 29, 53, 183
BMW, 33
Booz Allen Hamilton, 14, 17, 77
brand
  archetypes, 31
  classifying, 31
  day-to-day engagement with, 49–50
  design, 140–141
  differentiating, 176–180
  engagement session, 65–66
  engagement with company's brand
    strategy, 50
  identifying, 30–37
  personal and emotional engagement with,
    49
  touchpoints, 88–92
  types, 31–37
brand-building, xviii–xxi
  "brand-as-business" management
    approach to, xix

brand-culture fusion, xv–xviii, 180–181, 186
   assessment of current state of, 45–50
   and authenticity of brands, xv
   need for, xxiii–xxvi
   strategies to achieve, xxii
Brand-Culture Fusion Assessment, 16, 30,
    32, 52
brand identity, xii, 152, 164–165, 170
   developing, 173
Brand Touchpoint Wheel, 78, 89–91
Branson, Richard, xiii, 6, 29
Braun, Eduardo, 61
Brown, Andrew, 25
Brown, Michael, 132
Bucher, Amy, 131
Buffer, xvii
Burke, Katie, 113, 116
Burkus, David, 132

C
caring, 42, 171
Chernatony, Leslie de, 12, 105
Chevron, 129
Chouinard, Yvon, 163
City Year, xxv, 132–133
Cleveland Clinic, 81
Clio, 113–114
Cloudflare, 129
College Hunks Hauling Junk, 130
Collins, Jim, xiv, 9–11, 13
compensation experience, 115
competition, 42, 171
Conley, Chip, 133
conscious brands, 32, 34
consistency, 42, 171
The Container Store, 61
continuous improvement, 42, 171
Cooper, Brant, 131
core values, 13–24
   congruence, achieving and sustaining,
    21–24
   customer perception of, 17–18
   drafting, 20
   in hiring decisions, 69
   identifying, 16–21, 42–44

   importance of setting, 14
   information from, 19
   as operating instructions, 14
   tangible benefits of, 14–15
   uniqueness of, 16–17
Corkindale, Gill, 79
countercultures, 25
Covey, Stephen R., 45
creativity, 42, 171
Crossroads Church, 15
culture, xiii
   as an antidote to threats, xiv
   audit, 39, 41, 44
   cultivating healthy, xxiii
   healthy, significance of, xiv
culture-aligned operations, 86
culture-building, xviii–xxi
culture change, 77–78
customer experience (CX), 96, 100–101, 103,
    107, 118–120
customers, xii

D
Deal, Terrence, 127
Denison, 37
design, 42, 171
desired culture, xxi–xxii, 16, 25, 27, 30,
    38–39, 44, 48, 51–52, 60, 62–64, 66–68,
    70, 76, 78, 80–83, 85–86, 92–93, 101,
    103, 107–108, 110–112, 116, 120,
    123–124, 127–128, 130–131, 134,
    136–137, 141, 144–150, 157, 159, 161,
    170, 181, 185
discernment, 42, 171
disruptive brands, 24, 31
distinct culture, 182
distinction, 42, 171
Dreamforce, 123
drivers of business, xiii–xv
Drucker, Peter, 27

E
Ecomagination, 166
Eisingerich, Andreas, 147
Ellinghorst, Arndt, 59

Ellison, Marvin, 86
empathy, 43, 171
employee brand engagement, 48–52, 146–148
  communications campaigns, 154–158
  experiences, 148–154
  investments in, 160–161
  toolkits for, 158–160
Employee Experience Architecture, 107
employee experience–customer experience
    integration, 47–48, 52
employee experience (EX), 95
  aligning and integrating brand and culture,
    120
  designing, 103–116
  employee interactions, 106–109
  employee segmentation, 103–106
  integrating with customer experience
    (CX), 118–120
  involving employees in designing, 116–118
  prioritizing, 101–103
  programs, 101
  rules of, 99
  three-category design model, 109–110
  understanding, 98–99
  vs employee engagement, 100
employee interactions, 106–109
employee policies and procedures, 40, 124,
    134–140
employee segmentation, 103–106
employer branding, 147
employment branding, 147
engagement experience, 114
enhancing subcultures, 25
enjoyment, 43, 171
entertainment, 43, 171
Erickson, Tamara, 110, 112
EX, see employee experience (EX)
excellence, 43, 171
experience brands, 32, 35
experimentation, 43, 171

F
Facebook, 7–8, 13
fairness, 43, 171
FedEx, 25–26, 33

Ferry, Korn, 77
Fields, Mark, 65
Five Whys exercise, 9
Flynn, Nancy, 137
Ford, Henry, 8
Ford Motor Company
  core values, 64–65
  leadership actions at, 58–60
  turnaround of, 55–58
Forman, Jennifer, 149–150
Franklin, Benjamin, 148
Frei, Frances X., 81
Friedman, Nick, 130
Frito-Lay, xiv
frozen middle, 67
fusion, xiii

G
Gardner, Jeremiah, 131
Gartenberg, Claudine, 67
Gazelles, 18
GE, 69, 166–168, 170
Gentle Giants, 130
Gill-Simmen, Lucy, 147
Gittell, Jody Hoffer, 79
Global Brand Leaders, 84
Google, 18–19, 81–82, 137
Gratton, Lynda, 110, 112
Great Recession of 2008, 55
Griffin, Michael, 140

H
Hagerty, 11
haka, 127
Hastings, Reed, 23
Hatfield, Tinker, 4
Hewitt, Aon, 66
high commitment, 43, 172
H&M, 19
Hoffman, 64–65
Howard, Joy, 164
HubSpot, 113, 116–117
Hughey, Cheryl, 185
Human Synergistics, 37
humility, 43, 172

I

IBM, 16
ideological inconsistency, 22
Illumina, 18
Immelt, Jeff, 166
inconsistencies, 22
Ind, Nicholas, 19
innovative brands, 32, 34
internal brand alignment, 48, 52
inventiveness, 43, 172

J

Jackson, Eric, 25
Jannard, Jim, 178–180
JCPenney, 65, 86
Jobs, Steve, 9
Johnson & Johnson, 8
Joie de Vivre, 133, 138
Journal of Brand Management, 147

K

Katzenbach, Jon, 93
Kelleher, Herb, xiv, 183
Kennedy, Allan, 127
Kerr, Michael, 128
Kleinberg, Adam, 139
Kmart, 80
Knight, Phil, 3, 5

L

Laird-Magee, Tyler, 84
Lambert, Eddie, 80
leadership
    for achieving brand-culture fusion, 70–71
    actions, 64–66
    communication skills, 60–64
    in decision-making, 68–70
    diversity and inclusion (D&I) efforts,
        67–68
    for fostering culture, 58–60
    hiring and firing decisions, 70
    and level of engagement, 66–68
Lederman, Gregg, xvi, 148
Lencioni, Patrick, 21
Leverich, Nicole, 26, 82

Levy, Mark, 96, 117, 183
Lindeman, Jeff, 82–83
LinkedIn, 26, 82
Lorsch, Jay W., 93
lower-level management, 66–67
luxury brands, 32, 35

M

Makower, Joel, 166
Martin, Jason, 125
Meister, Jeanne, 100
MGM Grand, 144
MGM Resorts, 143–146, 148, 183
Michelman, Paul, xix
middle management, 66–67
Miles, Bryan, 27, 129
mission statement, 6–7
Mitchell International, 149
The Mitchell Way Day, 149–150
Morgan, Jacob, 101
Morris, Donna, 76, 82, 114
Morris, Steve, 13
Motley Fool, 139
Mulally, Alan, 56–58, 65
multi-dimensional brand engagement
    experiences, 151–154

N

Natura, 78, 86–87
NCR, 106
Netflix, 22–23
Nike, 3–4, 179
    brand-culture fusion, 5
    inspiration and innovation, 5, 8
    "Just Do It" tagline, 4
    mission and maxims, 4–5
nonprofit organizations, xxv–xxvi

O

O2, 154–157
Oakley, xiv, 178–180
OCAI, 37
office hours experience, 115
Ohana culture, 123, 125–126, 131
on-boarding experience, 113

operationalize culture, xxii, 67, 77–78
#OptOutside campaign, 177–178, 180
organizational culture, 27
   artifacts, 131–134
   identifying, 37–45
   policies and procedures, aligning, 134–140
   rites and rituals, 125–130
Organizational Culture Profile, 37
organizational design, 78–85
   brand touchpoints, analysis of, 92
   bridging culture-change efforts, 93
   design principles, 79–80
   goal of, 80–81
   integrating and aligning culture and brand, 85–87
organizational roles, 82–85
organizational standards, 81–82
organizational structure, 81
organizational subcultures, 25
organizational values, common, 42–44, 171–172
organization's hierarchy, 66–68
originality, 43, 172
orthogonal subcultures, 25
overarching purpose, 5–13, 95
   crafting a meaningful statement, 11–13
   pinpointing, 9–10

P
Palmisano, Sam, 16
Parker, Mark, 4
Patagonia, 163
   brand identity, 164
   environmental efforts and philosophy, 165
People First Leadership: How the Best Leaders Use Culture and Emotion to Drive Unprecedented Results (Eduardo Braun), xiii
performance brands, 32, 35
performance review experience, 114
Photoshop, 75
Plant With Purpose, xxvi, 114
Polman, Paul, 174, 176
Porras, Jerry I., 9–11, 13
pragmatism, 43, 172

Prince, Matthew, 129
purpose and values integration, 46–47, 52
"purpose-driven" company, 5
purposefulness, 43, 172

Q
Quicken Loans, 159
QuikTrip, 68

R
Rabobank Nederland, 110
"Rally Cry" campaign, 154–156
Random Corporate Serial Killer game, 9–10
recruiting experience, 113
Red Bull, 179
Red Jacket Society, 133
REI, 176–178
REVPAR, 146
Rhoades, Ann, 17, 64, 69
   Built on Values, 69
Ridge, Garry, 185
RightNow, 88
risk-taking, 43, 172
rituals, xxii, 41, 47–48, 123–130
Ritz-Carlton Hotel Company, 31, 113
role-based segments, 104
Rosenberg, Jonathan, 81
Rossman, John, 53

S
Sabin, Scott, 114
Saginaw, Paul, 134
Salesforce, 123–125, 131
San Diego Regional Airport Authority, 82–83
   "Let's Go" campaign, 83
Sartain, Libby, 157
Schmidt, Eric, 81
Schultz, Howard, 29, 169
Schumann, Mark, 157
Seabra, Antonio Luiz da Cunha, 86
Sears, 80
Serafeim, George, 67
service brands, 32, 34
SHOW acronym, 144–145

Siebel Systems, 133
Skylofts, 144
small businesses, xxv
Smith, Gillian, 132
Somma, Mark di, 12
Sony, xiv, 11, 88
sophistication, 44, 172
Southwest Airlines, 53, 64, 78–79
Southwest Airlines, culture of, xiv
Squarespace, 11
standard operating procedures (SOPs),
    135–136
standing out, 44, 172
Starbucks, 29, 53, 169–170
start-ups, xvi–xvii, xxv
status, 44, 172
Stritzke, Jerry, 177
style brands, 32, 35
Supervielle, Patricio, 20
symbolic inconsistency, 22

T
Takumi, Brian, 178–179
Tarjeta Naranja, 173–174
Telefónica, 154
Telenor, 153
Tencent, 115–116
Tenet Partners, 147
Thematic Apperception "Test" (TAT), 10
Think. Feel. Do exercise, 10
Tindell, Kip, 61
Toister, Jeff, 114
Tome, Brian, 15
Tomovich, Lilian, 144–145, 160, 183
Tower, 115
Traction, 139
training experience, 113–114
transparency, 44, 172

U
Uber's organizational culture, xvii–xviii
Umpqua, 84

unifying employees, 24–27
Unilever, 174–175
"Unilever Sustainable Living Plan" (USLP),
    174–175
uniqueness of company, 52–53
USAA, 31

V
value brands, 32, 34
value congruence, 21–22
values, see core values; organizational
    values, common
Valve, 115
Vanderbloemen, William, 113
Vanderbloemen Search Group, 113
Virgin enterprise, 29
Volkswagen, 59–60

W
Ward, Jonathan, 116
WD-40 Company, 17, 185
Weinzweig, Ari, 134, 136
Welch, Jack, xiii, 61, 69
Welch, Suzy, 69
well-known brands, xvii
Williams, Ardine, 26, 183
workplace environment experience, 115–116

X
Xradia, 11

Y
Yates, Darin, 15
YouGov BrandIndex, 98

Z
Zappos, 11, 16, 18
Zingerman's, 124–125, 134–135, 140–141,
    184
    Staff Guide, 135–136
ZingTrain, 135
Zuckerberg, Mark, 7–8, 13